♦ The Two-Week Traveler Series ♦

THE BEST
OF
BRITAIN'S
COUNTRYSIDE

NORTHERN ENGLAND AND SCOTLAND
A Driving & Walking Itinerary

◆ The Two-Week Traveler Series ◆

THE BEST OF BRITAIN'S COUNTRYSIDE

NORTHERN ENGLAND AND SCOTLAND
A Driving & Walking Itinerary

Bill and Gwen North

THE
MOUNTAINEERS

THE MOUNTAINEERS: Organized 1906 ". . . *to explore, study, preserve, and enjoy the natural beauty of the Northwest.*"

8   7   6   5   4
5   4   3   2

Published by The Mountaineers
1011 S.W. Klickitat Way, Suite 107, Seattle, Washington 98134
Published simultaneously in Canada by Douglas & McIntyre, Ltd.,
1615 Venables Street, Vancouver, B.C. V5L 2H1

Manufactured in the United States of America
Edited by Nick Allison
Maps by Karen Galley
Cover photograph: Yorkshire Dales
All other photographs by the authors
Cover design by Elizabeth Watson
Book design by Barbara Bash
Photos: page 2, Yorkshire Dales; page 5, Skye; page 6, Dovedale; page 9, York;
page 37, Kilnsey Crag, Wharfedale

Library of Congress Cataloging in Publication Data

North, Bill, 1947–
    The best of Britain's countryside : northern England and Scotland
  : a driving and walking itinerary / Bill and Gwen North : [maps by
  Karen Galley].
        p. cm. — (The Two-week traveler series)
    Includes bibliographical references.
    ISBN 0-89886-205-1 — ISBN 0-89886-205-1 (pbk.)
    1. Great Britain—Description and travel—1981– —Tours.
  2. Scotland—Description and travel—1981– —Tours. 3. England,
  Northern—Description and travel—1981– —Tours. 4. Automobiles—Road
  guides—Great Britain. 5. Landscape—Great Britain—Guide-books.
  6.Walking—Great Britain—Guide-books. I. North, Gwen.
  II. Title. III. Series.
  DA650.N58   1989   90-5455
  914.104'858--dc20   CIP

For my father,
who dreamed of faraway places . . .
oh, how he dreamed.

B.N.

Contents

PART ONE

Introduction

About This Guidebook

*T*his book is for independent, adventurous travelers who are short of time but still want the best of Britain.

After years of living, working, and traveling in Britain, we've found one timeless truth: The best way to enjoy the *real* Britain is to get off the tourist treadmill and experience the countryside—the emerald meadows and heather-clad hills, the ageless stone villages, cozy pubs, and warm people. When you visit Britain, that's what you remember most fondly.

But these days few people have the time to discover the out-of-the-way places that are Britain's best. That's where this book comes in. During a relaxed, but richly varied sixteen-day itinerary, you'll experience:

- ◆ Two of Britain's most fascinating **medieval cities**;
- ◆ Several of its best **ancient sites**;
- ◆ Three of its most scenic **national parks**;
- ◆ Three spectacular **wild areas**;
- ◆ Several magnificent **cathedrals, abbeys,** and **castles,** both ruined and intact;
- ◆ Two pastoral **river valleys**;
- ◆ One of Britain's most magical **islands**; and
- ◆ Many of its most picturesque and friendly **villages,**

But that's not all. Any book can tell you what and where things are. This book explains why—with a wealth of illuminating, sometimes quirky details about people, places, and things along the way—why this village seems so perfect, why that castle is in ruins, why the landscape changes so dramatically, and so on.

We also offer tips on how best to prepare for your trip and a whole section on how to understand British culture—from pubs to pounds sterling.

Then, each chapter covers a different day of the itinerary. You can follow the route closely or just use it as an outline and fill in the details yourself. To encourage you to explore, we've included a seductive array of optional side trips and special attractions for each day.

In addition, while you'll spend much of your time tooling along scenic country roads in a rented car, we slow you down to walking speed every other day or so. Britain has thousands of miles of protected footpaths through some of the world's most beautiful countryside. We've selected some of the best, ranging from the impossibly pastoral to the breathtakingly dramatic. And you don't have to be a climber or even a regular hiker to enjoy them; if you're in average shape, you'll do just fine.

Two weeks later you'll return with your head and your heart filled with secret places, magical experiences, sweeping vistas, and memorable people.

In short, the best of Britain.

Bill and Gwen North

How This Book Is Organized

Each chapter covers a different day in the itinerary and includes:

1. ORIENTATION. An opening page or two that sets the scene for the day's explorations—a description of the landscape through which you'll travel, some historical notes on the area, and so forth. Just enough to give you a taste of what's to come.

2. THE ROUTE. Directions to guide you through the day's drive (or walk), along with a running commentary full of details chosen to illuminate the passing scene.

  This symbol indicates driving portions of a day's trip.

  This symbol indicates walking portions of a day's trip.

3. SIDE TRIPS. Optional short detours from the main route of the day to places of special interest.

❖ This symbol indicates side trips.

4. DIVERSIONS. Alternatives to the main route, provided so that whatever your mood (or the condition of the weather) you have more than one way to spend each day.

5. CREATURE COMFORTS. Guidance on where to stay (Daily Bed) and where to have dinner (Daily Bread).

The Itinerary at a Glance

DAY 1: Arrive in London and travel north, by rented car or train, to **York.** Walk the medieval walls for great afternoon views of the old town. Dinner at a pub.

DAY 2: Visit the **Jorvik Viking Centre,** an underground archeological dig with Disneyland-like exhibitions. Take the free **guided walking tour** of old York. Visit soaring **York Minster.** Lunch in a pub built over a **Roman bath.** Walk through York's **"snickelways"**—narrow, twisting medieval alleys. Optional visits to the **National Railway Museum** and the **York Castle** historical museum. Optional dinner aboard a historic train through the **North York Moors.**

DAY 3: Visit the haunting ruins of **Fountains Abbey,** then drive into the **Yorkshire Dales National Park.** Afternoon walk along the pastoral River Wharfe in **Wharfedale.** Optional scenic climb to the top of **Buckden Pike.**

DAY 4: Morning drive to spectacular **Malhamdale;** walk to **Gordale Scar** gorge and the limestone cliffs of **Malham Cove.** Afternoon driving tour across the moors to **Brontë** parsonage and a visit to the riverside ruins of **Bolton Abbey.** Optional circular drive through western and central Dales.

DAY 5: Drive through **Wensleydale** and **Swaledale,** via **Aysgarth Falls** and **Butter Tubs Pass,** into **Lake District National Park.** Orientation stop at the National Park Centre near **Windermere,** then north to the high mountains and secluded **Borrowdale** via **Grasmere** and ancient **Castlerigg Stone Circle.** Optional stop at Wordsworth's home, **Dove Cottage.** Possible afternoon walk in Borrowdale.

DAY 6: Hike deep into the Lake District's most spectacular mountains, with three alternative summits to ascend—**Great**

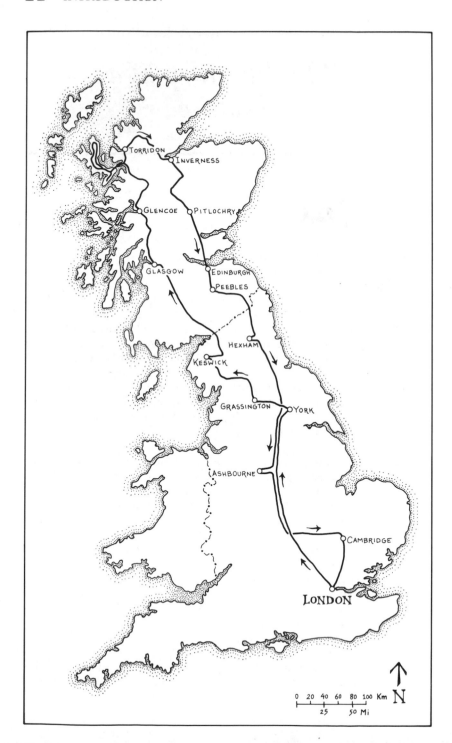

Gable, Scafell, and **Glaramara.** Craggy fells (cliffs), crashing forces (waterfalls), tumbling burns (mountain streams), twinkling tarns (glacial ponds), and sweeping vistas. Easier alternative walks over the fells to **Watendlath, Castle Crag,** and **Langstrath** valley. Afternoon circular drive around remote **Buttermere** and **Crummock Water.**

DAY 7:   Drive north into **Scotland,** along the "bonnie banks" of **Loch Lomond,** and into the **Highland** wilderness of **Glencoe.** Afternoon walk to a **hidden valley** high in the fells. Optional side trips to **Glasgow** and **Inveraray Castle.**

DAY 8:   Three alternate routes through the remotest **Highlands.** Visit **Bonnie Prince Charlie's** haunts, **Iron Age fortresses,** or **Eilean Donan,** the quintessential Scottish castle. Then by **ferry** to Skye, the "Isle of Mists" and ancestral home of the MacDonalds and MacLeods.

DAY 9:   Two alternative walks into Skye's wild **Black Cuillin** mountains. A visit to the **Talisker** whisky distillery. An afternoon **driving tour** of Skye, and an optional walk into the volcanic pinnacles of the **Quiraing.**

DAY 10:   Back to the **mainland** and north over the **Pass of the Cattle** into the world's oldest mountains—the **Torridon** wilderness. Afternoon walk in the Torridon hills.

DAY 11:   Drive across the Highlands to **Inverness.** Visit **Culloden** battlefield, where the Bonnie Prince was finally defeated, then drive south through the **Grampian** mountain range to quaint Victorian **Pitlochry.** Optional side trip to **Loch Ness** and **Castle Urquhart.**

DAY 12:   To **Edinburgh** for a car tour of Georgian **New Town** and a walking tour along medieval **Old Town's "Royal Mile."** Visit the **Palace of Holyroodhouse,** the **castle** on the mount, and everything in between. Afternoon drive into the pastoral valley of the **River Tweed,** and a visit to **Traquair House,** Scotland's oldest continuously occupied fortified mansion. Possible walk along **Southern Upland Way.**

DAY 13:   South across the **Scottish Borders,** with optional stops at **Borders Wool Centre,** Sir Walter Scott's **Abbotsford,** and the serene ruins of the borders **abbeys** at **Melrose, Dry-**

burgh, and **Jedburgh.** Then across the moors to **Northumberland National Park** in England and Roman emperor **Hadrian's Wall.** Orientation at the National Park Centre, then an afternoon walk along the wall, visiting an excavated Roman fortress at **Housesteads** and the civilian settlement at **Vindolanda.**

DAY 14: Drive south either to **York** (for those who came by train) or toward London, stopping either at **Dovedale** in the **Peak District National Park** or **Cambridge.** Alternative afternoon walks through the limestone gorge cut by the River Dove, or around the colleges and grounds of Cambridge University.

DAY 15: A choice of either a tour through the twisting **Thames River Valley** or a day in London.

DAY 16: **Home.**

The eerie fractured landscape of "The Quiraing," Totternish, Isle of Skye

Preparations

Summer in Britain is the "high season"—that is, airfares are high, prices are high, rainfall is higher, and crowds are bigger. To be fair, summer's attractions are powerful: the long, golden English summer evenings are memorable, the landscape is impossibly green, and, on a practical note, everything is open (many stately homes, monuments, and the like are closed or have restricted hours before April and after October).

Still, as you plan your trip, consider late spring and autumn. For one thing, while the weather in Britain is always unpredictable, it is sunniest between April and the end of June, when many of Britain's gardens are also at their peak. The weather is quite stable in autumn as well, and you can wander freely in both spring and autumn and have little difficulty finding a place to stay, even in the most popular areas. So, as with all things in this book, be adventurous in choosing when to go.

RENTING A CAR

To find Britain's most wonderful nooks and crannies, you'll need a car—the trains and buses aren't what they used to be. (For tips on driving on the "wrong side" see Driving in Britain.)

Here's what you need to know about renting ("hiring") a car in Britain.

THE BEST RATES. As a general rule, you'll get a lower weekly rental rate if you arrange for your rental car *before* you leave for Britain. Most major North American car rental companies also operate in Britain, either under the same name as in the U.S. (Hertz, Avis, Budget) or in partnership with a British or European car rental company (National is Europcar-Godfrey Davis, Dollar is InterRent). Simply call their 800 numbers and ask for their unlimited mileage rate schedule for Britain.

In addition to the major international rental companies, many airlines offer discounted car rental rates through companies that represent large British car rental companies. But before you rent from either a British or an international company, be sure they have a large number of branches or affiliates scattered around the country, should you have to exchange the car for some reason. And if you plan to pick your car up at one location and leave it at another, be sure they won't add a hefty "drop charge."

THE RIGHT SIZE. Remember that European cars, even larger ones, may be smaller than you're used to. There will also be British car brands you may not recognize. In general, you will find British cars well made and a lot zippier than you'd expect from their size. As elsewhere, rental cars in Britain come in different size classes, from tiny two-seaters to vans and "estate wagons" (station wagons).

British rental cars typically come with standard, manual-shift transmissions. A small car with an automatic transmission will cost as much as a much larger standard-shift car. However, if you've never driven a standard shift, this is not the time to learn. You won't want another distraction while you're getting used to driving on the left.

INSURANCE. All cars come with coverage from either the British Automobile Association (AA) or the Royal Automobile Club (RAC). But this is just for on-the-road mechanical breakdowns. As elsewhere, car rental companies will want you to buy additional insurance protection against collision, physical injury, and sometimes loss of personal effects. You can avoid the collision damage waiver (CDW) if your own insurance company will cover international car rentals *or* if you rent the car with either an American Express Card or a MasterCard or VISA "Gold Card" (check the fine print; terms vary). If you don't have one of

Driving "on the wrong side" will be second nature in no time at all.

these cards, pay for the extra insurance. Nothing turns a holiday into a disaster faster than a wrecked car for which you are responsible. (**Note:** Unless you use a credit card to rent your car, be prepared to make a sizable deposit before you drive away.)

VAT. You will be charged Britain's 17.5 percent value-added tax (VAT) on the total cost of your car rental. Again, when you get price quotations, be sure to ask if VAT is included. Unlike the gifts you buy to take home with you, the VAT on car rental is not refundable.

WHAT TO TAKE WITH YOU

OFFICIAL DOCUMENTS: You'll need a valid passport to enter Britain, but not a visa, so long as you're a citizen of the United States or a Commonwealth nation. Others should check with the nearest British consulate. You do *not* need an international driving license to drive in Britain, just a valid license from home. If you plan to stay in youth hostels, join the International Youth Hostel Federation, either through the American Youth Hostel Association (P.O. Box 37613, Washington, DC 20013) or through the IYHF itself (Midland Bank Chambers, Howardsgate, Welwyn Garden City, Herts., England). If you have new camera equipment, get customs to give you a receipt for it on your outbound trip to avoid paying duty on it when you return.

MONEY: For maximum safety and greatest ease, carry traveler's checks *in pounds*. You cannot cash traveler's checks in dollars except in banks, leaving you at the mercy of your memory and the sometimes fickle hours of rural bank branches. With traveler's checks in pounds, you can pay for meals, purchases, and hotels (but generally not bed-and-breakfasts) simply by endorsing a check.

Credit cards are accepted in shops throughout Britain, even in quite remote areas. They also come in handy if you find yourself suddenly in need of a cash advance.

How *much* money you take depends, of course, on the style of travel you choose. At this writing, with an exchange rate of £1 to $1.60 (U.S.), a high-season Advance Purchase Excursion (APEX) coach round-trip ticket to London from the East Coast costs $500 to $600; rental of a small car for two weeks, including VAT and gas ("petrol"), is about $450; B&Bs run between $20 and $30 per person per night (higher in cities, higher for classy "country house" B&Bs); dinner for two at a good pub runs about $30 with drinks; dinner for two in a really fine restaurant, with wine, ranges between $50 and $75. Take enough money to cover estimated costs, then add a cushion for the occasional splurge.

CLOTHES. Our rule for packing for Britain is *take one of everything*— one bikini, one down-filled vest, and so forth. Seriously, remember that Britain's weather is fickle. You may spend the entire time in shorts and a T-shirt and come home with a tan, or you may spend the entire time in a turtleneck, wool slacks, and rainwear and come home with mold. The chances are about even. For the days you spend car touring and visiting historic sites, dress comfortably and have a light sweater and rain jacket handy. For evenings, remember that the British are a bit more formal at dinner—men should avoid jeans and pack a jacket and tie and women should pack a skirt. The overall guidance is to keep the bulk down. If you find you need a really heavy sweater, buy it there; after all, who makes better, cheaper wool sweaters than the British?

WALKING GEAR. As a general rule, for spring and summer trips pack loose, comfortable clothes—midweight cotton or lightweight wool slacks (not jeans, which are heavy and chafe when wet), T-shirt, cotton turtleneck, flannel overshirt, lightweight sweater, wool or cotton-wool blend socks, and polypropylene sock liners. Plan on somewhat warmer clothes in autumn.

Above all, even if you don't do a lot of hiking at home (we don't either), invest in first-class rain gear—a jacket (and slacks if possible) made of breathable waterproof fabric, and walking shoes (boots are not really necessary unless you have them) that are lined with breathable waterproof fabric. You can get away with cheaper materials and with walking shoes that aren't waterproof, but unless you live a particularly charmed life it *will* rain and the difference between disappointment and outright discomfort will be determined by whether you invested in real waterproofs.

A few other items, packed in the kind of small knapsack students use to carry books, will make your walks more pleasant: a small Swiss Army knife with a sharp blade (for cutting bread and cheese), corkscrew (for the occasional bottle of wine), and can opener (for canned paté, when fresh is unavailable); a small tablecloth; and collapsible cup(s). In addition, take small adhesive bandages and moleskin for blisters and, if you plan to take some of the more ambitious hikes, a small flashlight, a compass, and an emergency whistle. (More detailed suggestions are included in each day's itinerary.)

BOOKING ACCOMMODATIONS IN ADVANCE

Even in high season, you need not make advance reservations for most of the stops on this itinerary. There are, however, a few exceptions. Knowing where you're going to stay in York will make your first few days, when jet lag makes you cranky anyway, a bit more comfortable. A reserved room in Edinburgh is useful any time of year, but is virtually mandatory during the International Festival in August. And of course, a prearranged reservation in London will mean you'll have that much more time to sightsee. For the rest of the itinerary—and even for York, Edinburgh, and London, if you wish—be adventurous. Explore and find your own favorite places to stay; if you follow the guidance in the Creature Comforts section of each day's chapter you can't go wrong.

OTHER BOOKS TO READ

The whole point of this guidebook, of course, is to put virtually everything you'll need or want to know between two covers. For more detail, however, see Further Reading in the back of the book.

COPING WITH JET LAG

No matter who you are, where you come from, or how you modify your diet, you *will* be affected by jet lag during your first few days in Britain. You can minimize the effect by taking a daytime flight that gets you into Britain in the afternoon instead of the morning, but there are relatively few such flights available. There are over-the-counter "anti–jet lag formulas" that purport to help, but no independent information is available on them.

The only tried and true way to limit how long you are affected by jet lag is to "tough it out" the first day. If you arrive in the morning, *do not under any circumstances* retire to your hotel room in the afternoon for "a nice little lie-down." Push through "The Wall" by staying active until dinnertime, eat a reasonable meal, and go to bed, perhaps a little earlier than usual. The next day, you'll find that the worst is already over.

OLD TREES ARE
LIABLE TO SHED
BRANCHES AND
THE PUBLIC ARE
ADVISED NOT TO
SIT UNDER THEM

Understanding Britain

THE PEOPLE

The British have an international reputation for being cold and aloof. Nothing could be more unfair or undeserved. What the British are is polite. Bump into an Englishman on the street and he will invariably say "sorry," as if it were his fault. The British maintain a certain dignified initial reserve. But don't take it at face value. Remember, this is the nation that produces more eccentrics per capita than any other, the nation that produced the Monty Python troupe and scores of other outrageously silly comedians.

Getting to know the British, then, requires a strategy. Begin by being unfailingly polite. Address the people you meet formally, until you get a signal that something more familiar is appropriate. Get used to saying "sorry" and "thank you" whether it's appropriate or not. Meet them on their own ground, the pub—Britain's public living rooms. A discreet question, perhaps about the best local beer, will very likely put you on the road to an evening of warm, often hilarious, and occasionally lasting friendship.

THE LANGUAGE

George Bernard Shaw once described Britain and America as "two nations separated by a common language." Certainly some British regional dialects can be impenetrable (those of Yorkshire and the Scottish Highlands in particular). But for the most part, you'll find that British English is a bit more musical than North American English, with inflection and emphasis coming in different places. Pronunciation often differs as well (*schedule* is "shed-ewe-el"). Also, never assume any British placename is pronounced as spelled; centuries of colloquialization render many of them unrecognizable (Hawick is "hoik," for example). And sometimes common words have uncommon meanings: "cookie" is old British slang for a "lady of the night," for example. Say "biscuit" instead.

A Practical Guide to British English

BRITISH	U.S. EQUIVALENT
At Hotels/B&Bs:	
twin	= two single beds
double	= one double bed
bathroom	= little room with a bathtub in it
loo, toilet, w.c. (water closet)	= bathroom
flannel	= washcloth
torch	= flashlight
fortnight	= two weeks
porridge	= hot oatmeal
fully cooked breakfast	= fried egg, bacon, sausage, etc.
At Restaurants:	
cream tea	= tea with scones, jam, clotted cream
clotted cream	= a bit like whipped cream
jam	= jelly, preserves
jelly	= Jell-O
chips	= french fries
crisps	= chips (potato)
sweet, pudding	= any dessert
bill	= check

BRITISH	U.S. EQUIVALENT
Shopping:	
chemist	= drugstore
plaster	= bandage
jumper	= sweater
pinafore	= jumper (dress)
tights	= pantyhose
braces	= suspenders
suspenders	= garters
waistcoat	= vest
vest	= undershirt
pants	= underpants
trousers	= pants
plimsolls	= sneakers
trainers	= running shoes
first floor	= second floor
ground floor	= first floor
off-licence	= retail liquor store
Transportation:	
queue ("cue")	= line
return	= round-trip ticket
single	= one-way ticket
Underground	= subway
subway	= underground walkway
Miscellaneous:	
football	= soccer
American football	= football
redundant	= laid off, idled
cheers	= thanks/good-bye
"a nice cuppa"	= tea, solution to all ills

DRIVING IN BRITAIN

Otherwise confident adults are often reduced to quivering masses of Jell-O (jelly) at the prospect of driving on the "wrong side of the road." Relax. You'll spend more time giggling about British road signs (What could HEAVY PLANT CROSSING mean?) than trembling over driving on the "wrong side." Ask for a complete run-through of your car's features before you leave, and be sure there's a manual in the glove compartment and a good spare tire (tyre) and jack. Spend a few moments tooling

A typical major thoroughfare in rural Britain

around the parking lot for familiarity, then set off . . . carefully. You'll be surprised at how quickly driving on the "wrong side" becomes second nature.

BRITISH DRIVERS AND DRIVING ETIQUETTE. British drivers, like the British character, range from the punctiliously correct to the Monty Python loony. They are aggressive, drive a good deal faster than the speed limit (except in towns), and will pass (overtake) on blind curves. On the other hand, they will always come to a full stop as lights turn red, stop at pedestrian crossings (marked by white stripes on the road), and yield the right of way when approaching traffic circles (roundabouts) to cars already in the circle.

Because you are *expected* to follow these rules, chaos (or worse) erupts if you don't. In keeping with British reserve, horns are almost never used; you blink your lights to signal that you want to pass. On the one-lane roads that lace the countryside, passing areas are placed at regular intervals. When you encounter someone coming toward you, whoever is closest to a passing area reverses back to it and blinks his lights to signal that the other driver should come ahead. You pull into the passing area if it's on your side or wait opposite it if it's on the other. When driving well-lit urban streets at night, the British keep their headlights "dipped" (that is, drive with parking lights only); do the same unless you feel uncomfortable doing so. Note: Seat belts are mandatory in the front seat and police regularly use breath analyzers to check for drunk drivers; punishment is swift and stern.

BRITISH ROADS. Well-paved roads have been a tradition in Britain since the Romans built their splendid road system, and macadam paving was invented by a British civil engineer named—what else?—McAdam. In general, there are four classes of roads in Britain: *M, A, B,* and *unclassified*. Limited-access, six-lane, high-speed motorways—"M" roads—are the newest (Hitler first invented the idea). They cut across all the major regions of the country except the Highlands of Scotland, have their own distinctive blue-and-white signs, and are numbered with either single or double digits (e.g., M1, M25, etc.). "A" roads are major "arterials," a word that comes from the recognition by twentieth-century planners that roads were the lifeblood of industrial growth. You can tell how major "A" roads are by whether they have one, two, or three numbers after the A; the more numbers, the less important the road. "B" roads connect smaller villages with nearby market towns and are generally two lanes wide. Unclassified roads, with no letter or number, run through the most rural areas and are often a single lane with passing places. *All* roads, no matter how remote, will be well paved.

Unless otherwise marked, the speed limit on motorways and divided highways (dual carriageways) is 70 m.p.h. (112 km./h.), 60 m.p.h. (96 km./h.) on other open roads, and 30 m.p.h. (48 km./h.) in built-up areas.

GASOLINE. Gasoline (petrol) is expensive (roughly two to three the U.S. price) and sold in imperial gallons. One imperial gallon equals 1.2 U.S. gallons or about 4.5 liters. Octane ratings are 2-star (90 octane), 3-star (94), and 4-star (97). You'll be expected to use either 4-star or premium unleaded, and the car will perform more reliably if you do.

CAR TROUBLE. Get instructions from your rental company about how to handle accidents or mechanical problems. You'll have emergency breakdown coverage from the AA or RAC, each of which maintains special call boxes (yellow for AA, blue for RAC) along motorways and other major roads. If the problem is serious and you are near a rental agency branch, you may be able to exchange the car. In case of an accident, follow the agency's instructions and call them as soon as possible. You should expect your damaged car to be replaced promptly.

A Driver's Glossary

bonnet	= hood	*lay-by*	= pull-over
boot	= trunk		place
car park	= parking area	*lorry*	= truck
cul-de-sac	= dead end	*petrol*	= gasoline
diversion	= detour	*roundabout*	= traffic circle
dual carriage-	= divided high-	*silencer*	= muffler
way	way	*tailback*	= traffic jam
estate car	= station wagon	*windscreen*	= windshield
flyover	= overpass	*zebra*	= crosswalk
give way	= yield		

BRITISH HOTELS AND B&BS

The best British accommodations fall at the two extremes: lavish and expensive country-house hotels and charming and inexpensive bed-and-breakfast establishments in private homes. If cost is no object, by all means go the country house route; you'll be treated like royalty. On the other hand, at a good B&B you'll be treated like family, and that can often be even nicer. B&B prices can range from about £12 per person in the countryside to as much as £20 in major cities, popular tourist spots, and especially luxurious country B&Bs. You can expect a clean, and often quite charming, bedroom, typically with a sink and mirror but generally with bath and toilet down the hall, and a substantial breakfast in the morning (see below).

In between these two extremes are all manner of hotels and guesthouses, which will typically cost much more than a B&B and offer no more—and often less—in the way of comfort, charm, and friendliness. As a general rule, skip hotels and guesthouses in favor of B&Bs.

WHEN AND WHERE TO START LOOKING FOR A ROOM. Except in those cases where you've reserved in advance (see Booking Accommodations in Advance), start looking for a place to stay by 5:00 P.M. (earlier in autumn and winter when daylight is shorter). There are more B&Bs and other accommodations in holiday areas, near famous sights, and in national parks than elsewhere. In towns and cities, B&Bs will mysteriously cluster in one or two neighborhoods. If you're using one of the accommodation guidebooks recommended in this book, phone ahead from a public telephone, even if you're some hours away. Your hosts will be happy to hold your reservation until the time you expect to arrive; but if you're delayed, call to reconfirm. And *never* simply fail to show up.

PICKING A GOOD B&B. In some popular vacation areas, the choice of B&Bs can be bewildering. Always follow this rule: *If the place is well cared for, you'll be well cared for.* It's that simple. If the indicators are good, knock (or ring) and ask if the room you need (single, double, twin, or "family") is available. If there's a vacancy, you'll be asked if you'd like to look at the room. Use this opportunity to "case the joint" (screaming infant? indeterminate musty smell?) and to frame a gracious exit line. Be sure to sit on the bed; there's nothing quaint about an antique mattress.

The British Tourist Authority has established standards for B&Bs and you'll often find oval commendation signs (with little crowns) in the front window. Unfortunately, the number of crowns tells you absolutely nothing about how charming or well decorated or friendly the place is, or how inspired the breakfast is (see below). All it tells you is whether rooms have sinks, TVs, tea and coffee makers, and so forth. So put your trust in the appearance rule instead. There *are* quality differences, and you'll be surprised at the difference a pound or two sometimes makes.

Many of the most scenic B&Bs, and the ones with the nicest hosts, are farms. You get to wander around and see the animals, take long evening walks in the countryside after dinner, and enjoy excellent meals, and you can expect a special solitude not available in town.

THE UBIQUITOUS BREAKFAST. At some point in the dim past, the word went out that the second *B* in B&B would include: juice or cornflakes (but not both), fried egg (two for men, one for women), lean bacon (sometimes grilled, sometimes steamed), a link of sausage (an acquired taste), a piece of bread fried in the drippings, possibly grilled tomato and mushrooms, toast (in little tin cooling racks), marmalade, and tea (coffee, if requested in advance). Massive and sustaining, it is a terrific bargain, if something of a bore after a week or two. The rigidity of the menu has begun to change, more so in the cities than in the country.

DINNER. Especially in the country, many B&Bs offer dinner too. You usually have to let them know in advance (easier if you're staying for two nights), but this option is often an excellent value. Ask about what's planned and make your choice accordingly. You can buy a bottle of wine to accompany dinner at an off-licence (liquor store) or wine merchant.

BRITISH PUBS, BEERS, AND PUB GRUB

> *There is nothing which has yet been contrived by man by which so much happiness is produced, as by a good inn or tavern.*
>
> —Dr. Samuel Johnson

Pub is short for public house, a name that hearkens back to the days, hundreds of years ago, when ale making was a domestic activity and those known to make especially good ale began selling it by the pitcher from a "public room" in their own house. Some of the ale makers grew beyond their own pubs and became brewers, and by the 1800s *tied houses*—pubs owned by the breweries—emerged. Today more than 80 percent of Britain's pubs are owned by breweries; the rest are *free houses* (where the owner, not the beer, is free).

Tied or free, the pub is Britain's common room, a community or neighborhood's gathering place, where folks go to get together, not to get drunk.

Traditionally—and this is still the case in some country pubs—there were two faces to a pub: the "Public Bar," with bare floor and walls and simple furnishings, designed originally to serve workingmen, and the "Saloon" or "Lounge Bar," carpeted, with more comfortable chairs and more luxurious furnishings—lamps, paintings, shiny brasses, and other decorative flourishes—for gentlemen and ladies. It is in the more formal

The timeless charm and welcoming warmth of Britain's pubs disprove instantly the claim British are "aloof."

Lounge Bar that visitors get the warmest welcome. (**Note:** Small children are generally barred from pubs, though you may find an accommodating landlord. In popular holiday areas, many pubs will have a "family room" that does not have its own bar.)

THE MYSTERIES BEHIND THE BAR. Even in a tied house the range of beer taps—not to mention bottled beer—behind the bar can be bewildering. Don't give up in despair and order something that looks like American beer. British ales (technically, they're not "beer") are darker, more varied, less gassy, and have smooth, rich, and distinctive flavors, each one slightly different from the next. As you approach the bar, you'll notice an array of taps, some with long handles, others with little levers. The taps with the long handles are for fresh, unpasteurized, "cask conditioned" traditional ales that are "pulled" up from their cellar casks by the vacuum created when the pump handles are pulled down. The taps with the little levers deliver "keg beer"—mass-produced, pasteurized, artificially carbonated ales that are less distinctive than the "real" ales. By the late 1960s the big breweries had nearly replaced traditional ales with the mass-produced stuff when a consumer rebellion, led by the Campaign For Real Ale, turned the tide. Today the big breweries have brought back their traditional ales and many small breweries (some serving only one pub) are flourishing.

Whether real or keg, British ales fall into several categories: "bitter," the traditional cool, mildly carbonated light brown ale (which is nutty, not bitter, in taste); "best bitter," the brewery's premium product, with a slightly higher alcohol content (and higher price); "strong," which is a bit stronger still and often has a slightly sweet aftertaste; and "mild," a dark, creamy, malty ale that, as its name suggests, has less alcohol than other ales. All are made strictly from malted barley, hops, water, and yeast and, contrary to reputation, are neither warm (they're served at 55 degrees) nor flat (all have varying degrees of natural or artificial carbonation). You'll also find "pale" and "light" ales (generally in bottles), which are slightly more carbonated and less rich in taste; "stout" and "porter," the dark, strong, malty drink favored in Ireland; and European "lagers," the closest thing to American beers (and the least interesting).

Cider—alcoholic and ranging from sweet to quite dry and refreshing—may also be on tap, as are various soft drinks. Many British women favor lagers sweetened with either lemon soda (called a "shandy") or Rose's Lime Juice (both drinks are disgusting).

There are, of course, hard liquors. When ordering Scotch, ask simply for a "whisky" and specify your brand. Ordering a "martini" will get you a glass of Martini-brand vermouth, unless you are more specific. A gin and tonic will come with a slice of lemon, not lime. And all mixed drinks and soft drinks may come without ice unless you ask for it—ice cubes are measured out as if they were a precious commodity.

PUB GRUB. Most pubs have a bar menu—a selection of inexpensive but often excellent meals ranging from sandwiches to traditional steak-and-kidney or shepherd's pies, roasts, game dishes, various sausages and regional specialties, fish, and even more sophisticated dishes. City pubs will have their most lavish meal selection at lunchtime (when they get their biggest crowds), and may serve no food in the evening.

In a few pubs, many inns, and most hotels there will also be a more formal dining room. Except for the ones that have a reputation for fine food, however, hotel dining rooms can be deadly dull and meals expensive and boring. The pub will almost always be a more convivial place, and the food will often be a better value.

THE CURRENCY

British currency is the pound sterling—just think of pounds as fat dollars, worth between $1.50 and $2.00 during the last few years. Bank notes (wonderfully colorful) come in denominations of £5, £10, £20 and £50 (£1 notes are still in use in Scotland). There are 100p (pronounced "pee" and short for *pence*) in a pound. Coins come in denominations of 1p, 2p, 5p, 10p, 20p, 50p, and £1. The 1p and 2p coins are copper, the 5p through 50p coins are silver, and the £1 coin (in England) is thick and a brassy gold color. The 20p and 50p coins are six-sided. Life is not made any easier by the fact that the 20p coin is much smaller than the 10p, and the £1 coin is smaller than either the 10p or 50p coins. You may still come across 1 and 2 shilling coins, equal to 5p and 10p respectively, left over from the days before coinage went to the decimal system.

THE PHONE SYSTEM

A new phone system is almost completely installed throughout Britain. You are likely to encounter two kinds of public phones: those that take 5p, 10p, and 50p coins, and those that take only Phone Cards (which you can buy at most post offices for anywhere between £2 and £20). In coin-operated public phones (the most common), you put money in first and then dial. When you get through, a digital readout tells you how much money you're using up as you talk (creating remarkable levels of anxiety). When you get to zero you either add more money or hang up. If you haven't used up all your money and you have another call to make, don't hang up; just press the "Redial" button and dial the next number. The subtraction process resumes when your next call is answered.

Most British phone numbers today include both the local number (anything from three to seven digits) and the dialing code within Britain, usually printed in parenthesis. If all you have is a town name and number (e.g., Anytowne 123), dial the operator (100) and ask for help (no coin is required). If you need a number anywhere in Britain, dial Directory Enquiries (also a free call); the number is 192 outside London, and 142 in London. The international operator is 152 and U.S. Directory Enquiries is 155. Emergency (police, fire, ambulance) is 999—a free call, and one that can usually be made even from nonworking phones. (**Note:** Some public phones cannot receive incoming calls, but there's no way of knowing which ones.)

THE WEATHER

It's very simple, really: Wherever you go, it will always have been sunny *last* week.

WALKING IN BRITAIN

There may be no nation on earth that offers as much scenic variety for walkers as Britain, and there is certainly no nation that guards its footpaths more jealously. There are more than 120,000 miles (193,000 kilometers) of protected rights of way in England and Wales alone, and uncounted more in the open moors and uplands of Scotland. The truth is you cannot really appreciate the glory of the British countryside—the heady fragrance of a Yorkshire meadow, the crisp clarity of the Lake District air, the soft sea mists on Skye, the unearthly quiet of the ancient Torridon hills—from your rented car. You have to take it at walking speed.

The walks in this guidebook include three national parks and a variety of national scenic areas and wildlands owned by the National Trust, the Nature Conservancy, and the Forestry Commission, among others. Walks described as **easy** involve generally level or gently undulating ground, often on well-maintained and popular paths. The **moderate** walks involve some steady climbs or generally easy terrain with occasional steep slopes, again on very well marked paths. The only **difficult** walks included are summit climbs in the Lake District; they will tend to be steep and occasionally involve scrambles through scree. Except for these summit climbs, all the walks included in this itinerary can be made by reasonably fit folks, including retirees. They are stunningly beautiful, full of variety, and occasionally breathtaking—in more ways than one. So take your time; you're on holiday, after all.

MAPS AND TRAILS. The maps included in each chapter, and the narrative that accompanies them, are all you really need to take these walks. Nevertheless, additional maps (usually 1:50,000 Ordnance Survey maps available in local stores) and recommended guidebooks are suggested at the beginning of each walk for those who wish more detail. All the routes are well marked, usually with wooden marker posts painted with directional arrows but occasionally by cairns at higher altitudes and in rocky areas.

SAFETY. None of these walks is dangerous, but accidents happen. In all but a handful of cases, you'll seldom be very far from a public phone (dial 999 for police and rescue assistance). In remoter areas, tell the people with whom you are staying what your planned route is (they'll

Carefully maintained footpaths make walking in Britain's countryside a joy for even the most inexperienced visitor.

frequently have good advice), and carry either an emergency whistle or a flashlight. Six blasts on the whistle, or six flashes, is the International Distress Signal (three is the answering response).

WEATHER. Jokes about British weather aside, being wet and cold as well as tired is not only miserable, it's dangerous. A few of these walks involve significant altitude gains and even in midsummer that can mean low temperatures and high winds. Layered clothes and thoroughly waterproof outer garments and walking shoes can make the difference between comfort and hypothermia.

THE COUNTRY CODE. Much of Britain's most scenic countryside, while privately owned, is looked after by the Countryside Commissions of England and Wales and of Scotland. Ultimately, however, *you* are responsible for its upkeep, and most of what you need to know is common sense—like closing gates behind you, not climbing on stone walls, leaving livestock and machinery alone, taking your litter home, and staying on the public footpath (assume the rest of the property is private). In short, follow the official **Country Code.**

The Country Code

◆ Enjoy the countryside and respect its life and work.
◆ Guard against all risk of fire.
◆ Fasten all gates.
◆ Keep dogs under close control.
◆ Keep to public paths across farmland.
◆ Use gates and stiles to cross fences, hedges, and walls.
◆ Leave livestock, crops, and machinery alone.
◆ Take your litter home.
◆ Help to keep all water clean.
◆ Take special care on country roads.
◆ Make no unnecessary noise.

The Itinerary

Traveling through
Time to Medieval York

LONDON ◆ YORK

- ◆ **A guide to coping with London airports**
- ◆ **How to find your rental car or the train to York**
- ◆ **Reading the landscape en route**
- ◆ **A walk along York's medieval city wall**

I was the giant, great and still
that sits upon the pillow-hill,
and sees before him, dale and plain,
the pleasant land of counterpane.
　　　　　　　　—Robert Louis Stevenson
　　　　　　　　A Child's Garden of Verses

The first inkling of the delights ahead comes early in the morning as your jumbo jet noses down into its gradual descent to London. Outside, the high thin clouds part and far below a softly rumpled counterpane of patchwork greens and browns stretches to the horizon. The morning mist lingers in the low spots. Black and white cows are scattered willy-nilly like toys across a quilt. Neat brown villages cluster in the folds and creases of the earth or straggle out along narrow, winding hedge-lined lanes. As the plane descends through 10,000 feet and makes its final approach, you can almost smell the greenness of the damp earth, the sharp scent of coal fires burning in chintz-decorated parlors, and the soothing fragrance of tea in delicate china cups.

The abrupt bump as the wheels touch down, and the chaos as three hundred or so stiff, cranky passengers lurch simultaneously from their seats, bring you abruptly back to the twentieth century. You will travel back through time today, from modern London to medieval York, but the toughest part of the journey lies immediately ahead: navigating the international arrivals area at the airport.

Virtually all travelers to Great Britain arrive at either **Heathrow**

Airport, just west of London, or **Gatwick Airport,** south of the city in suburban Surrey. If you do not plan to spend time in London and want to concentrate just on the sights of Northern England and Scotland, there are a few airlines that fly into **Prestwick Airport,** just west of Glasgow. In that case, just pick up in the middle of this itinerary as it passes Glasgow on the way to the Scottish Highlands.

HOW TO LOCATE YOUR RENTAL CAR OR GET INTO LONDON

There is no fast route through the international arrivals process at either Heathrow or Gatwick, so be patient and follow the signs to baggage and customs. What you do after clearing customs depends upon whether you intend to rent a car at the airport and drive to York, or take the train from London to York and rent a car there. (**Note:** If you plan to spend a few days in London before driving north, consider returning to the airport when the time comes to rent your car; it will simplify returning it the day of your flight home.)

Here are the steps to follow for either locating your rental car or reaching London (or the train to York) from each airport.

HEATHROW. After customs, simply follow the WAY OUT signs through the doors to the arrivals hall. An airport information desk is straight ahead, along with a Bureau de Change where, for a fee, you can cash some of your traveler's checks. If you've chosen to **drive to York,** you'll find several of the major car rental agencies arrayed along the wall. Other companies can be called from a bank of phones ahead near the "Meeting Point." The car rental company will pick you up outside, at a designated area, in a well-marked minivan.

If you choose to **take the train** from London to York (or if you plan to spend a few days in the city before beginning your tour) you have two choices for getting into the city or to Kings Cross Station (from which BritRail trains depart for York): cab or subway. If you have three or four individuals traveling together, a cab isn't a bad deal; they're incredibly roomy, the drivers are unfailingly polite (remember to say "please" when asking to be taken somewhere), and the total fare (nearly £40) will be more than twice the subway fare for everyone in your group—well worth it for the convenience and the above-ground views.

If only one or two people are traveling together and cost is a concern, the subway—called the "Underground" or, more colloquially, the "Tube"—is the best bet. It is a fraction of the cost of a cab and the station is beneath the airport. Moreover, the line that connects Heathrow to London—called the "Picadilly Line" and marked in navy blue on

Tube maps—goes to the Kings Cross train station; the trip takes about an hour (roughly the same as the cab in rush hour) and you won't have to change subway lines along the way. Just push your baggage cart down the ramp marked for the Underground and, in a few minutes, you'll be in the Tube station.

When you reach the Tube station, go to the ticket booth and ask for as many one-way tickets as you need, or buy them from self-service machines if you have the correct change. And don't throw your ticket away; you'll need to give it to an attendant when you reach your destination. (If you plan on staying in London for a few days and expect to be using the Tube a lot, save money by purchasing a tourist pass— several types are available; check restrictions. A one-day pass, for example, will only be marginally more expensive than your one-way ticket into the city.)

GATWICK. Though smaller than Heathrow, Gatwick has a more spacious, less frantic feel. As you leave customs, ahead are a British Tourist Authority information booth, a Bureau de Change, and several major car-rental company desks. Public phones to call rental companies not in the terminal are available in several places in the hall.

If London is your immediate destination, head toward the far right-hand corner of the terminal as you come through the customs doors, following signs for the BritRail express train to London's Victoria Station. Gatwick is a long way from London; cab rides take forever and cost a fortune. The BritRail express, on the other hand, is fast (less than a half-hour), leaves every 15 minutes, and is a bargain at £8 as of this writing. When you get to Victoria Station, take a few minutes to visit the British Tourist Authority office and bookstore in the station. It's a great place for specialty guidebooks on Britain and information about London. Buy the official London map for 50p if you plan to be in London anytime during your trip; it's far superior to the free ones. Also, if you haven't booked London accommodations ahead of time, the tourist authority runs an exceptional booking service for a very modest fee.

If you're heading directly for York via Kings Cross Station, a different train (*not* the Victoria-Gatwick Express) will take you there from Gatwick. Ask at the BritRail ticket counter.

KINGS CROSS STATION. All trains to York depart from Kings Cross Station on London's north side. A vast glass-and-iron station, Kings Cross seems straight out of a World War I spy story. The only thing missing is the clouds of steam.

Trains depart for York nearly every half-hour on weekdays and almost as frequently on weekends. Most transatlantic flights land between 6:00 A.M. and 9:00 A.M. Allowing generously for customs

York's best-known landmarks—its soaring Minster and its medieval city walls.

delays and transportation to London, you should be able to make any train from midmorning on. The standard return (round-trip) fare at this writing is £57, but if you travel after 9:30 A.M. and not between 4:30 P.M. and 6:30 P.M.—which is, after all, when you are *likely* to be traveling—the discounted "Saver" return fare every day but Friday is only £32. Buy a return ticket, not a single (one-way), if you'll return to London from York at the end of your trip; the ticket is good for a month (three months for standard fares) and the combined fare is much lower than if you purchased one-way tickets each way. Also, don't bother with first class tickets; the difference isn't worth the expense. The trip normally takes just under three hours, but two-hour express trains depart at 10:30 A.M., 12:00 noon, and every hour on the hour thereafter until 5:00 P.M., Monday through Friday, and somewhat less regularly Saturday and Sunday.

🚗 EN ROUTE FROM LONDON TO YORK

Distance: About 210 miles/338 kilometers (from Heathrow); 250 miles/402 kilometers (from Gatwick)
Roads: Motorways (freeways) all but the last few miles
Driving Time: About 4–5 hours, depending upon airport
Map: Michelin Map #404 and #402
By Train: 2–3 hours from Kings Cross Station, London

GETTING OUT OF THE LONDON AREA. London sits, vast and sprawling, in a huge shallow bowl, surrounded by a rim of chalk hills. Only a few million years ago, the London metropolitan area was a broad saltwater bay. What few hills there are in the city and its suburbs were once gravel sand bars. Slowly the land lifted and the water retreated. Marshy, choked with vegetation, and no doubt foggy even then, the area would have been the last place prehistoric Britons would have chosen for speculative real estate development. Too bad, really; they would have made a killing when the boom came.

Like most major cities, London is encircled by a highway—the **M25** motorway. It runs around the outer suburbs of the city, just inside the chalk hills that form the rim of the bowl. Whether you landed at Gatwick or Heathrow, **your immediate objective is to get on the M25 heading north (clockwise) in the direction of the M1,** the principal motorway leading north to the industrial cities of England's Midlands.

From **Gatwick,** ask the car rental agency for directions or simply follow the well-marked blue-and-white motorway signs to the **M23.** Head north through a gap in the chalk hills and down into the London basin for about 12 miles and then turn onto the **M25,** curving first west (clockwise around London) and then around to the north. Ignore exits for the motorways to the West and Northwest—the M3, M4, and M40—and continue around until you reach the exit for the **M1** near Watford. Follow signs for **The North** and you're on your way.

From **Heathrow** the drill is less involved. Ask for directions, or simply follow signs, to the **M4** (just outside the airport) heading west, away from London. After just a few miles, follow signs for the **M25 north,** traveling clockwise around London and, in roughly 20 miles, turn onto the **M1,** heading north.

For the first few miles, the M1, England's first motorway, parallels the A1, England's first long-distance highway. Both the M1 and A1

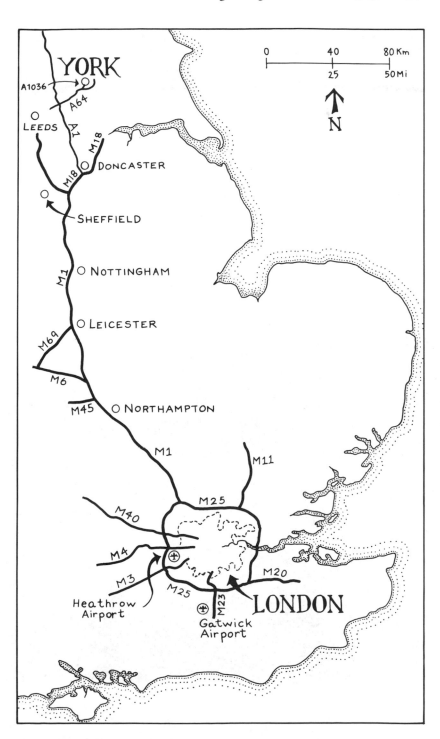

(and the rail lines as well) climb up out of the bowl of London through gaps in the bowl's northern rim that have been used for centuries as access routes to the north. In fact, as you approach **Exit 8** on the M1, you are following closely the route the Romans took when they built Watling Street, 2,000 years ago, to link Londinium to their northern settlements and forts. (Years later, Watling Street became the unofficial border between the Norse and Saxon tribes.) Running perpendicular to these routes, near **Exit 10,** is an even older highway—the Icknield Way—part of a prehistoric trade route that once ran along the tops of the chalk ridges all the way from Norfolk, near the east coast, to the late Stone Age religious centers at Avebury and Stonehenge in Wiltshire.

Routes like the Icknield Way, and the Ridge Way to which it is connected south of the Thames, explain where the word *highway* came from in the first place. In prehistoric times, routes for the movement of

Medieval field patterns, like these long ridges and furrows, can be seen right along the edge of the M1 motorway in Leicestershire.

people, and of traded goods such as flint and salt, avoided marshy lowlands and kept to the more thinly forested, and generally drier, higher elevations—thus "high ways."

One of the great joys of travel in Britain is the extraordinary variety of landscapes and village types that exists within very short distances. In the space of a few hours you can experience places so different in look and feel that you have the sensation of having visited several foreign countries in a single day. There are social and historical reasons for some of these differences, of course, but the principal reason is geologic. There are few places on earth more geologically varied than Britain. Torn by cataclysmic events, worn by millions of years of erosion and the repeated advance and retreat of glaciers, submerged beneath ancient seas and then heaved upwards by colliding continents, the Britain of today is a portrait of the history of the earth. But it's an abstract portrait, understandable only if you know how to read the clues.

On the M1, near the **Watford Gap** service area beyond **Exit 16,** is one of these clues. Look at your map for a moment and you'll notice that the M1, the A5 (built upon the Roman Watling Street), and the rail line to Coventry and Birmingham all come within a few hundred yards of each other as they squeeze through a gap in the ridge you have been approaching. Even the Grand Union Canal (the "motorway" of the Industrial Revolution) must fit in here, though it tunnels through the ridge part of the way.

The ridge is the reason the farms and villages along the motorway have changed suddenly from brick to golden-gray stone. It is part of a long arm of rock—sandstone here and limestone further to the southwest—formed at the bottom of a vast prehistoric sea by the buildup of the skeletons of marine life (in the case of the limestone) and by wind- and waterborne sediments (in the case of the sandstone). At some point, during a more violent period, the sea bottom was thrust above the surface, creating the long low ridge dead ahead—a convenient source of the building stone from which the some of the prettiest English villages are built.

The M1 now dips down into the broad **Midlands plain,** England's industrial heartland. But even though industry is not far off, it is remarkable how pastoral the scenery is. Farming persists here, as it has for centuries. In fact, particularly in Leicestershire, there are fields along the motorway that look oddly like green corduroy, or an undulating sea. The long ridges and furrows were created by the plowing patterns of medieval farmers.

Roughly 20 miles (32 kilometers) north of **Leicester,** above **Exit 22,** the M1 climbs up to the crest of another ancient relic—**Charnwood Forest.** A dense forest in the Middle Ages famous for hunting, Charnwood today is a sprawling natural area of bracken and occasional clumps of trees all clinging to the tops of a buried 600-million-year-old mountain range. You can see the dark granite and slate peaks—some of the oldest rocks in Britain—poking out of the thin soil like reefs exposed at low tide.

North of Charnwood, the landscape changes again, flattening out as it approaches **Nottingham** and the valley of the River Trent. From here north to Sheffield, you are in the energy center of Britain. Hundreds of feet beneath your wheels as you drive north of **Exit 27,** coal is being mined to fuel electricity generating stations throughout the area.

A little over 30 miles (48 kilometers) further, the motorway splits at **Exit 32.** Instead of following the M1 as it branches west toward Leeds, take the **M18** east toward **Doncaster.** After about 18 miles (29 kilometers), at **Exit 2,** leave the M18 and take the **A1** north, bypassing Doncaster and eventually entering into the broad and pastoral Vale of York, following the same route the Romans once took to get to their northernmost defense, Hadrian's Wall. A few miles north of **Aberford,** turn east onto the **A64** and, roughly 40 miles (65 kilometers) later, watch for the turnoff for the **A1036** into York.

ORIENTATION IN YORK

As you approach the center of York on the **A1036** (which as you enter the city is called, maddeningly, first **Mount Vale Street,** then **The Mount,** and finally **Blossom Street**), the traffic is directed sharply left onto **Queen Street** (which becomes **Station Road** as it passes the train station) and continues in a clockwise direction around the outside of the massive city wall and moat. The road, and the wall, cross the River Ouse at **Lendal Bridge.** Dead ahead, the massive twin towers of York Minster loom majestically above the slate and terra cotta roofs of the old city. You follow the traffic over the bridge and into **Museum Street,** then turn left onto **St. Leonard's.**

Around the bend, on the right-hand side of the street, is the **York Tourist Information Centre.** Find a place to park nearby and make this your first stop. (If you arrive from another direction, just follow the blue-and-white "i" street signs pointing to "Tourist Information.") Pick up an official city guide with map. You might wish to consider the more comprehensive *AA Town and City Guide* for York, and the delightful and beautifully illustrated *Walk around the Snickelways of York* by Mark W. Jones, also available here. Then take a moment to orient yourself. The area immediately around you—the vicinity of the Minster—will be the focus of your visit to York; everything you'll want to see is no more than a few blocks away. What you need to do is get settled into a hotel or B&B as close as possible to this spot.

Luckily, a major guesthouse/B&B neighborhood is only a couple of blocks away down **Bootham Road** (see map and Creature Comforts).

Bootham Bar, the oldest of the gates through York's ancient city walls

If you have difficulty finding a room for the next two nights, or came by train without an accommodation reservation, the information center will arrange a booking for you for a small fee. Specify that you want someplace near Bootham Road. The center is open during the tourist season Monday through Saturday from 9:00 A.M. to 8:00 P.M. and Sunday from 2:00 P.M. to 5:00 P.M. Out of season, from October to May, hours are Monday through Saturday 9:00 A.M. to 5:00 P.M., and closed Sunday.

Once you get settled, do not—repeat *do not*—give in to jet lag and the urge for a "quick nap." You'll only lengthen the period of adjustment by doing so, get a lousy night's sleep later, and miss a great opportunity.

🚶 Walk the Medieval City Walls

Distance: 2.5 miles/4 kilometers
Difficulty: Easy and mostly flat; some stairs
Attractions: Many great views of the old city
Gear: Comfortable shoes, rain gear
Map: Any city guide

A circumnavigation of the city walls is a wonderful way to stretch your legs and learn the layout of the old city. The walk is mostly flat, only two and a half miles around, and takes an hour or so. Begin at Bootham Bar, the city gate a few steps from the information center, and walk clockwise. By this route you begin with closeup views of the Minster and end with the picture-perfect longer-distance view of the city at **Lendal Bridge,** with the Minster in the background—the view you had when you drove in but were too busy to appreciate. Remember that Phil Stanley, the official Keeper of the City Walls, locks the fifteen gates and doors along the wall each evening at dusk. When "dusk" arrives is apparently strictly up to him.

CREATURE COMFORTS

Daily Bed

Oddly enough, for a city that attracts hordes of visitors, fine hotels and restaurants are relatively few and far between in York. On the other hand, there are an exceptional number of reasonably priced bed and breakfast guesthouses a stone's throw from the Minster, on side streets branching off Bootham Road—the road that comes out of the city wall at Bootham Bar a few steps from the Tourist Information Centre.

You'll find the best selection on **Bootham Terrace** and **Bootham Crescent.** The crescent overlooks a playing field, while the terrace leads down to the river, providing a delightful riverside walk to the heart of town. A handful of accommodations are also available on Marygate Road (first left as you head up Bootham Road), and they have the added feature of overlooking the ancient ruins of St. Mary's Abbey and the lovely Museum Gardens along the river. What's more, the gate in the abbey walls opens early in the morning, offering a garden shortcut to the Minster.

As noted in part 1, be choosy about where you stay. The quality can vary even though the prices typically do not. What looks good from the outside generally will look good on the inside as well. Also, since you'll be spending two nights here, ask if there is a price break for more than one night's stay.

Daily Bread

There are several fine pubs within walking distance, one or two on **Marygate** and a few along **Bootham Road** near Bootham Bar. But for more formal dining, you'll need to wander a bit farther afield. The only street that seems to have a small cluster of really fine restaurants is tiny **Grape Lane.** To get there, walk straight down Bootham Street and through the gate in the city wall. At this point the road changes names to High Petergate. Just beyond the intersection with pretty Stonegate, turn right into a narrow alley—Grape Lane. Two or three excellent restaurants are at the end of the block, including—appropriately enough, given the street name—a wine bar that serves light meals.

Exploring the Ancient Walls and Snickelways of York

◆ **Highlights of a walking tour of the old city**
◆ **A visit to newly restored York Minster**
◆ **A walk through York's medieval "snickelways"**
◆ **Optional visits to three excellent museums**

The history of York is the history of England.
—King George VI

T he compact city of York sits at the confluence of two rivers, the Ouse and the smaller Foss, on a broad gravel mound left behind 20,000 years ago by a retreating glacier. With rivers on two sides and a dense forest on the third, it presented an exceptional strategic position—a point lost on no one, apparently, in the past 2,000 years. Time and again, York has been settled, sacked, and resettled by folks with a keen eye for real estate. The result is an extraordinary historical richness, a palpable sense of the weight of the centuries. It's there in the jumble of architectural styles caught in the embrace of the city's walls, in the maze of narrow passageways, and in the city's oddly foreign vocabulary, in which a street is a "Gate" (from the Scandinavian *gata*), a gate in the city walls is a "Bar," an alley is a "Yard," and a yard is a "Court."

York was probably first settled by **Iron Age** tribes, but its urban history really begins officially in A.D. 71, when the **Roman** military governor of Britain, Quintus Pestilus Cerealis, established a fifty-acre fortress on the site, calling it *Eboracum*. Over some 300 years, it became perhaps the finest Roman settlement in Britain; indeed, Constantine the Great was proclaimed emperor in York in A.D. 306. Archeologists have uncovered portions of the settlement, including a red-clay-tiled section of the original fortification that can be seen at the base of the Multangular Tower in the Museum Gardens, and a massive bathhouse that was discovered (and is on view) in, of all places, the basement of a pub—called, naturally, "The Roman Bath"—on St. Sampson's Square. York Minster itself is built upon the site of the *Principia,* or regimental headquarters, and a section of the original Roman building was discovered 20 years ago during a restoration of the foundations (you can see it in the Minster's Undercroft Museum).

The Romans withdrew in the fourth century A.D., and were suc-

York Minster from narrow Stonegate, the route by which the Minster's builders brought stone from riverside barges

ceeded by the Germanic **Angles** and **Saxons** in the seventh century and then by the Scandinavian **Vikings** in the eighth. The Norse name for the settlement, *Jorvik,* stuck, evolving to become *York.* Finally, in the eleventh century (by which time the Vikings had been almost completely absorbed into British life), the **Normans** invaded from France. The two most characteristic features of York—the city walls (which were encircled by a moat crossed by drawbridges at each bar) and the minster—are actually medieval newcomers. The walls were built by the Normans after a great fire destroyed the city in 1069, and the minster was begun two centuries later, as York's wealth grew with the medieval wool trade. Many of the oldest stone and half-timber buildings that dot the old city date from this period.

Among all its architectural features, it is the narrow, winding streets that give York its old-world flavor. The best window-shopping streets, stone-flagged Stonegate and Petergate, follow the same routes as the Roman *Via Praetoria* and *Via Principalis.* The Viking and Saxon periods are represented in Coppergate (street of coopers) and the Shambles (from *fleshammels,* or meat shelves, on which butchers displayed their products). Linking them all is a maze of narrow medieval alleys, "snickets," and "ginnels"—originally shortcuts to church, markets, and less respectable pleasures—dubbed **snickelways** by writer and local historian Mark Jones, some of which we'll explore later today.

A 2,000-YEAR WALK THROUGH HISTORY

After an early breakfast, hurry over to the **Jorvik Viking Centre** in Coppergate. Be there by 8:45 A.M., 15 minutes before opening. It's not that this is the most important thing to see in York, it's just that at this hour there should be little or no line. (See today's Diversions section for details.) The tour takes an hour, depending on how long you linger in the exhibition area, and you'll be ready to really start the day at 10:15 A.M. with the city's free guided walking tour.

🏃 A Walking Tour of the Best of Old York

Distance: 1–2 miles/1.5–3 kilometers, but allow 2–3 hours
Difficulty: Easy
Gear: Sneakers, comfortable shoes, rain gear or umbrella
Map: Any city guide

The tour begins in the middle of the little plaza **across from the Tourist Information Centre** on St. Leonard's, near Bootham Bar. (**Note:** Tours are also offered at 2:15 P.M., April through October,

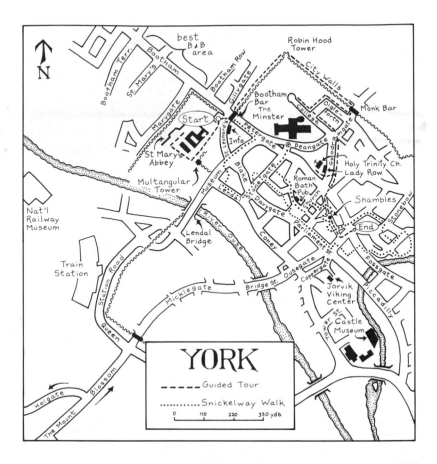

and 7:00 P.M. in July and August.) A tip: if you arrived a few minutes late, head for the Multangular Tower in the **Museum Gardens** (behind the plaza in the direction of the river); that's where the tours go first. Then, after a bit of Roman history, your volunteer guide will backtrack to climb the steps up to the top of the city wall at **Bootham Bar,** the oldest of the city's original four great gates—the others are a mere seven hundred years old, but there has been a gate at Bootham for two millennia! Each of the bars was equipped with vast wooden doors, sharply spiked portcullises, and a barbican—a pair of parallel walls running out perhaps 50 feet from the gate—installed to pen in visitors so it could be determined whether they were friend or foe.

Then the tour passes through the bar and heads northeast along perhaps the prettiest section of the **city walls.** High above the city's chimney pots, the wall slips under the arching branches of sycamore trees, bends around the carefully tended formal gardens of many of the city's grandest houses, and provides splendid views of the Minster and its associated Treasurer's House, Deanery, Grays Court, and Chapter House. The outer edge of the wall-top path is protected by a six-foot-high crenelated fortification, with periodic waist-level openings convenient for pouring boiling oil on would-be attackers. The inner edge had no wall, but today an iron railing has been added in places to keep bemused sightseers from tumbling into picturesque back gardens. Impressive year round, the wall is prettiest in the spring, when the grassy mound upon which it is built is embroidered with daffodils and narcissus.

The tour continues around the wall to Monk Bar, then climbs down a narrow stone staircase into busy Goodramgate. Looking back at Monk Bar you can see a tiny door and platform high above the street from which town criers once delivered proclamations—the news anchormen of their day. Then you turn right into Ogleforth Street (originally "Ugle's Ford" in Viking Danish), past York's oldest brick building, built with bricks that had once been ship's ballast, and then left into Chapter House Street, in the shadow of the great cathedral. It was near here that one Harry Martindale, an apprentice plumber working in the basement of Treasurer's House a few years ago, heard a trumpet and was somewhat surprised to see a phalanx of Roman soldiers march through one wall, across the basement room, and out through the opposite wall, without benefit of doors. When, some time later, he finally mustered the courage to confide his experience to city authorities, an excavation confirmed the existence of a Roman street three feet below the basement floor—thus explaining why Harry could only see the soldiers from the knees up. (He now leads evening "ghost walks.")

After a loop through the Dean's Park at the back of the Minster, the tour curves around to the East Front with its tennis-court-sized stained-glass window. It was here, after Minster officials discovered that the walls were leaning dangerously outward, that the task of shoring up the cathedral led to the discovery of the remains of the Roman headquarters. A Roman pillar discovered in the excavation stands reassembled near the Minster gates.

From here, walk down cobbled College Street, passing the handsome half-timbered St. Williams College, but pausing briefly to peer closely at the right-hand oak door to the inner courtyard to find the carved mouse that is the trademark of one of Yorkshire's most famous woodworkers, Robert "the Mouseman" Thompson.

Reaching Goodramgate at the National Trust Gift Shop (a great place to buy Christmas gifts and support the nonprofit National Trust's preservation work too), you turn right and walk down the shop-lined pedestrian street, past the Angler Arms pub (from which the ghost walks begin), until you draw even with a graceful brick arch and ironwork gate on the opposite side. The gate, built in 1766, frames the distant West Tower of the Minster, but, more importantly, leads to one of York's smallest gems—**Holy Trinity Church.** Although the church was first mentioned in 1082, the current building was begun in 1250 and completed in 1500. It is full of curiosities, including boxed family pews with seats facing in both directions so parents could keep an eye on their youngsters; a "squint" or "hagioscope" (a small angled window cut into the stone wall of the chapel to permit a priest to see what was going on over in the high altar); and another smaller hole in the wall into which unused wine from the service would be poured to flow down to the foundation and "reconsecrate" the church. Holy Trinity no longer holds services, but it is carefully maintained and sits in a quiet grassy park that backs up to **Lady Row**—the oldest timber-framed buildings in York, built in 1316—just to the left as you face the iron gate.

The tour now retreats back out through the gate, turns right onto **Goodramgate** again, and then left across **King's Square** into the picturesque **Shambles**—the street of butchers. If you look closely at the fronts of the street's dizzily leaning buildings, you'll find that several still have their trademark butchers' meat hooks and storefront display shelves.

At the bottom of the Shambles, you turn sharply left into **Whipma-Whop-ma-Gate,** the shortest street in York with the longest name. The tour ends near the corner by a large street map to help you get to wherever you need to get next.

Given the hour, your thoughts will, no doubt, have turned to lunch (shame on you, after that breakfast!). Opportunities abound, but the most interesting would be to turn right into Parliament Street and walk a block or two to **St. Sampson's Square.** Because of its proximity to the marketplace, there were once seven pubs here, but now there are only two. Choose either, but do not fail to visit The Roman Bath public house to see the ruins on display there. Once you are suitably refreshed, it's time for York's centerpiece.

York's Magnificent Minster

Technically, it is "The Cathedral and Metropolitical Church of St. Peter in York." But to the people of Yorkshire—indeed to all of England—it is simply "The Minster" (*mynster* is early Anglo-Saxon for an evangelical mission). A spectacular composite of every Gothic architectural style, York Minster's creamy Tadcaster limestone towers shimmer brilliantly in the sun like some great ship sailing through the choppy

The Minster's magnificent west front, opposite of which our
"Snickelways" sampler begins.

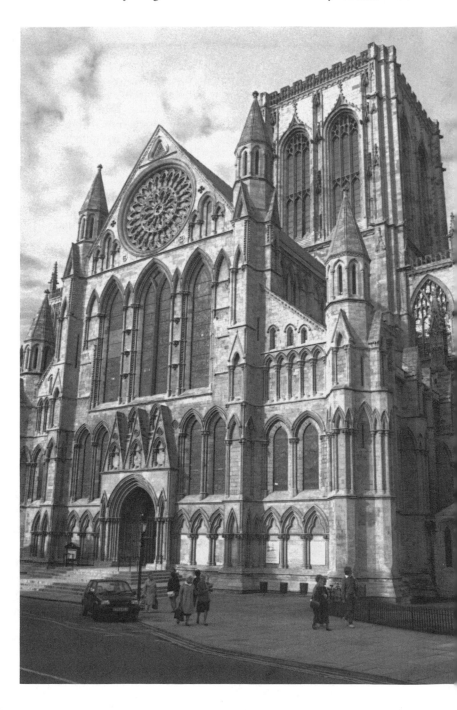

rooftops of the old city. It is Britain's largest medieval cathedral, and only one, Canterbury, is more important to the Church of England.

The first Minster, a primitive wooden affair, was built as part of a bargain struck in A.D. 627 by pagan King Edward of Northumbria with his Christian wife, Ethelburga. After narrowly avoiding an assassination attempt by the king of the West Saxons, Edward set off to conquer his would-be murderers. His wife urged him to pray to her Christian God for victory and he agreed, promising to build a place of worship if he was victorious. Successful in the battle, he converted to Christianity and established the first Minster in what was then the Anglo-Saxon trading center, *Eoforwic*.

The present cathedral (from *cathedra*, throne of the archbishop) is either the fourth or fifth on the site; historians are unsure. It was begun in 1220 and completed in 1472, and is a sumptuous study of the changing styles of the Gothic period. For the proper introduction to York Minster, head for the **Great West Door,** festooned with carvings of the story of Adam and Eve. Inside, the vast nave stretches out ahead of you, the massive pillars supporting the vaulted roof as it marches east to the central transept and on to the choir and the Lady Chapel, some 486 feet away. On sunny days, light and color slant through the dimness like

The open-air market in the heart of medieval York

rays breaking through clouds, and the quiet is startling and awe-inspiring.

Which is almost a pity, actually, because in the fifteenth century the mood would have been very different indeed. To fully appreciate the spirit of the Minster in those days, you must close your eyes and imagine the nave not as a place of hushed reverence, but as a kind of secular bazaar, noisy and noisome with jugglers, circus performers, pickpockets, merchants, and moneychangers all working the crowd. That's why there is an intricately carved stone screen just beyond the intersecting transept; it permitted the clergy to pursue holier pursuits in the Eastern Arm beyond, in relative peace.

Do not fail to take one of the guided tours, or pick up either the "Walk Round York Minster" brochure or the more comprehensive guide *York Minster*, by Lucy Beckett and Angelo Hornak, in the Minster bookstore.

⚡ A Walk Through York's Medieval Snickelways

Distance: 1–3.5 miles/1.5–5.5 kilometers, depending on how curious you are
Difficulty: Easy (unless you get turned around easily)
Gear: Same as above
Map: Mark Jones's superbly illustrated *A Walk around the Snickelways of York* (£2.95 at the Tourist Information Centre and local bookstores)

A visit to York without a sampler of snickelways would sacrifice much of the medieval flavor of the place, the sudden surprise views, the tiny architectural details. Not all snickelways are picturesque; one or two are even a trifle squalid. But taken together they illuminate the essential character of York, something too many tourists miss. And following them is a delightful adventure, a kind of grownup's hide-and-seek.

A complete tour of the snickelways is a twisting, turning 3.5 miles (5.5 kilometers) long, but you can start or stop anywhere. Assuming you're outside the Minster at this point, you might consider beginning at **Minster Gates,** the sixteenth of Jones's snickelways, directly opposite the newly restored South Transept (page 42 of Jones's book). The walk takes you past the many elegant shops of **Stonegate** (so named because it was the route by which stones for the Minster were transported from the banks of the river), then turns left under the leering gaze of a bright red, hand-carved printer's devil, into **Coffee Yard.** Named after a coffee roasting oven once located here, Coffee Yard is, according to

Jones, "the quintessence of the Snickelways"—it is medieval, has a headroom of only 5'10" at one point, has a minimum width of 2'11", is long, and contains three tunnels, a yard, and a ginnel.

From here, the walk wanders back through **St. Sampson's Square;** cuts through **Silver Street** to the Marketplace; then dodges in and out of the **Shambles;** heads down to the River Foss by way of **Whip-ma-Whop-ma-Gate, St. Saviorgate, High Hungate,** and **Black Horse Passage** (passing through a notorious Victorian red-light district); then returns to the center of town and Parliament Street by way of **Straker's Passage, Cheat's Lane,** and **Lady Peckitt's Yard.** From here you have two choices: the long choice swings out to York Castle Tower and the York Castle Museum (see Diversions, below), then along the banks of the River Ouse, finally returning to St. Sampson's Square again. The shorter alternative takes you back down Parliament Street one block to St. Sampson's Square, where you cross to **Hornpot Lane Nether.** From this point, it's only a few more twists and turns (with a powerful potential detour at famous Betty's Bakery and Tearooms on St. Helen's Square) to Bootham Bar and home.

DIVERSIONS
The York Castle Museum

England's largest folk museum, York Castle explores how ordinary people lived from Stuart times until the 1950s. Exhibits include two reconstructed period streets, Victorian and Edwardian, complete with shops, fixtures, costumes, cobbled streets, and vehicles appropriate to the times, among many others. Open Monday through Saturday from 9:30 A.M. to 6:30 P.M. and 10:30 A.M. to 6:30 P.M. Sundays, from April to October; and from 9:30 A.M. to 5:00 P.M. Monday through Saturday and 10:00 A.M. to 5:00 P.M. Sundays from November to March.

The Jorvik Viking Centre

Set below ground amidst the largest and most complete Viking-period dig in Britain, this museum combines archeological accuracy with a Disneyland-like ride back through time—literally. Small electric cars move you backwards through history to a fully restored Viking village (complete with the sights and sounds—and smells—of the marketplace, wharves, streets, and primitive homes of Viking Jorvik). Then they move you forward to the present to the dig itself and a handsome and well-explained exhibition of the artifacts recovered, many in superb condition. Open seven days a week from April 14 through October from 9:00 A.M. to 7:00 P.M., and from 9:00 A.M. to 5:30 P.M. from November through March.

The National Railway Museum

The British love their trains, and the National Railway Museum, opened in 1975 and visited by more than a million people each year, does them up proud. Located on the west bank of the River Ouse, a short walk along Leeman Road from graceful Lendal Bridge, the museum is a lively monument to iron and steel and a superb collection of gleaming, and occasionally steaming, locomotive monsters. Housed appropriately in an old train depot a few hundred yards from York's magnificent Victorian train station, the heart of the museum is two huge engine turntables around each of which some two dozen tracks radiate. On display is everything from rail pioneer George Stephenson's quirky-looking little *Agenoria*, built in 1829, to the ornate and astonishingly vulgar private car Queen Victoria used whenever she commuted between London and Balmoral Castle in northeast Scotland. Open 10:00 A.M. (11:00 A.M. on Sunday) to 6:00 P.M. every day of the year except January 1, Good Friday, and December 24–26.

CREATURE COMFORTS

For lovers of baked goods, the sights of York are rivaled only by the sinful smells wafting from the city's many small bakeries and tearooms. Today, plan a tea break at midafternoon, or at least a quick munch of some of Yorkshire's specialties. There are melt-in-your-mouth **Yorkshire curd tarts,** made of curds, currants, and other things you don't want to know about; **Yorkshire parkins,** a sharply spicy ginger cake; **slab cake,** black currants sandwiched between sweet pastry; and—best of all—**Fat Rascals,** an inspired (and big) bit of bakery crossbreeding that combines the best traits of scones (golden top and lots of currants and raisins) and the sweet crumbliness of shortbread, with bits of orange and lemon rind blended in for good measure. They are available, alas, only at one of Yorkshire's oldest and most famous bakeries—Betty's, on St. Helen's Square, near the bottom of Stonegate.

Here is another tip. If you already have your rental car, and seek a dinner experience that is at once romantic and historic, consider an evening ride through the North York Moors pulled by a smoke- and cinder-belching, whistle-tooting restored steam engine, complete with dinner. The train departs from the headquarters of the nonprofit North Yorkshire Moors Railway in Pickering, only 25 miles (40 kilometers) northeast of York, via the A64 and A169. On one of northern England's long summer evenings, with the setting sun burnishing the moor tops, the excursion and dinner—at roughly £20 per person—could be one of life's great bargain experiences. Reservations are required; write North Yorkshire Moors Railway, Pickering, North Yorkshire YO18 7AJ, or telephone Pickering 72508.

Reservation required

Into the Wild Heart of the Yorkshire Dales

YORK ◆ FOUNTAINS ABBEY
UPPER WHARFEDALE

◆ A visit to a spectacular ruined abbey
◆ A dramatic ride across Yorkshire's wild fells
◆ A driving tour of pastoral Upper Wharfedale
◆ Afternoon walks along the River Wharfe or to the top of Buckden Pike

In all my travels, I've never seen a countryside to equal in beauty the Yorkshire Dales.
—J. B. Priestley

Nowhere in all of Britain does the turbulence of English history lie so gently or so beautifully on the landscape as in the Yorkshire Dales. Romans, Angles, Saxons, Vikings, Normans, and marauding Scots have simply been absorbed into the timeless rhythms of the region's whaleback ridges and deep green valleys.

There are clues to their passing, certainly: crude stone circles and primitive fortifications left on strategic hillsides by the earliest tribes; ruler-straight roads built by the Romans to speed them across the wind-swept moors; clustered stone settlements that signal their Anglo-Saxon origins with names ending in *-worth* (a homestead), *-ham* (a settlement), and *-ton* (an enclosure); and the brooding castles and soaring abbeys left behind by the Normans. But it was the Norse Vikings who captured the stark character of the landscape in the blunt monosyllables that are the voice of the Dales: *crag, fell, scar, beck, gill, mere, rigg,* and *tarn.*

This is a world of rock and water, a place where the bones of England's spine—the rugged Pennines—poke through the surface like the skeletons of ancient dinosaurs, worn by the rain and bleached white by the sun. On the dozen or so summits over 2,000 feet (600 meters), the

Lonely Dales barn high above Kettlewell, Wharfedale

wind whistles through the heather and cotton grass, the mournful cry of the curlew hangs in the air, and the ridges roll on to the horizon like the swells of a great green sea. Far below, on the flanks of the fells, layers of gleaming limestone stacked in deep horizontal beds terrace the hillside.

The dales themselves—broad Wensleydale, sinuous Swaledale, pastoral Wharfedale, secretive Coverdale, bleak Ribblesdale, dramatic Airedale, and a dozen smaller ones—were gouged out of this layered landscape by glaciers that covered the region a million years ago, then refined by the meandering rivers from which each dale takes its name, a process that continues today. The result is a perfectly proportioned blend of round-shouldered hillsides, weathered limestone crags, deep valleys punctuated by widely dispersed farmsteads and closely clustered villages of warm gold-gray limestone, glittering streams tumbling down staircase waterfalls, and elegant stone walls enclosing small green meadows and lonely stone hay barns.

Much of this region, some 700 square miles, is today part of the Yorkshire Dales National Park, established in 1954. But the name is misleading; as with other segments of the British National Park System, it is neither nationally owned nor a "park." Virtually all the land within the park boundaries is privately owned and in use. Instead, the designation acknowledges the importance of the area to the nation and establishes a management system designed to ensure that its unique characteristics are carefully conserved. The system seems to work; the Yorkshire Dales are a delightful and often dramatic harmony of the works of nature and man.

🚗 ACROSS THE VALE OF YORK TO FOUNTAINS ABBEY

Distance: About 35 miles/56 kilometers
Roads: Major roads; minor road last few miles
Driving Time: 1 hour
Map: Michelin Map #402

The morning begins with a visit to one of the finest and most moving ruins in all of Britain—Fountains Abbey. By midday, you'll drive deep into the heart of the Yorkshire Dales to Upper Wharfedale.

Begin by backtracking a bit along the route you took coming into

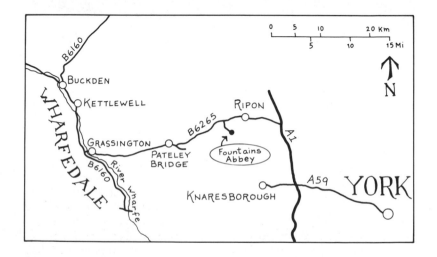

York two days ago. Cross Lendal Bridge heading west, follow **Station Road** around past the York train station, and turn right onto **Blossom Street** and then right again onto **Holgate Road**—the **A59.** After about 15 miles (25 kilometers), turn north onto the **A1** (taking the same route along a limestone ridge as the Roman Dere Street). Shortly thereafter, take the **B6265** west into **Ripon,** a lovely old market town. From the center of Ripon, simply follow well-marked signs for **Fountains Abbey.** The route takes you further west on the **B6265,** then south on a minor road past the entrance to **Studley Royal Gardens,** before dipping down into a leafy swale, passing the abbey entrance, and crossing a narrow bridge over the tumbling River Skell. Parking is on the left and right.

𝕏 A WALK THROUGH MAJESTIC FOUNTAINS ABBEY

Distance: 1–2 miles/2–3 kilometers; allow 1 hour
Difficulty: A leisurely saunter on maintained paths
Gear: Comfortable shoes
Map: None necessary

It was just two days after Christmas in 1132 when thirteen bedraggled Benedictine monks from York arrived at this remote site, a barren piece of land given to them by the archbishop when they seceded from York's Abbey of St. Mary's to protest what they felt had become a

The vast, evocative ruins of Fountains Abbey

dissolute and corrupt life. What they found when they got here was a wilderness "thick set with thorns ... fit rather to be the lair of wild beasts than the home of human beings."

Yet within two years they had begun building what would become the most beautiful abbey in Britain, naming it after a "fountain" or spring on the site. They dedicated it not to the Benedictines, but to the Cistercians—an austere monastic order typically found in remote locations, committed to contemplation and manual labor.

Fountains soon became a major agricultural and wool-producing enterprise that was so successful that it was able to fund an almost continuous building program for the next 300 years. At the height of its

Sheep are a common (and incredibly stupid) road hazard in the Dales.

prosperity, Fountains held sway over 1,000 square miles of land and some 15,000 sheep. By the thirteenth century it was possible to travel west for nearly 30 miles without leaving the abbey's property.

The approach to the abbey could hardly be more theatrical. Initially, the path parallels the beautiful River Skell, rising gently as it passes Fountains Hall (built in 1611 by a wealthy iron producer, it has lovely old oak paneling and a small exhibit). Then it drops down a treelined slope to a long, narrow plain hemmed in by limestone crags and ledges from which gnarled trees grow. In the center of the plain, on a bend in the river, the romantic remnants of the abbey—once the richest in Britain—soar above the landscape. It is a huge, almost fantastic edifice more dramatic as a ruin, perhaps, than in its original form, and reminiscent, in its rugged setting, of the lush, almost exaggerated canvases of many nineteenth-century landscape painters.

The Gothic details of the great Chapel of the Nine Altars are impressive even today, but perhaps the most remarkable thing about Fountains is how much of the entire abbey complex remains visible and comprehensible. The cloisters, chapter house, guesthouse, infirmary, dormitory, warming house (how bleak the winters must have been), refectory, and abbot's house are still in place 450 years after Henry VIII dissolved all of Britain's Roman Catholic monasteries and sold the buildings in a fit of pique over the pope's unsympathetic view of his romantic (and murderous) nature. Soon after, the entire complex became fair game as a quarry for precut building stone.

Fountains Abbey is a National Trust property (like national parks, the National Trust is not government-owned, but is a private nonprofit conservation and historic preservation organization). The abbey is open April through September from 10:00 A.M. to 8:00 P.M., and October through March from 10:00 A.M. to 4:00 P.M. The grounds also encompass Studley Royal, a famous English landscape garden; other walking paths abound.

🚗 OVER THE FELLS TO WHARFEDALE

Distance: About 40 miles/65 kilometers
Roads: Minor 2-lane roads with breathtaking views; *watch for suicidal sheep!*
Driving Time: 1.5 hours
Map: Michelin Map #402

From Fountains, backtrack just a bit to pick up the **B6265** again, turning west in the direction of **Pateley Bridge,** a former linen-making center in lower Nidderdale that was rendered obsolete when coal-fired, steam-powered mills further south forced the dale's water-powered mills out of business.

Coming out of Pateley Bridge, still on the **B6265,** you climb higher and higher to the top of Craven Moor, eventually reaching **Greenhow**—at 1,300 feet (396 meters) above sea level, one of the highest villages in Britain. The rain-lashed moors here are so brutally bleak that it's hard to understand why anyone would willingly settle in this wild,

Along the Dales Way

inhospitable place, especially given that pastoral Fountains and civilized York are only a few dozen miles away. The original attraction was lead ore deposits; today it is **Stump Cross Caverns,** just west of the gritty village, one of many undergound grottoes in the limestone dales.

Beyond Greenhow, the B6265 tips over the edge of the moor and slides diagonally down the fellside through **Hebden** and into **Wharfedale,** perhaps the prettiest, most welcoming of all the dales and a terrific base for exploring the region.

Upper Wharfedale's unofficial capital is the lovely village of **Grassington,** where the B6265 crosses the River Wharfe. Dating back to Anglo-Saxon times, if not earlier, Grassington's name evolved from the ancient word *garth* (an enclosure). It prospered initially because it was on an old monastic route from Malham (over the fells to the west) to Fountains Abbey, was later sustained by lead mining, and today is a bustling small market town. Its narrow, winding streets and tiny cobbled squares abound with shops, good pubs, and restaurants. In addition, Grassington possesses a **National Park Information Centre** (on the left just before the center of town). Stop in and pick up a free copy of *The Visitor* for information on what's happening in the park, and the locations and themes of dozens of guided walks; columns on farming, forestry, and wildlife issues; a diary of local events; hours and admission costs for museums, castles, gardens, and other special attractions; ads for accommodations, restaurants, and bicycle rental centers; and much more. The center also offers exhibits, maps, brochures, and books, and helpful people who can provide a wealth of inside advice.

Before you set off to explore Upper Wharfedale, perhaps after a late pub lunch, there's one bit of business to get out of the way: arranging for someplace to stay for the next two nights. Wharfedale can be a busy place and unless you make arrangements now—either in Grassington itself, or in charming Kettlewell, tiny Starbotton, or Buckden, all just a few miles ahead in the Upper Dale—you stand a good chance of being stranded this evening. See Creature Comforts below for what to do and get settled early.

TWO AFTERNOON WALKS IN UPPER WHARFEDALE

How you spend this afternoon will depend upon what kind of an afternoon it is and how much of it is left after your initial exploration of the dale. If the weather is good—in fact, even if it is misty—dump your things wherever you choose to stay and walk; this is some of the finest (and gentlest) walking country in Britain. If the weather is simply unremittingly dreadful, consider a short driving tour of the surrounding landscape (see Diversions for details).

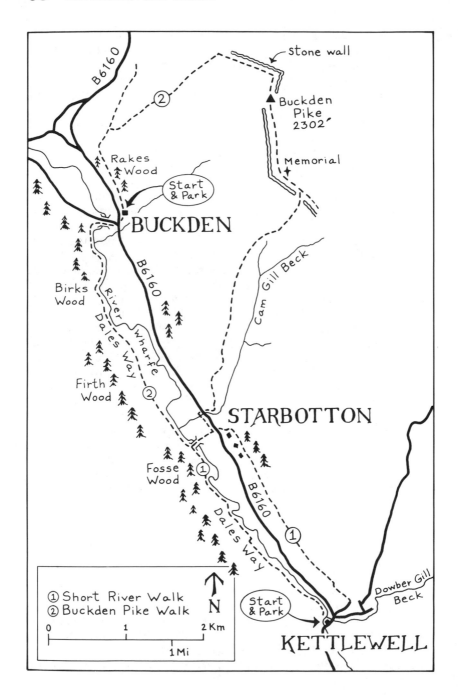

stone wall

B6160

②

Rakes Wood

Start & Park

BUCKDEN

▲ Buckden Pike 2302′

Memorial

B6160

Birks Wood

River Wharfe

Dales Way

Cam Gill Beck

Firth Wood

②

STARBOTTON

Fosse Wood

①

B6160

Dales Way

①

Dowber Gill Beck

Start & Park

KETTLEWELL

① Short River Walk
② Buckden Pike Walk

N

0   1   2 Km

1 Mi

𝕏 A Short Walk along the Banks of the River Wharfe

Distance: 4–5 miles/6.5–8 kilometers; allow 2.5 hours
Difficulty: Easy, level walk on well-marked path
Gear: Comfortable walking shoes/boots; sneakers
Maps: Ordnance Survey 1:25,000 Outdoor Leisure Map, Malham and Upper Wharfedale, or "Wayfarer Walks in Upper Wharfedale," Stile Publications, Otley, West Yorkshire

If you are running out of afternoon, at least take a short riverside walk before dinner to admire what many commentators have called the prettiest river valley in England. Because the Dales Way long-distance path parallels the river from Grassington north to Hubberholme and villages are evenly placed along the way, how far you go depends upon when and where you decide to turn back. One of the most scenic options takes in Kettlewell and Starbotton.

Begin by parking in the lot near **Kettlewell's** pretty arched bridge. Then walk into the village, over the smaller bridge crossing Dowber Gill Beck, and into the small pub-framed square. Go **left** around the Bluebell Inn and up a narrow village road, past handsome stone cottages. Where the road turns sharply right, continue **straight ahead,** over a stile, and then turn **left** along a wall.

From this point all the way to Starbotton, the path runs roughly straight ahead at the same elevation, partway up the hillside, staying just high enough to afford splendid views of the great limestone sills as they follow the contour lines along the opposite ridge, and of the river as it twists through bend after bend on its way downstream. Along the way, the path passes through dozens of small stone-walled hay meadows running down to the road and the river. From June onwards, the sweet, lime-rich soils in these meadows support an astonishing display of daisies, buttercups, and mountain pansies that even the Swaledale sheep can't keep ahead of. As you pass from field to field, you can generally expect the company of skylarks and, occasionally, a golden plover, while high on the fellsides above you the peregrine falcon is making a comeback from being nearly eliminated by pesticides a few decades ago.

Eventually, the path edges the downhill side of a **small wood.** On the other side, roughly just above the most southerly houses of **Starbotton,** you cut **left** down into the village near the Fox and Hounds Inn. When you reach the main valley road, turn **left** for a few yards to the end of the village, then **right** into a farm track heading toward the river. Cross the new footbridge and turn immediately **left,** onto the **Dales Way.**

The way parallels the river, which runs silkily over a bed of rounded stones, providing ideal habitat for trout, for which the Wharfe is famous. But except for moments when they flick the surface to grab a snack, they are all but invisible, as are the herons that sometimes lurk in the shadows before launching themselves into a slow-motion drift downstream. Generally more obvious are the frantic antics of the dippers, and the shy kingfisher as it speeds along the surface.

Wherever the river curves east toward the road, the Dales Way stays a straighter course, cutting across sheep and cow meadows and clambering over wall after stone wall through a succession of stiles and gates, until the river bends back again. Along the way, wildflowers proliferate, from the most common magenta cranesbills to the rare, early-June-flowering bird's eye primrose. Finally, all too soon, the Dales Way returns to Kettlewell.

⭐ A Longer Hike up Buckden Pike

Distance: About 6.5 miles/10.5 kilometers; allow 4 + hours
Difficulty: Moderate with some steep sections
Total Elevation Gain: 1,572 feet/479 meters
Gear: Water-resistant boots, rain gear, sweater (summit is often windy)
Maps: As above

If, by the time you've checked into your B&B, it's still only mid-afternoon and there are at least five hours of daylight before dinner, consider the hike to the top of Buckden Pike, which offers magnificent views of the entire southern Dales, as well as some historical points of interest.

Begin at the small national park parking area a few yards north of the Buck Inn (a classic old stone pub) in **Buckden,** the last village in what is formally Upper Wharfedale. A well-marked path—what's left of a Roman road that once ran from Ilkley, in Lower Wharfedale, to a fort in Bainbridge, north in Wensleydale—leads out of the **lower left** corner of the lot and up into Rakes Wood.

After less than a mile, the road breaks through the wood to the top of a limestone ledge—a great place to catch your breath and enjoy sweeping views of Upper Wharfedale and Langstrothdale, with the tiny village of Hubberholme far below. Just above this point, the farm track forks. Ignore the route curving round to the right, and go through the gate straight ahead. Here a signpost points the route uphill to the **right** to Buckden Pike (the path straight ahead goes to the village of Cray). The uphill path first follows the wall, then slants away to the **left** to a gate in the wall on the opposite side of the field.

From here, the route is clear: the path continues its gradual climb diagonally upward, curving gently around to the **right** across the face of the fells below the summit, passing beneath eroded and frost-shattered limestone crags. Slowly, the landscape begins to change; the rough grazing meadows give way to heather, carpeting the ground in magenta in August and September and intermixed in places with yellow tormentil and wild thyme, then yielding to plants that can survive in the wet, acidic peat that blankets the high moorlands, principally reeds and cotton grass.

Once past the crags, high above Cray, the path turns sharply **right** and traverses a series of narrow and often boggy plateaus, before climbing straight up along a stone wall to the summit (2,302 feet/702 meters). Marked by a modest cairn, the summit is less a peak than a long, high ridge. The path, such as it is at this point, follows the outside edge of a long stone wall running due south along the ridge top. The views, however, are magnificent—to the east, across Nidderdale and its reservoirs and beyond into the Vale of York, far away in the haze; to the south, the vast bulk of Great Whernside, capped by massive blocks of gritstone (coarse sandstone); and to the west, the dark, crouching shapes of Pen-y-ghent, Ingleborough, and Whernside.

The walk along the ridge is inevitably a kind of hopscotch as you try to avoid the boggier areas. Eventually, you will come across a memorial to the crew of a plane that crashed here during the last war *and* to the fox whose tracks the sole survivor followed to safety. Just beyond the memorial, there is a clear break in the stone wall. Turn **right** through the gap, and follow the well-worn path west, staying to the right of the valley formed by Cam Beck. After only a few hundred yards, a cairn ap-

Buckden's all-purpose village store is a good place to begin the Buckden Pike walk (and the pub next door is a good place to end it).

pears above another stone wall. Take the path to the right of the cairn and continue downhill along the ridge line that edges Knuckle Bone Pasture until the path drops steeply down into the village of **Starbotton,** just behind a carefully restored seventeenth-century farmhouse that now is an elegant bed and breakfast establishment called "Hilltop."

Once you reach the main road, you have three choices: turn right and walk the two miles back to Buckden along the roadside, return by way of the river and the Dales Way (go to the southern end of Starbotton, turn right and take the path to the footbridge over the river, then turn right again and follow your nose), or, if your feet or legs have had enough, hitchhike or flag down the occasional bus.

DIVERSIONS

🚗 A Short Driving Tour of Upper Wharfedale

Distance: About 10–15 miles/16–24 kilometers, depending upon
    where you choose to stay the next two nights
Roads: Fine 2-lane road along the river
Driving Time: Determined by how much film you have
Map: As above

Coming out of Grassington, take the **B6265** across the arched bridge over the River Wharfe and, a few hundred yards further, turn right at the T-junction onto the **B6160** heading up the dale toward Kettlewell. Up ahead, a massive outcropping of limestone, **Kilnsey Crag,** arches outward 170 feet above the road on the left, the remnants of climbers' ropes dangling forlornly from old pitons. A little further on, the road crosses the river again at yet another graceful stone bridge and enters tranquil **Kettlewell,** named either after a well belonging to Ketel, a local Irish-Norse chieftain, or after a *cetel wella,* Anglian for "a bubbling spring"—no one appears to be sure. Despite occasional peak season crowds, Kettlewell has a comforting, enfolding character. Handsome stone cottages line both of the narrow, leafy banks of Dowber Gill as it plunges down from the flanks of Great Whernside, a vast hulk of a peak looming 2,308 feet (703 meters) above the village.

Continuing up the narrowing dale, the B6160 hugs the east bank of the river, twisting through tightly clustered **Starbotton** and, a mile or two further up the road, **Buckden,** gathered around its small green. Ahead, the dale splits. The right fork follows Cray Gill, eventually dropping down into Wensleydale, near **Aysgarth.** But instead of going right, turn left in the direction of **Hubberholme,** in **Langstrothdale.** Hubberholme possesses a gem of a church filled with pews made by Robert "the Mouseman" Thompson and bearing his signature carved

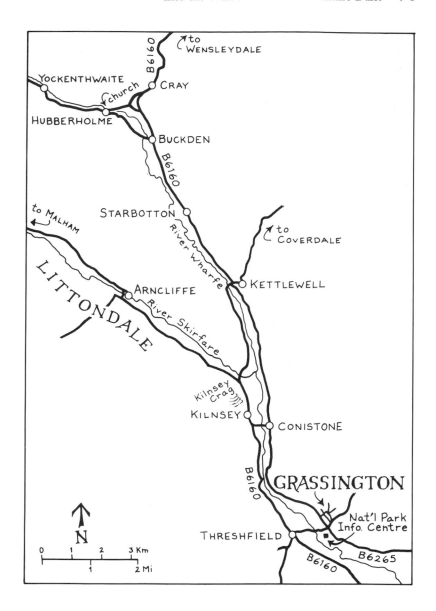

mice. The stained-glass windows record local history. Beyond Hubberholme, near **Yockenthwaite,** there are the remains of a crude stone circle erected during the Bronze Age. When you've finished exploring,
turn and drive back down the dale to wherever you decided to spend
the night.

CREATURE COMFORTS

Daily Bed

In general, because it is the largest town in the dale, Grassington offers more overnight accommodations than other villages. But Conistone, Kettlewell, Starbotton, and Buckden all have B&B accommodations to offer—one or two of exceptional quality—and have the benefit of more peaceful surroundings. So explore the options a bit before making a commitment. This is home, after all, for the next two nights. In addition, there are youth hostels in Linton (across the river from Grassington) and Kettlewell. For information, write YHA (Yorkshire Area), 96 Main Street, Bingley, West Yorkshire, BD16 2JH.

If you run into trouble finding someplace suitable, there are three sources of assistance. First, talk to someone at the **Waymarks Visitor Centre** on the second floor of Pletts Barn, at the upper end of Grassington village above the mountaineering shop. They have a good collection of brochures and business cards for local accommodations posted on their bulletin board, and the folks inside are exceptionally helpful. Second, check the ads in *The Visitor*, the national park newspaper. Third, ask for assistance at the **National Park Information Centre** in Grassington.

Daily Bread

There are three choices here, too. First, there are several freestanding restaurants in Grassington, as well as restaurants in a couple of hotels in the town that are "open to nonresidents"—people not staying in the hotel. Second, as always, there are the pubs, offering good food at fair prices in a convivial atmosphere.

Finally, ask about whether an evening meal is available where you're staying. Good country fare is offered at many B&Bs. What's more, increasingly these days (and in several places in Wharfedale), superb cooks who have fled the city are running delightful small "country house hotels" that are simply a classier form of B&B, often at prices only marginally higher than the run of the mill. Dinner here may run to three or four courses, offer an excellent wine list, and make you want to move in for good.

Of Grikes, Clints, Scars, and Coves: Exploring Malhamdale

WHARFEDALE ◆ ARNCLIFFE ◆ MALHAM COVE
WHARFEDALE VIA BOLTON ABBEY OR THE THREE PEAKS

- ◆ A breathtaking drive through Littondale and over Fountains Fell
- ◆ A half-day walk around the limestone gorges and cliffs of Malhamdale
- ◆ Two scenic alternative routes for returning to Wharfedale
- ◆ An optional drive to the Brontë homestead

I stayed there (not without shuddering) a quarter of an hour and thought my trouble richly rewarded, for the impression will last for life.

—Thomas Gray, poet,
writing about a visit to Malham Cove, October 1769

*P*art of the charm of the Dales is its capacity to surprise. Around every turn in the road, beyond every bend in the footpath, some new astonishment awaits—a thundering waterfall, a looming cliff face, a fast-moving stream that suddenly disappears into the ground, a gaping cave, a stunning patch of wildflowers. The reason for this visual diversity is geologic: here in Wharfedale, and throughout much of the Dales, the dominant feature—responsible both for the scenery and the richness of flowers and other forms of life—is limestone. Formed some 330 million years ago from the shells and skeletons of sea life when much of this area was a shallow ocean, deep beds of limestone alternate with sandstone and gritstone.

Because limestone is hard, the layers are exposed when softer rocks and soils erode away. But because, under the right circumstances, limestone also dissolves in rainwater, tiny irregularities and cracks in the rock can expand to form deeply fissured plateaus, sheer cliffs, plunging gorges, odd dry river valleys, spectacular caves, vanishing rivers, and, over time, sweet, rich soils that support an extraordinary array of wildflowers.

These features exist throughout the Dales (though the limestone tends to be buried deeper the farther north you go), but nowhere are they more dramatically displayed than in Malhamdale.

Strange limestone "pavements" atop spectacular Malham Cove

🚗 UP LITTONDALE AND OVER THE FELLS TO MALHAM

Distance: About 12 miles/19 kilometers from Kilnsey Crag
Roads: Narrow, mountainous, with great scenery
Driving Time: 30–45 breathtaking minutes
Map: Michelin Map #402

This morning, pack a comfortable pair of sneakers or walking shoes, a light lunch, the inevitable rain gear, and roughly three times as much film as you think you could possibly use in one day, and head for **Kilnsey Crag,** south of Kettlewell and north of Grassington on the **B6160.**

About ¾ of a mile (1.2 kilometers) north of the crag, turn onto a **minor road** signposted for **Arncliffe.** As the road wanders deep into Littondale, paralleling the River Skirfare, the valley grows narrower and massive limestone outcroppings beetle overhead. At Arncliffe—a charming cluster of houses, barns, and cottages facing a buttercup- and daisy-strewn green—the road turns **sharply left** towards **Malham,** following Cowslip Beck and zigzagging steeply up the eastern flanks of Darnbrook Fell with a spectacular scree-sloped valley plunging down on the left. As the road reaches the top, there is a beautiful view back into Littondale.

Next, the road traverses high moorland crisscrossed by ancient stone walls, some climbing directly up and over cliff faces, and then begins a gradual descent in the direction of Malham village. Beyond the entrance to the Malham Tarn Field Centre (located in a country home where Charles Kingsley wrote the classic *The Water-Babies*), **bear left,** continuing downhill. **Continue straight on** at the next intersection and descend into the village of Malham. Drive straight through the tiny village center and park at the **National Park Information Centre** lot on the right.

🚶 A WALK THROUGH DRAMATIC MALHAMDALE

Distance: About 7 miles/11 kilometers; allow 5 hours
Difficulty: Easy to moderate, with one short scramble
Total Elevation Gain: About 490 feet/150 meters
Gear: Sneakers or comfortable walking shoes/boots; lunch; rain gear; camera with oodles of film
Maps: Ordnance Survey 1:25,000 Outdoor Leisure Map, Malham and Upper Wharfedale; or "Malhamdale Footpath Map & Guide," Stile Publications, Otley, West Yorkshire

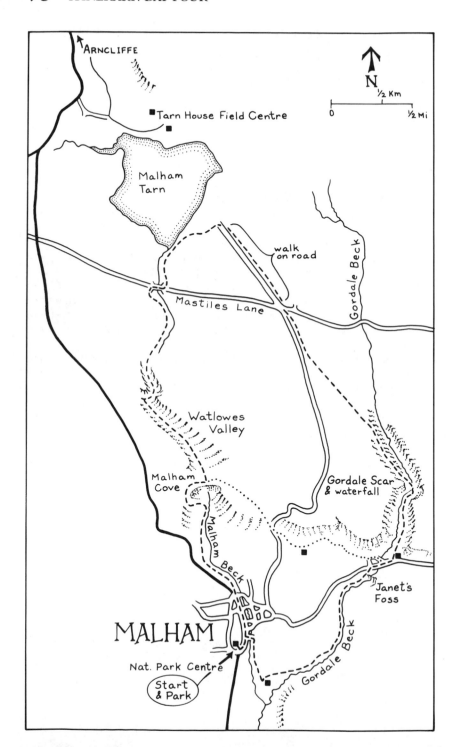

The tiny village of Malham manages to accommodate thousands of tourists, walkers, and climbers each year without compromising either its own quiet dignity or the impact of the scenic treasures that make it one of the most visually stunning places you'll visit during the entire trip.

After visiting the information center, cross the road and, near the Smithy, take the narrow **footbridge** over Malham Beck and **turn right,** following the well-maintained path (in fact, the **Pennine Way,** perhaps Britain's most famous long-distance path) a quarter-mile or so downstream. There, at a classic Yorkshire hay barn, **turn left** and follow Gordale Beck upstream.

JANET'S FOSS. The path crosses several flower-speckled fields, passes two more fine stone barns, then follows the burbling beck around to the left into a quickly narrowing, steep-sided little valley. Foliage overarches the path as it twists around the gnarled roots of sycamore and ash trees and clambers over limestone terraces and under outcroppings. The effect is romantic and slightly fantastic, a bit like walking into an Arthur Rackham illustration of Grimms' fairy tales. A wide variety of moisture-loving wildflowers, including white-flowering ramsons (a type of wild garlic), carpet the banks of the beck and huddle under the ledges.

After rounding another curve and scampering over a low ledge, the path reaches Janet's Foss (from *force,* or waterfall)—said to be the home of Jennet, a water sprite who lives in the shallow cave behind the falls. The falls themselves are modest but lovely, tumbling over a series of ledges. The main attraction here is the tufa apron that curves down from the edge of the main falls into the pool below. Tufa is a relatively rare kind of rock formed when the calcite in the stream water, dissolved from the surrounding limestone hills, precipitates from the spray onto the moss growing from the lip of the falls, gradually petrifying it.

GORDALE SCAR. A few steps above the falls, the path encounters the road from Malham village. **Turn right** for a hundred yards or so until you reach a signpost pointing **left** to the path to Gordale Scar, already visible.

The vast escarpment dead ahead, which runs west (left) to Malham Cove and beyond, is part of the Mid-Craven Fault, one of several massive geologic faults that shattered the thick limestone beds underlying this entire area. The matching half of the cliff face before you actually lies far below your feet.

Oddly enough, however, it is the slow work of water and ice, not violent earth movements, that has had the most to do with creating the fantastic landscapes around Malham. In the last few million years, the climate has changed several times. During cold periods the entire area

A precarious picnic high above Gordale Scar

was frozen solid and glaciers moved across the landscape scouring out valleys and shaving the fell tops. As warmer periods returned—but before the ground defrosted—stupendous amounts of meltwater rushed down from the heights, widening valley bottoms, exposing limestone ledges or "pavements," and creating massive waterfalls.

Gordale Scar, a ragged gash in the face of the escarpment straight ahead, was created some 15,000 years ago, by a raging meltwater torrent that cascaded over the edge of the fault line and gradually cut its way backwards, creating the twisting gorge that remains today. As you enter the gorge, the footpath parallels a much tamer, watercress-filled stream that picks its way through the rubble-strewn valley floor. The further up the valley you go, the narrower it becomes until, eventually, the overhanging cliffs soar, cathedrallike, some 400 feet (120 meters) above, blocking out the sun. You round a final bend and there, deep in shadow, in what could easily be the lair of some fearsome beast, a double waterfall cascades over a huge plug of tufa and the scar appears to dead-end.

Of course, it doesn't. The path to the valley above follows a route **up the left-hand side** of the sloping face of the falls. (Avoid the sharp-edged tufa as much as you can.) This climb is short, quite easy, and the only scramble you'll face all day.

(Should you wish to avoid the short climb, go back down the gorge to the road, turn right, cross a small bridge, and turn right again, following a slanting path signposted for Malham Cove. While you'll miss a good bit of the rest of today's walk, the consolation is that this route passes the remains of an Iron Age settlement dating from perhaps A.D. 300—see map p. 78.)

Above the falls, from which there are spectacular views of the chasm below, the path slants up to the **left** to the western edge of the dry valley of Gordale Beck. A few yards further on, the path finally reaches the top of the limestone plateau and follows a broad, shallow depression carpeted by thick, springy grass and populated, like as not, by sheep oblivious to the magnificent scenery around them. The path, such as it is at this point, travels up this little swale, eventually reaching a paved road.

But detour to the **left** out of the little depression just for a moment to see one of the other wonders of this landscape—the bizarre limestone "pavements" atop the escarpment plateau. Here and elsewhere in the area, the flat limestone bed is exposed to the elements and the result is a deeply and regularly fissured expanse of stone like some giant's patio, made of huge square blocks, called *clints.* The vertical fissures, called *grikes,* were cut by rainwater penetrating cracks in the limestone bed. If you walk along the top awhile, you'll discover that the clints "rock." They are separated from the bed below by horizontal fissures, also cut by water seeping through the planes of the limestone. In between the massive blocks, deep in the shadows, a wide variety of plants thrive—wood anemone, lily of the valley, wood sorrel, and several ferns—out of the reach of even the most determined sheep.

Back on the path in the shallow valley again, continue away from Gordale Scar, **slanting gently right** toward the paved road (which lies behind the long stone wall running left and right ahead) until you reach a **ladder stile** over the wall. Climb the stile, **turn right** (left leads back to Malham Village), and follow the road a few hundred yards to an intersection with another road—Mastiles Lane, the ancient cattle-drove road that once connected Fountains Abbey to Borrowdale in the Lake District. Cross the lane and continue straight ahead, following the gravel track over a rise and down toward Malham Tarn, roughly the halfway point of the walk.

MALHAM TARN. There are precious few lakes of any kind in the Dales for the simple reason that water has long since found underground routes to lower elevations through the honeycombed limestone. Malham Tarn (*tarn* is old Norse for "tear") is one of the rare exceptions. It exists because a layer of slate left behind by the last Ice Age acts as a barrier to keep the tarn, which is fed by springs, from dribbling away underground.

Just before you reach the small wood at the edge of the tarn, take the path leading **left** toward the tarn. After skirting the shoreline, the path turns **left** to follow the outflow stream from the tarn. When you reach Mastiles Lane again, **turn right** across a narrow bridge, then **left** again at the signpost, through the gate, to follow the right bank of the stream south. The stream, known as Malham Water, clatters merrily along through a pretty green meadow, twisting around boulders left behind by retreating glaciers. Then, quite suddenly, it is gone. One minute it is running fast and full, the next it simply disappears into the stony ground—following an invisible route down to a maze of underground channels, eventually to reappear far below Malham Village at a place called Aire Head.

The path continues down the gradually narrowing valley (follow the signpost for "Dry Valley"), then turns sharply **right** at a precipice overlooking Watlowes Valley. Like the valley above Gordale Scar, Watlowes was created by glacial meltwater thousands of years ago, but today is completely dry, its stream having long ago found a lower underground course. The path curves around and down to the scree-strewn valley floor, following an ancient dry stone wall.

MALHAM COVE. At the far end of the valley, the overhanging crags begin to widen and, after a pair of ladder stiles, the landscape opens upon an acres-wide, deeply fissured limestone pavement. The quickly expanding views of the hills and meadows of Malhamdale are the first clue that you have reached Malham Cove. Pick your way across the rocking clints of the pavement and the earth suddenly drops away, revealing the immense curving edge of Malham Cove, an extraordinary limestone cliff rising 240 feet (73 meters) from the lush green valley below. Like Gordale Scar, the cove was created by a combination of glacial action and meltwater working away at the edge of the thick limestone bed exposed by the Mid-Craven Fault. At one point, scientists speculate, there may have been a cataract here twice the size of Niagara Falls. On any good day, expect to see the brightly colored figures of technical climbers far below, picking their way up the smooth green-gray walls of the cove.

When you've had your fill of the view, move across the pavement to the **right** and rejoin the path (the Pennine Way again), which at this point is a series of maintained steps down to the green valley floor. At the bottom, **detour upstream** for a closer look both at the escarpment itself and the stream bubbling up from its foot. This is not the one you watched disappear into the ground near Malham Tarn, but one that en-

The beck that bubbles up from the foot of Malham Cove enters the ground miles away.

tered the ground much further to the northwest at Smelt Mill Sinks. With luck, blue-flowered Jacob's-ladder will be blooming near the cliff edges. Then follow the clear path **downstream,** across ancient grazing meadows, and into Malham village again, perhaps pausing at the pub in the village center before retrieving your car.

THE RETURN TO WHARFEDALE

There are several alternative routes by which to end the day and return to Wharfedale. The shortest is simply to return by the same route you took this morning. With a bit more time, there are two other possibilities.

🚗 Return to Wharfedale via Bolton Abbey

Distance: About 25 miles/40 kilometers (to Grassington)
Roads: Minor roads to start, then major 2- and 4-lane roads
Driving Time: Half-hour to Bolton Abbey
Map: Michelin Map #402

If you have a couple of hours available, one delightful alternative is to head south and take in the beautiful ruins of Bolton Abbey in Lower Wharfedale. From **Malham,** take the minor road south along the banks of the River Aire to **Kirkby Malham.** In the center of this pretty village, turn **left** onto another minor road to Gargrave by way of Airton. Below Airton, the road crosses the river and heads overland to Eshton, eventually passing through the pastoral grounds of Eshton Hall before dead-ending at another minor road. **Turn right** and drop down into Gargrave, cross the Leeds and Liverpool Canal, and turn **left** in the center of town onto the **A65** toward **Skipton.** The road follows the canal for a while, leaving it near Thorlby.

At the roundabout junction with the A59 outside Skipton, follow the **A59 east** (in the direction of **Harrogate**) through several more roundabouts. Five miles (8 kilometers) or so beyond the last roundabout, take the exit for the **B6160** and **Bolton Abbey.** The best parking area is just beyond the priory ruins.

For sheer romanticism, **Bolton Priory,** situated on a gentle bend in the River Wharfe amid meadows and woodlands, has few equals, especially late in the afternoon with the sun slanting through the trees and the uncompleted tower casting shadows across the meadows. An inspiration to Turner, Landseer, and many other painters, the priory is surrounded by parklands crisscrossed with paths and nature trails, including one upriver to **The Strid,** a narrow, rocky gorge, only six feet wide at one point, through which the river thunders, some 30 feet deep, before spreading out placidly above the priory. Despite the dissolution of the monasteries by Henry VIII, the nave of the priory (built in the 1100s) remains in use today as a parish church.

When you've finished exploring Bolton Priory, continue north on the **B6160** following the river through Barden and Burnsall, past pretty Linton to Threshfield and **Grassington.** From here, follow your nose to wherever you stayed last night.

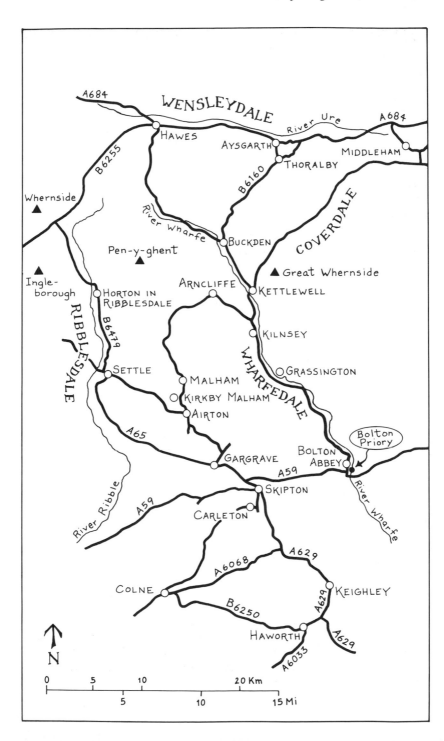

Yorkshire's Barns

One of the most distinctive visual characteristics of the York-shire Dales is the hundreds of handsome stone barns that sit at the edges or corners of the hayfields checkering the valley bottoms and slopes. The barns, or *laithes,* were built mostly in the 1600s to store hay harvested from each meadow and to provide winter pro-tection for four or five cows. They were sited in the fields rather than closer to home so the hay wouldn't have to be carried so far. The walls are two stones thick, tied together with "through stones." Inside, as much as three-quarters of the space was devoted to hay storage, the rest to cattle stalls. High windows were for pitching hay out to the ground below. Most of today's barns are used to store equipment; some have been converted to walkers' huts.

🚗 Return to Wharfedale via the Three Peaks

Distance: About 50 miles/80 kilometers (to Grassington)
Roads: Mostly minor 2-lane mountain roads
Driving Time: 2–3 hours, depending on stops
Map: As above

If you hunger for a wilder landscape and have perhaps three hours before dinner, consider a drive through the wide and lonely moors of upper Ribblesdale, under the gaze of Yorkshire's three most famous peaks—Pen-y-ghent (2,278 feet/694 meters), Ingleborough (2,376 feet/724 meters), and Whernside (2,416 feet/736 meters).

As above, head south out of Malham Village, but **turn right** in the center of **Kirkby Malham** onto a minor but scenic road across Scosthrop Moor and down into the market town of **Settle.** On a clear day, the views to the west and south are incredible: the Lake District is visible straight ahead and the humpbacked mass of Pen-y-ghent peak is off to the right. As you enter Settle, follow signs for the **B6479** and **Horton-in-Ribblesdale,** heading north. The road skirts the handsome little villages of **Langcliff** and **Stainforth,** following the course of the Ribble and the Settle-Carlisle rail line. Beyond Stainforth, the landscape begins to widen and takes on a decidedly industrial cast; from **Helwith Bridge** through **Horton-in-Ribblesdale** limestone and slate quarries, both active and disused, scar the bare fellsides.

As you pass Horton, the summits **Pen-y-ghent** (on the right) and

Ingleborough (far off to the left) rise above the moors like immense breaching whales, long stone walls hanging from their flanks like abandoned harpoon lines. Around them, a vast sea of heather and bracken rises and falls in broad greenish brown swells, turning choppy as you head further up the dale and encounter the lumpy drumlins and moraines left behind by passing glaciers thousands of years ago. There isn't a tree for miles.

At **Ribble Head,** where several small becks join to give birth to the River Ribble, the B6479 dead-ends. Ahead, the third and highest of the Three Peaks, **Whernside,** slopes up to the sky. Turn **right** onto what once was a Roman road (and now is called the **B6255**), heading for **Hawes,** about 10 miles (16 kilometers) ahead in Wensleydale. The road climbs up over Gayle Moor, across a hummocky landscape, then begins a long slide down steep-sided Widdale into Hawes.

Almost immediately after the **B6255** joins the **A684** at the edge of town, turn **right** and climb uphill on a minor road through the hamlet of **Gayle** (indistinguishable from the rest of Hawes). The road runs along the left side of a valley cut by Gayle Beck and then, after passing the last house, climbs even more sharply uphill. As it tops the rise, the road bears **right,** joining the route of the Roman road again, then turns abruptly **left** to cross a stretch of boggy moorland before dropping just as abruptly down into **Langstrothdale** and passing through the tiny settlements of **Oughtershaw, Deepdale,** and **Yokenthwaite.** At **Hubberholme,** the upper reaches of Wharfedale open up again, green and pastoral, and you simply follow the **B6160** south until you reach wherever you chose to stay last night.

DIVERSIONS

🚗 A Brontë Pilgrimage, via Malham and Bolton Abbey

Distance: About 60 miles/97 kilometers; time varies with stops
Roads: Mix of minor and major roads; some city driving
Driving Time: All day, with several long stops
Map: Michelin Map #402

If bad weather rules out the half-day walk to Malhamdale, here is an alternative. Follow the directions to **Malham Village** in "Up Littondale and Over the Fells" (p. 77). Stop at the National Park Information Centre in Malham, grab your umbrella, and take the short walk up to **Malham Cove.** Then return to the car and follow the directions to **Skipton** in "Return to Wharfedale via Bolton Abbey" (p. 84). Skipton, a major wool and cotton cloth-producing center in the last century, has a handsome and still-occupied Norman castle that is worth the visit.

From Skipton's town center, follow signs to **Carleton** and take the road to **Colne** over the summit of **Pinhaw Beacon.** Just outside of Colne, turn **left,** cross the A6088 road to Keighley, and take the **B6250** over the moors to the Brontës' home, **Haworth.** Along the way, you'll pass a twin-pillared gate on the right leading to a cluster of seventeenth-century buildings known as Wycoller Dene. One of the buildings, the ruined Wycoller Hall, is said to be the "Ferndean Manor" of Charlotte Brontë's *Jane Eyre.* Further on, near the village of Stanbury, you pass Ponden Reservoir, with Ponden Hall, "Thrushcross Grange" in *Wuthering Heights,* on the far shore. When you reach Haworth, follow signs to the Tourist Information Centre for information on walks to places featured in many Brontë classics, or go directly to the Brontë Parsonage itself (which has a large car park nearby).

After Haworth, follow signs to the **A629** and **Keighley,** 3 miles to the north. Stay on the A629 to **Steeton,** then turn **right** onto the **A6034** through **Silsden** on the banks of the River Aire. Turn **right** onto the **A65,** go through Addingham village, then turn **left** onto the **B6160** and drive roughly 3 miles (5 kilometers) to **Bolton Abbey,** whose priory ruins, on a bend in the River Wharfe, are among the most romantic in Britain (see "Return to Wharfedale via Bolton Abbey" above for details).

To return to **Upper Wharfedale,** simply head north on the **B6160** until you reach home again.

CREATURE COMFORTS

See last night's listings.

Through Herriot's Yorkshire to Wordsworth's Lake District

WHARFEDALE ◆ WENSLEYDALE ◆ SWALEDALE DENTDALE ◆ THE LAKES

- ◆ **A drive through three very different but very beautiful northern dales**
- ◆ **A spectacular introduction to the heart of the Lake District**
- ◆ **An optional side trip to Wordsworth's Dove Cottage**

I do not know of any tract of country in which, in so narrow a compass, may be found an equal variety in the influences of light and shadow upon the sublime and beautiful features of the landscape.
——William Wordsworth, *Guide to the Lakes*, 1810

*I*n a nation which is a bit short in the lake department, it was probably inevitable that the "sublime and beautiful" northwest corner of England would be called the "Lake District." And yet somehow the name seems ill suited. It's a bit like calling the Rockies the "forest district"—it misses the essence.

Yes, the Lake District has lakes, sixteen major ones and countless smaller ones—some broad and serene, others dark, sinuous, and brooding. But it is the raw, primitive power of the district's mountains that holds the key to the region's soul. So stark and massive are they, so different from the gentle Dales, that it comes as a shock to discover that the highest Lakeland peaks are only just over 3,000 feet (915 meters).

THE MOUNTAINS

Geologically speaking, the Lake District is really three regions. The northern mountains, hulking and round-shouldered from erosion, are the oldest, composed of slates formed from sediments that accumulated at the bottom of a shallow ancient sea some 520 million years ago. Skiddaw, the district's fourth highest peak at 3,054 feet (931 meters), squats humpbacked and brooding in the center of this slate area, just north of Keswick.

A mere 20 million years later, violent eruptions ripped open the earth south of today's Keswick, creating a wide expanse of lava and ash now called the Borrowdale Volcanics. Harder and more resistant to erosion and glaciation than the soft slates of Skiddaw, the jagged fells in this central region—Scafell Pikes, Great Gable, Eagle Crag, and the Langdale peaks—have a wild, primitive feel.

Next, about 400 million years ago, another sea laid down a new layer of sediments that later became the slates of the southern Lake District, near Haweswater. Of the three regions, this one is the most civilized: a softly rumpled, tree-clad landscape spread out at the foot of the central peaks like some vast green picnic blanket.

Then, only 10 to 20 million years ago, the entire area was raised up in a huge dome. Runoff created streams, then rivers, radiating from the center of the dome. Finally, in the last Ice Age, towering glaciers carved out the region's distinctive U-shaped valleys and formed and filled the lakes.

THE LAKES

Three of the smallest of the lakes—Elter Water, Rydal Water, and Grasmere—cluster near the center of the ancient, eroded dome. The thirteen other major lakes radiate around this hub, as Wordsworth himself noted, like the spokes of some great wheel.

Pointing due north, Thirlmere, man-made and almost unnaturally still, mirrors the seasons as the changing colors of bracken, larch, and mixed hardwoods punctuate the deep green of the conifer plantations that cloak its slopes. Clockwise, just to the east, Ullswater threads its way between the fellsides from Patterdale to Pooley Bridge, more like a river than a lake. A little further around, sickle-shaped Haweswater marks the lonely eastern boundary of the Lakes. In the south, Windermere, longest, most famous, and most crowded of the lakes, promenades the 10.5 miles (17 kilometers) from Ambleside to Newby Bridge with the stately, unhurried grace of a Victorian matron, averting her eyes from the boisterous commercialism along the shore. A few miles away, pocket-sized Esthwaite Water is virtually ignored by the throngs visiting the nearby home of children's writer Beatrix Potter. Also in the south, touristy Coniston Water cradles the ghost of Donald Campbell, who died in 1967 trying to break his own world speedboat record and was never found. To the west, deep, dark, barren Wastwater broods in the shadow of mighty Scafell, while Great Gable guards its northern shore. Ennerdale Water marks the remote western edge of the Lake District and, nearby, Buttermere, Crummock Water, and Loweswater are linked like pearls on a string running from the wild and wooly Honister Pass to the pastoral farmlands of the west. Coming back to the north, little-visited Bassenthwaite Lake and broad, popular Derwent Water recline under the protection of massive Skiddaw.

THE LANDSCAPE

The result of all this mountain building and lake forming, and subsequent centuries of wear and tear, is a region of unparalleled natural beauty and physical variety. Gaunt, scree-covered peaks thrust violently up out of the floors of valleys rich with wildflowers in the spring and aglow with color in the fall. On the heights, dark crags loom so gnarled and tortured that it seems the lava cooled only yesterday. Dozens of crystalline high-mountain tarns spawn icy streams that tumble down the fellsides in graceful silver threads to feed the long-fingered lakes.

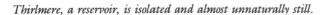

Thirlmere, a reservoir, is isolated and almost unnaturally still.

Ancient stone walls defy gravity as they climb up and over the steep fells, looking for all the world as if they had grown directly from the stony earth. Mossy stone farm buildings hunch together against the elements when it storms, which is often, or bask in the rarer good weather, their dark slate walls soaking up the sun as if to tide them through the hard winters.

Like the Dales, this is sheep-rearing country. But instead of the creamy Swaledales that predominate to the east, a hardier stock grazes the fells of the Lake District—the Herdwick, its rock-gray wool as tough and wiry as its constitution.

High above the fells, buzzards and other, rarer birds of prey—including the occasional golden eagle—patrol the updrafts. The woodlands on the lower flanks of the fells are rich with wildflowers and provide shelter for the tiny roe deer. Dippers skim stream surfaces like tiny daredevil barnstormers, and herons haunt the stream banks, lifting soundlessly from the water and ghosting just out of sight around the next bend.

In the end, the great attraction of the Lake District is the harmony that exists between the natural and the man-made landscapes. It is not wilderness, but it can be very wild indeed. It is well used, but it has been used well. A day's walk or climb can be as challenging as any on earth, but the comforts of a cup of tea and a warm fire are never very far away. Best of all, even on the most crowded bank holiday or summer weekend, a ten-minute walk away from any road presents a breathtaking landscape of absolute solitude. It is, quite simply, a walker's paradise. But first, you'll need to get there—an exceptionally pleasant task. This morning's transition from the Dales to the Lakes is a zigzagging, sometimes breathtaking roller-coaster ride through towns, villages, and countryside made famous by best-selling writer/veterinarian James Herriot. Lovers of his books, and the television series based upon them, will feel right at home.

🚗 THROUGH HERRIOT'S DALES TO LAKELAND

Distance: A little over 100 miles/160 kilometers
Roads: Mostly 2-lanes, single lane on moor tops
Driving Time: About 3 hours (more for stops) to Brockhole
Map: Michelin Map #402

Bid farewell to Wharfedale by heading north on the **B6160** through Buckden, Cray, and Newbiggin. Then turn **left** onto a minor

Footbridge over the River Wharfe at Starbotton

road for **Thoralby,** whose houses were built in the 1600s and are
among the oldest and best preserved in the Dales.

Continue to **Aysgarth,** turn **right** onto the **A684,** and, near the end
of town, turn **left** onto a minor road signposted for **Aysgarth Falls.**
The road pitches steeply downhill into the gorge cut by the river Ure,
past lovely St. Andrew's Church and an old mill (now a museum), before crossing a humpbacked stone bridge with the falls cascading over

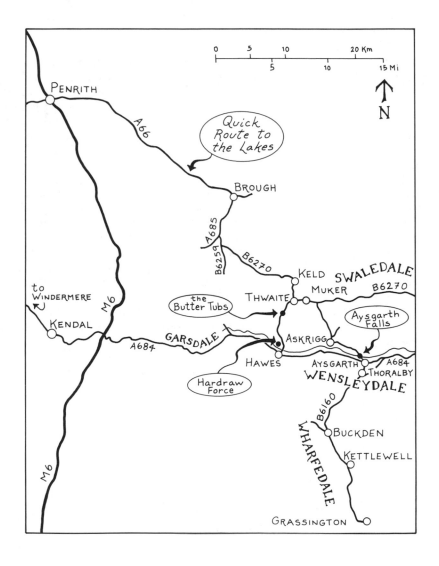

broad limestone ledges both left and right. Near the top of the hill a National Park Information Centre and parking lot are on the left. A short footpath at the back of the lot goes to the upper falls, while another path below the center leads to the more dramatic middle and lower falls (worth the short walk).

After visiting the falls, turn **left** out of the parking lot, then **left** again when you reach the T-junction. From here another minor road runs along the northern side of Wensleydale, into **Askrigg** (site of Herriot's "Skeldale House"). Where the road turns sharply left as it enters the town, you turn **right,** up a steep minor road. This road climbs the side of the valley (stay **left** at the fork), providing magnificent views backward, then abruptly enters the wild, heather-clad expanse of Askrigg Common.

Eventually, the road reaches the edge of the next ridge and there, far below, is Swaledale—narrower and more remote-feeling than Wensleydale. When you reach the main road, the **B6270,** turn **left** and you'll soon reach two of the most charming villages in Yorkshire—**Muker** (with one-lane bridges pinching off each end of town) and **Thwaite**— their hard-edged names echoing Viking origins.

A Shortcut to the Lake District

Those eager to reach tonight's base in the Lake District, and perhaps take in an afternoon walk, can be there in about an hour from this point. Just stay on the B6270 through Keld to Kirkby Stephen, turn right onto the A685 and drive 4 miles (6.5 kilometers) to Brough. Then turn left onto the mostly four-lane A66 for a fast 40-mile (65-kilometer) run through Penrith to Keswick. See the end of this chapter for information on Keswick, directions to Borrowdale, and suggestions on accommodations. Then see Diversions in the next chapter for afternoon walks.

After exploring Thwaite, backtrack a few yards beyond the lower bridge and turn **right** up the steep minor road to **Hawes,** passing the strange limestone holes called "the Butter Tubs" at the summit, then winding across the moors until, just before the road widens again, a sweeping view of upper Wensleydale opens before you. The road plummets downhill and dead-ends at a T-junction. Turn **right** for a few hundred yards and, if you have the time, take in **Hardraw Force,** a 100-foot (30-meter) waterfall that makes a sheer drop from an overhanging semicircle of rock cliff to a dark pool below, a short walk from the road. Access to the falls is through the Green Dragon Inn. Then go back beyond the T-junction and take the first **right** into Hawes.

From Hawes, take the **A684** west through narrow, steep-sided **Garsdale** to **Kendal,** a distance of about 20 miles. From Kendal's town center, follow signs for the **A5284** and the **A591** heading for **Windermere.**

🚗 AN INTRODUCTORY DRIVE IN THE LAKE DISTRICT

Distance: About 60 miles/97 kilometers
Roads: Generally 2-lanes
Driving Time: 3–4 hours, depending upon stops
Map: Michelin Map #402

A student of Lakeland poets encountering Windermere for the first time might be excused for wondering whether Wordsworth's handwriting hadn't been misread by his publisher: surely it was the phrase "I wandered only in a crowd," not "lonely as a cloud," that began his famous poem about daffodils. According to the British Tourist Authority, the Lake District plays host to an astonishing 12 million tourists each year, and on a sunny midsummer's day it can seem as if all 12 million of them have converged upon Windermere and its neighbor Ambleside. To really appreciate the Lake District, avoid Windermere completely.

The A591 from Kendal comes perilously close to Windermere and its crowds before it turns **north** toward **Ambleside.** But we risk the traffic for a good reason: the National Park Visitors Centre at **Brockhole,** a treasure trove of information on the park itself, as well as Lakeland history, geology, flora and fauna, sheep rearing, dry stone wall building, vernacular architecture—and, of course, the Wordsworths. Take in the audio-visual introduction to the Lake District (offered several times each day) and stock up on information on local events. Then, when you're ready to leave, turn **left** onto the **A591** for perhaps a mile, then turn right onto a minor road signposted for the hamlet of **Troutbeck.** As you climb steeply through rhododendron-clad hillsides above Windermere, the road offers one of the finest prospects of Windermere in the area. Far from the madding crowd, it becomes only too clear how this graceful sliver of a lake, shimmering in the afternoon sunshine, became beloved by so many.

After climbing up from the lakeshore, the road tops a ridge, then drops into Troutbeck. Straggling along the mile-long ridge from Town End to Town Head, Troutbeck is a village-sized museum of Lakeland vernacular architecture—from the rather grand Town End Farm

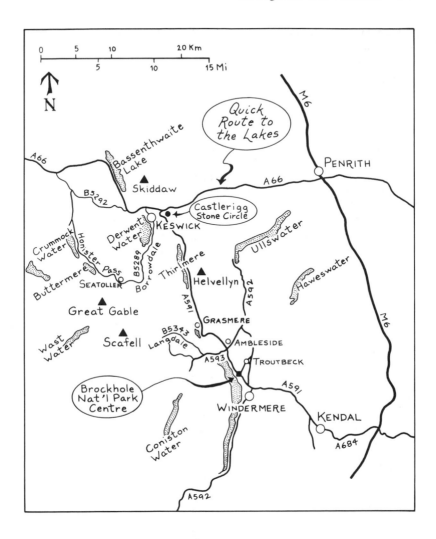

(c. 1628) to bank barns with spinning galleries, and "longhouses" that are part barn, part residence. Despite the appearance of antiquity (perhaps it's just the hard winters), few of the buildings you see here or elsewhere in the Lake District are much older than the 1700s, the period in which the area's timber-framed buildings were replaced with stone. Lakeland's stone buildings have an inherent integrity—solidly constructed, minimally ornamented, with doors and windows deep-set in the thick walls—they seem *of* the surrounding landscape, not just on it.

About Those Stone Walls

Throughout the Lake District, there are stone walls— "running like live things about the fells," as novelist Hugh Walpole once noted. A few of these walls date back more than 800 years, to the land development programs of the rich abbeys at Furness and Fountains that owned these lands. But most were built in the late eighteenth and early nineteenth centuries, after the passage of the Enclosure Acts, when teams of itinerant wall builders roamed the fells creating walls so well crafted that many remain intact today.

Each wall is really two walls that lean gently into each other, separated at the base but joined together at the top. No mortar is used. Instead, the two walls are tied together in places by long "through stones," and the space in between filled with rubble. The stones are set at a slight angle to shed water and prevent ice from forming in the center. The walls are capped with "cam stones," set on edge and sloping downhill. Stiles are often built into the structure so you can cross the wall without damaging it, and small triangular "cripple holes" permit sheep to move from field to field.

From the T-junction at Troutbeck Town End, turn **left** and follow the road north toward the Kirkstone Pass. Directly opposite the Kirkstone Pass Inn, turn sharply **left** onto a minor road that drops steeply down into the north end of the bustling shopping town of **Ambleside.** At the bottom of the hill you'll run into the north-south A591. Here, Wordsworth fans should turn right in the direction of Grasmere (see Diversions below).

Others should turn **left,** drive **south** through the town on the one-way section of the **A591,** and then, just as two-way traffic resumes, turn **right** and follow the signs toward Skelwith Bridge and the **B5343** to **Langdale.**

Great Langdale is a classic Lakeland glacial valley, so perfectly U-shaped that you can almost see the towering glacier that filled the valley millennia ago. The valley floor is full of glacial rubble, deeply cut by the meandering Langdale Beck. Roughly two-thirds of the way up the dale, the valley opens up to a huge glacially formed bowl framed by the massive Langdale Fells. As the road begins to draw near to the end of the valley, it turns sharply **left** and climbs up and over Side Pike on the south rim. Here the road is so steep and so haphazardly laid out that it looks as if someone simply poured macadam down the mountainside.

Near the rim there is a small cleared parking area. Stop and take a moment to look backward. Far below, one lonely farmstead crouches in the lee of the Langdale Fells, in splendid isolation.

Although this is one of Britain's premier natural areas, the truth is the hand of man is everywhere, and has been for centuries. Stone Age Lakelanders, who lived mainly on the coast, learned that the extremely hard, easily chipped crystal structure of the volcanic rocks near Langdale was ideal for ax blades, and a number of ax workings have been found here. After taking the blades to the coast to be sharpened on quartz sands, these early land developers returned to the mountains to begin clearing the trees that once filled the valley before you and clad all but the highest peaks. Their domestic animals, and those of their successors, grazed the ever-widening clearings even as they do today, ensuring that, once cleared, the land remained that way. The result, some 4,000 years later, is the sweeping alpine vistas that are an essential part of the Lakeland's "natural" landscape today.

Other residents left their marks as well. Bronze and Iron Age settlers left enigmatic monuments and strategically sited forts. The Romans built a road from Kendal in the east over the fells to Ravenglass on the western coast, and protected it with forts en route. High atop the Hard Knott Pass, scarcely 3 miles (5 kilometers) southwest of where you stand, the remains of one of these forts still exist today. As in Yorkshire, however, it was the Norse, who migrated to this region from Ireland and the Isle of Man, who left the most lasting impression, through language. The names of places and landscape features here are similar to those with which you are already familiar—*thwaite* (a clearing in the woods), *dale, beck, fell,* and many others.

Returning to your car and leaving Great Langdale behind, follow the road as it slips through a narrow gate, crosses a cattle grid, and then traverses a high plateau. Off to the right, ringed with rhododendron and framed by tall pines, silvery Blea Tarn (a delightful place to take a short walk if time and weather permit) sparkles in the sunshine. After another gate, the road then drops down into **Little Langdale,** which owes much of its pastoral charm to Beatrix Potter's willingness to use the royalties from her children's books to purchase many of the farms and fells in the valley. Turn **left** at the T-junction and follow this road to its end at the **A593,** turning **left** again past the landmark Three Shires Inn, with its stone-flagged "walkers bar," toward Skelwith Bridge and back to **Ambleside.** The entire circuit of the Langdales should take only an hour.

Regaining the one-way traffic pattern in Ambleside, turn **left** onto the **A591** again, heading north toward **Grasmere** and **Keswick,** and almost immediately you're in the heart of Wordsworth country. The road skirts the eastern shores of reed-edged Rydal Water and Grasmere, both immortalized by Wordsworth, whose principal homes—Dove Cottage

and Rydal Mount—are here (see Diversions below).

As you continue north on the A591, the road climbs sharply up the Dunmail Raise, a bleak, wind-swept saddle between the crags and open fells, of which one of the early eighteenth-century visitors to the Lakes wrote, in the breathlessly overwrought prose of the period, "The whole view is entirely of the horrid kind. With a view to adorning such a scene with figures, nothing could suit it better than a group of banditti. Of all the scenes I ever saw this was the most adopted to the perpetration of some dreadful deed."

What timid folk they must have been—the wind up here is bracing, the views backward toward Grasmere breathtaking, and on a misty day the effect is positively magical.

Pressing on, the A591 soon hugs the eastern edge of **Thirlmere,** its shoreline trimmed in larch and fir plantations. Then the road reaches a high plateau and turns west. Just before it drops into Keswick, the market town for the northern lakes, watch for a tiny National Trust sign on the right pointing to **Castlerigg Monument.** Turn in, and follow the lane a few hundred yards through high hedgerows to a small car park.

Castlerigg is one of Britain's more mysterious stone circles. Thought to have been built about 1400 B.C. by Bronze Age settlers, oval-shaped Castlerigg originally was composed of some sixty rough-hewn stones, of which about thirty-eight remain today. The monument sits atop a high plateau at the juncture of three valleys and possesses a commanding 360-degree view. Whether its purpose was strategic, political, or religious is anyone's guess. But on a stormy afternoon, with dark clouds scudding over the felltops and the wind howling across the plateau, a primitive magic radiates from the stones and no explanation seems too fanciful.

Then, **return** to the main road, turn **right,** and continue a mile or so into **Keswick,** nestled cozily at the northern tip of broad **Derwent Water,** its blue-green slatestone buildings filled with welcoming bakeries, pubs, restaurants, and outdoor equipment shops.

The quirky Moot (meeting) Hall in the center of town, built in 1813, now houses a good National Park Information Centre for the northern Lake District. Parking is available in front of the hall or in the large lot nearby—just follow the blue P signs. Inside the hall, a wealth of free information and sage advice is available, as well as a wide variety of the best, most detailed maps and guidebooks for the area. Pick up the National Parks' "What's On" guide, and consider Hunter Davies's definitive, opinionated, and funny *Good Guide to the Lakes.* In addition, you may wish to purchase an A. Wainwright *Pictorial Guide to the*

The hidden valley of Borrowdale is an idyllic base for exploring the Northern Lake District.

Lakeland Fells for the area you've chosen to hike tomorrow. These beautifully handwritten and hand-illustrated guides are the definitive step-by-step sourcebook on Lakeland walks, and a splendid keepsake. The Moot Hall also is the starting point for a number of guided walks and, in the evenings, plays host to slide shows and talks by local naturalists.

If time permits, Keswick is the place to stock up on picnic supplies for tomorrow's walk. Even more important, if you have thus far been hiking in sneakers, several of the outdoor outfitters in town rent high-quality boots for between £5 and £6 per week. You'll need them.

But if the day is growing late and the shops are closing, press on—there will be time to return to Keswick in the morning, if necessary. Your objective this afternoon is **Borrowdale,** a few miles to the south—arguably the finest base for walking in Britain and unquestionably one of the most beautiful valleys in the land.

Returning to the car, head toward Derwent Water, following signs for the **B5289** and **Borrowdale.** The narrow two-lane road twists along the shoreline, bounding over ledges too big for the road builders to remove, then flattens out briefly toward the southern end of the lake where silt and stone from the spring floods of the River Derwent have formed a broad delta. Further along, a side road on the right crosses a picturesque humpbacked stone bridge to the pretty village of **Grange**—centuries ago a grain storage site for the Cistercian monks of Furness Abbey, far to the south.

Continue **straight ahead** on the main road past the bridge and down the quickly narrowing valley. Up ahead, the slopes of Grange Fell reach down to meet the glowering face of 900-foot (274-meter) Castle Crag, and the valley seems to come to an abrupt end. You have reached "The Jaws of Borrowdale." Here the road narrows to a ribbon, clinging to the cliff side and squeezing through a cleft cut by the River Derwent until, all at once, you are deposited at the northern end of a serene, hidden valley rimmed by massive fells that seem to leap directly out of the valley floor. Accessible only by this narrow passage through the mountains and, at the far southern end, by one of the steepest passes in Britain, Borrowdale is an ideal base for touring, walking, and climbing in the Lake District.

There are four tiny settlements in the valley. The first you'll encounter, and the largest, is **Rosthwaite,** a compact cluster of stone houses and farmsteads, a one-room general store—cum—post office (in what was once an inn of dubious reputation), and a few small hotels ringing Miller How, a lump of rock that dominates the village. The road was clearly an afterthought here, and it has to squeeze between the store and a barn before proceeding. A half-mile or so further along, a side road branches left up one of the two narrow, south-pointing fingers of the Y-shaped dale to the ancient hamlet of **Stonethwaite.** Perhaps another mile beyond the turnoff for Stonethwaite, a second left

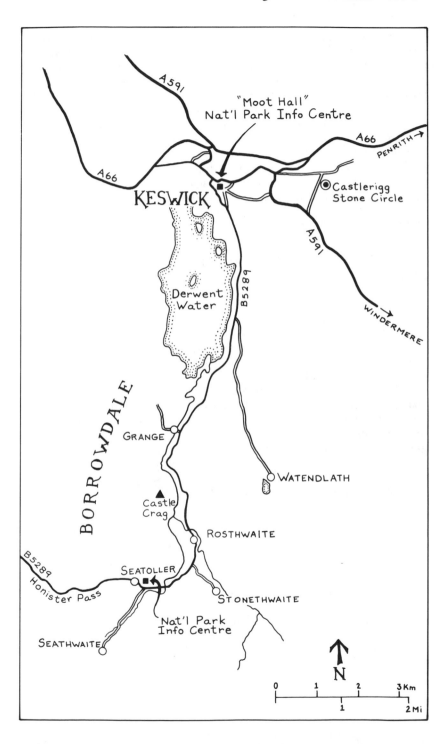

turn will take you to **Seathwaite,** little more than a farm and a few out-buildings at the end of the other finger of the valley. The main road, the B5289, continues a hundred yards or so farther to the fourth settlement, **Seatoller,** a tiny jumble of dwellings at the foot of the Honister Pass. At Seatoller's Dalehead Base (in a beautifully converted old stone barn) is yet another of the National Park Authority's information centers, though its hours are more limited than the Keswick center's.

With a little luck, if you arrive late in the day in midsummer, the setting sun will be coating the slate rooftops and fields of wildflowers with a rich honey gold, the fells echoing with the bleat of sheep, and the air will be tinged with the sharp antique smell of a coal fire in the parlor of the B&B in which you'll spend the next two nights.

DIVERSIONS

Wordsworth's Dove Cottage and Grasmere Village

Dyed-in-the-wool Wordsworthians will want to stop at William and Dorothy Wordsworth's **Dove Cottage** (open March through October) in Grasmere, just a few miles north of Ambleside on the A591. Turn left at the first signpost for Grasmere Village and follow the signs to the parking areas. Dove Cottage and the Wordsworth Museum are back on the other side of the A591.

Afterwards, walk past the parking lot in which you left your car and take a stroll into Grasmere Village to visit two Lakeland institutions: the gallery of the superb Lakeland watercolorist **Heaton Cooper,** and the **Grasmere gingerbread shop,** where a flat, crumbly, sharply sweet ginger cake has been made since 1855 (the recipe is kept in a local bank vault).

CREATURE COMFORTS

Daily Bed

Finding a cozy, friendly spot at the upper end of Borrowdale to spend the next two nights is relatively easy, though arriving much after 4:00 P.M. in high season or on holidays can be risky. There are at least four ways to handle arranging accommodation:

1. USE THE BOOKING SERVICE AT THE MOOT HALL in Keswick. For a small fee they'll call ahead and find you exactly what you're looking for—from a posh hotel on the banks of Derwent Water

Stonethwaite Farm, Borrowdale

to a B&B in Borrowdale. You don't get to check out the accommodations ahead of time, but that's a small price to pay for peace of mind if you're running late—and you only have to commit for one night.

2. STOP IN AT THE YEW TREE RESTAURANT at Seatoller and ask for a placemat. Yes, a placemat. For years the Yew Tree has printed a map of Borrowdale on their placemats with a complete listing of all the B&Bs and guesthouses in the valley. Bang on the door (it is closed between lunch and dinner) and ask for one. Then walk to the pay phone down the hill by the car park and start calling.

3. PICK YOUR OWN. Unless it's very late, you can hardly lose. There are a few small hotels and guesthouses in Borrowdale, but it's hard to beat the B&Bs in this little valley. The working farms are the best bet. Several, in Stonethwaite and in Rosthwaite, date back to Norman times. They have thick stone walls and low ceilings, big, sustaining breakfasts, and hospitality as warming as evening tea. And if you get up early enough you're likely to be pressed into service bottle-feeding the orphaned lambs or letting the cows out into the meadow for the day.

4. CHOOSE A YOUTH HOSTEL. There are some thirty youth hostels in the Lake District and two impressive ones are in or near Borrowdale—Loughthwaite Hostel, just behind Seatoller, and Honister Youth Hostel, at the top of the pass. For information on Lakeland hostels, write to the Lakeland Regional Headquarters, Elleray, Windermere, Cumbria.

Daily Bread

Evening meals are offered at some B&Bs (especially farmhouses) by prior arrangement; ask your hostess about tomorrow night, if evening meals are offered. Elsewhere in Borrowdale, dinner meals are available, usually by reservation, at several of the small hotels and at the only restaurant in the valley, the Yew Tree in Seatoller. A much wider choice of restaurants and pubs is available back in Keswick, only 15 or 20 minutes away.

Wherever you choose to dine, look for local trout and lamb, and for one particular Lakeland speciality: grilled Cumberland sausage.

Hiking the Lakeland Fells

BORROWDALE AND VICINITY

- ◆ A grand circuit of Seathwaite Fell with three alternative peaks for the more adventurous
- ◆ A circular walk across the lower fells to a remote, picturesque hamlet
- ◆ A steep but easy scramble to a fantastic viewpoint
- ◆ A lowland stroll through a dramatic glacial valley
- ◆ A rainy-day drive around the most pristine lakes

. . . they
Who journey thither find themselves alone
With a few sheep, with rocks and stones, and kites
That overhead are sailing in the sky.
It is in truth an utter solitude . . .
—William Wordsworth

*E*arly in the morning, with the sun peeking over Stonethwaite Fell, the cows' bells clanking as they return from milking to the meadows bordering the beck, and the sheep bleating their halfhearted complaints far up on the fellsides, Borrowdale, enveloped by its jagged fells, feels protected and timeless.

In fact, much of this land *is* protected. As you swing your eyes around the enclosed valley, a great deal of the land and all of the most important natural features you see are actually owned by the National Trust. Much of the credit for the care with which these treasures have been preserved goes to Canon Rawnsley, vicar of Crosthwaite, near Keswick, at the turn of the century. Rawnsley, who with Beatrix Potter helped protect the Herdwick sheep breed, was one of the three founders of the National Trust, the nation's largest conservation organization. The land in Borrowdale may look like it is privately owned, but much of it is actually leased by the trust back to the families and individuals who work it, under strict stipulations. Thus the land is both preserved and in economic use, a combination which seems to work to the benefit of all concerned.

Borrowdale sits precisely at the point where the soft slates of northern Lakeland meet the hard volcanics of the central region. The result is a landscape of sharp contrasts—of gentle folds at the northern end and jagged peaks in the south. The undulations in the broad valley floor are *moraines* (gravel sand bars) left behind where retreating glaciers paused. Since then, the valley floor has been shaped and reshaped by repeated floods, and the wire-enclosed stone barriers built at bends in the River Derwent and Stonethwaite Beck attest to the continuing threat.

THE RAINIEST PLACE IN ENGLAND

The chances are good that when you get up this morning it will be overcast, perhaps even raining. Don't let it dampen your spirits. Even brilliantly sunny days start out this way in Borrowdale. While Seathwaite has the highest rainfall in England, in excess of 130 inches in an average year, you are just as likely to have spectacular sunny weather, at least part of the day, as you are to be rained upon.

It all has to do with having a bunch of high mountains dead in the path of incoming Atlantic weather patterns. To get up over the mountains, the clouds have to shed some weight. It just so happens that they usually do it above Seathwaite. But the clouds themselves tend to be only the thinnest of layers; often, as they scud across the peaks, the blue just above them is tantalizingly visible. Just as often, it may be pouring where you are and brilliantly sunny someplace else *within sight*. Change, not rain, is the meteorological constant in the Lake District. For the record, the driest months are June and September.

PREPARING FOR A DAY ON THE FELLS

The two elemental forces in the Lake District—geology and water—have created a landscape rich with spectacular walking experiences accessible from Borrowdale, and this chapter offers four ways to experience the Lakeland fells at walking speed, ranging from a circuit of the higher fells (from which may be taken several of the most challenging—and rewarding—climbs in Lakeland) to three shorter, less difficult—but still breathtaking—routes within Borrowdale itself. A bit of time spent at either the Dalehead Base Information Centre at the end of the valley in Seatoller (open only from Easter through September) or the Keswick

Looking back at peaceful Watendlath in the Borrowdale fells

Moot Hall (open until January) is not just wise, it's a necessity. The staff will have up-to-the-minute weather information, suggestions on the times you should budget for each route, and additional maps and guidebooks, if required.

Some cautions are in order. First, tell the folks with whom you're staying where you're going and roughly when you expect to return. While the Lakeland peaks are hardly wilderness, they *are* wild and accidents happen. Second, dress sensibly. Don't strike out on a daylong midsummer hike with only shorts and a T-shirt. The Lakeland mountains can be ferocious weather breeders. Violent storms, impenetrable fogs, wind, and sharp temperature drops can develop quickly.

On the other hand, you're not mounting an expedition to Everest either. Unless it's the depth of winter, lightweight hiking boots (preferably lined with waterproof material) will be perfectly suitable for the more rigorous hikes. And if the weather has been dry for some time (droughts *do* happen here, really), the new generation of walking shoes will also suffice for most walks. Rain gear, on the other hand, is mandatory. Properly protected, you'll find that the mists cloak the hike in romantic mystery and that even the occasional downpours are bearable; unprotected, you'll just be miserable. In addition, take a sweater, even in the summer; temperatures on the heights can be bone-chilling. As a general rule, *underestimate* your endurance. You'll end the day happier and healthier.

If you didn't have time to buy picnic supplies in Keswick yesterday, do it first thing this morning and hurry back; while the "core" hike

The River Derwent near the turnoff for Seathwaite, Borrowdale

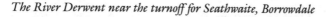

today takes only four hours, scaling Great Gable takes two additional hours and surmounting the giant—Scafell Pike—will take four hours. That's no problem in late June or early July, when it is still light at 9:00 at night, but at other times of the year Scafell requires an early start.

Finally, if you have been cursed with a morning of unrelenting, heavy rain, don't despair. A marvelous circular tour of the most remote and pristine of the Lakes is presented in Diversions later in this chapter. As always, the guiding rule on such days is "Be adventurous"—drive until you get lost and have a grand time finding your way back home.

⚡ A DAY IN THE MOUNTAINS: THE GRAND CIRCUIT OF SEATHWAITE FELL

Distance: Circuit only, about 6 miles/9.7 kilometers; allow 4 hours
Difficulty: A short, steep scramble near the beginning, easy to moderate ascents and descents thereafter; side trips to peaks steep but routes clearly marked
Total Elevation Gain: 1,592 feet/485 meters
Gear: Good walking boots/shoes, extra sweater, rain gear, lunch; for side trips to peaks add compass, flashlight for emergencies
Maps: Ordnance Survey 1:25,000 Outdoor Leisure Series, The English Lakes, NW; A. Wainwright, *Pictorial Guide to the Lakeland Fells*

This dramatic but only moderately difficult walk plunges you into the very heart of the central Lakeland fells, the huge volcanic peaks that were thrust out of the ancient sea millions of years ago, fought off the onslaught of the glaciers, and today contain some of England's most formidable climbing areas. A. Wainwright, the chronicler of Lake District hiking, calls it "the finest fellwalk" in the Lake District. The walk begins at the last outpost of Borrowdale: the tight little cluster of farm buildings known as **Seathwaite.**

Seathwaite in winter is a lonely place—the end of the road in a bleak landscape. One is moved to wonder which are the hardier, the sheep or the people who live here, patiently waiting for spring. After mid-November, not even the sun pays a visit. By then, it is too low in the southern sky to top the fells. It does not return until March.

But on a frosty fall morning, with the russet hills gleaming in the sun, or on a midsummer afternoon, with the meadows sparkling with daisies and buttercups, Seathwaite is stunning. It can also be busy. This is the "staging area" for some of the most scenic walks and most rigorous climbs in Britain, and on high-season weekends and holidays walkers tumble out of the buses that travel almost hourly between Kes-

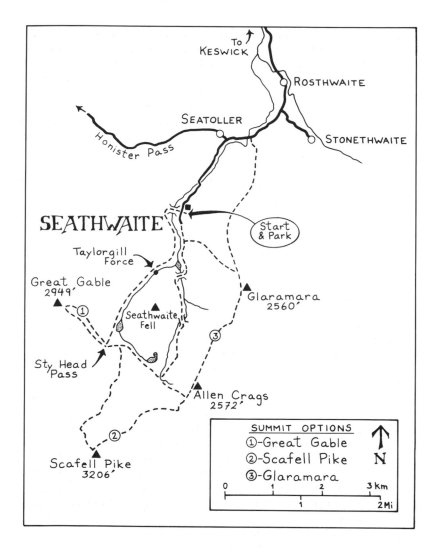

wick and Seatoller, and cars pile up at the end of the road, just outside the cobbled forecourt of Seathwaite Farm. So it's best to be there early. But don't worry about the crowds; the casual day-trippers won't get much further than a picnic up at Stockley Bridge or Sour Milk Gill Waterfall. After half an hour of walking you'll wonder where everyone disappeared to.

Many walkers, in a hurry to take the most direct route to Scafell Pike, head due south through the courtyard of Seathwaite Farm, past the somewhat sobering Mountain Rescue Post, and up the well-beaten farm track toward the head of the valley. Don't follow them. Instead, turn **right** through the **archway** connecting two farm outbuildings on the west side of the courtyard and follow the lane toward the river.

Grazing in the walled meadows on each side you are likely to find an odd mix of sheep—some pure black, others brown, and still others a stony gray. They are, in fact, all Herdwicks, one of the oldest and hardiest breeds in England. They roam the fells year-round and are collected twice a year for shearing. The colors of their wool are indications of their age (and occasionally the breeds with which they've been interbred, chiefly Swaledale). The black sheep are very young. As they mature, their coats begin to change to brown. At maturity, the wool will be long and deep gray. Sheep farmers in Borrowdale typically hold the

Seathwaite Farm, starting point for many of the most dramatic walks in the Lakeland mountains

youngest sheep, and the orphans, in valley-floor meadows before releasing them to the fells.

A stone and wood bridge—new, and further proof of the destructive force of the spring floods—spans the River Derwent at the foot of the fells. Immediately after you cross the main bridge, turn **left** and follow a well-worn path southward up along the right bank of the Derwent toward the head of the valley.

After a few hundred yards, just beyond a small larch plantation, the river swings across the valley floor to the east and the path veers away from the bank, heading gently to the right across a gradually steepening hillside strewn with huge boulders—chunks of the fells above that have given way to the subtle destructive forces of freezing and thawing on the heights.

The ground underfoot immediately softens, and soon you are squelching across a curious bit of landscape: a bog on a steep angle. Bogs form either because there is insufficient drainage or because there is insufficient evaporation. Here, in the wettest place in England, both are a problem. The water from the fellsides drains down to this rocky slope so profusely that it can neither drain away nor evaporate fast enough. Over time, soggy dead plants become so acidic that bacteria can no longer survive to break them down, and layer after layer of vegetation builds up, ultimately becoming peat. In dry weather the thick mat of sphagnum moss created by this process puts a delightful spring in your step, and you find yourself bounding across the slope. In wetter weather, it's more like a game of hopscotch, as you pick your way around the boggiest spots.

If you know how to read them, there are clues to wet and dry routes hidden in the flowers and plants that flourish here. The wettest areas stand out because of the tall tussocks of sedge and cotton grass. Another giveaway is leaf surface. Plants in the boggiest areas—the cotton grass, for example—have long, reedy leaves that reduce transpiration. The bog water is so acidic that the plants take little of it up and, consequently, can afford to give little of it off to the air. In contrast, the drier areas, generally well trimmed by sheep, are carpeted with broadleafed daisies, deep-magenta thistle, and bright pink foxglove. Fernlike bracken, a curse for farmers because neither sheep nor cattle will graze it, spreads in clumps across the drier areas of the hillside, brilliant green in the early summer and a rich bronze in the fall.

Following the "path" here, therefore, can be a haphazard affair if it has been raining. In general, you want to keep climbing **diagonally uphill** across the ever-steepening hillside toward the right part of the fork in the valley created by **Seathwaite Fell,** the huge mass of rock dead ahead to the south. As you approach this fork, the slope steepens, and a little bit of hand-over-hand scurrying is required. This is the most strenuous part of the entire walk, but it is a route followed often by senior citizens' walking clubs, so anyone in reasonably good shape should have no difficulty.

Up ahead—*straight* up—is "the gate in the sky," a startling wooden gate in a bit of stone wall that seems to grow out of the cliff face and that, from this angle, looks for all the world like it leads directly to the clouds. What you discover on the other side is almost as dramatic: a thin path clinging to the steep slope directly opposite **Taylor Gill Force,** one of the finest waterfalls in Lakeland.

A little care is needed here. The narrow path traverses an area of scree that slopes off steeply some 50 feet (15 meters) to the foot of the falls. A few scrawny and unfriendly holly bushes edge the uphill side of the path and two stunted oak trees perch like vultures on the downhill slope, their clawlike roots dug into what appears to be solid rock.

At the head of the falls, a small wood of pine and larch creates a tranquil oasis amid the exposed and rocky fells. In the misty backwash from the falls, bright green mosses carpet the ground around the trees and cloak the rocks.

Then, quite suddenly, the path emerges upon an entirely different landscape: a broad, boulder-strewn glacial valley, devoid of trees, with **Aaron Crags** on the left, hanging from the western edge of Seathwaite Fell, and the flanks of **Base Brown, Green Gable,** and **Great Gable** on the right. In between, **Sty Head Beck** clatters merrily northward through the gill before flinging itself over the edge of the falls. In a matter of minutes you have gone from pastoral England to an environment so bleak and wild that it might easily be Mongolia.

Farther up this valley, a well-worn path crosses a small bridge from the left, having come up from Seathwaite via Stockley Bridge and skirted the foot of Seathwaite Fell—a faster but far less interesting ascent. Up ahead, the path skirts the right bank of Sty Tarn and ends at **Sty Head,** a high saddle of open land between Great Gable and Great End that is the Grand Central Station of central Lakeland. From the dark green, wooden Mountain Rescue Box in the center of the stony meadow, paths branch off in all directions. To the west, and straight up, two paths climb to the top of **Great Gable** (2,949 feet/899 meters), perhaps the most rewarding peak to climb in the area for its magnificent views. Due south, another path picks its way beneath the steep face of Great Gable and down into **Wasdale,** to the beckoning pub at Wasdale Head far below on dark, lonely Wast Water. To the southeast, partway up the hill, a path follows the Corridor Route to **Scafell Pike** (3,206 feet/977 meters), the highest peak in England. To the east, a broad trail leads to another major intersection at Esk Hause, where paths branch off for a second route to Scafell Pike, for the less-frequented ridge walk to **Glaramara** (2,560 feet/780 meters), and for descents into Eskdale, Langdale, and Borrowdale via Langstrath Beck.

Sty Head is the place to conduct a "reality check." Have your knees developed an odd wobble? If so, skip the side trips outlined below. Discretion, in a place as remote as this, is more than just the better part of valor, it is the preventer of serious injury. Going down will take a greater toll on your thighs, knees, and ankles than going up and is when most injuries happen.

Perhaps even more important, *look up:* if you can see the summit of Great Gable and you are still bursting with energy and ambition, by all means scale it or, if you have another five or six hours of daylight, scale Scafell Pike (see Side Trips below). There is no getting around the unexplainable exhilaration of a completed ascent. But if Great Gable is shrouded in cloud, why not explore more of the fells by taking a longer route home, say over Glaramara and then down into Seathwaite, or back to Borrowdale by way of the vast and lonely Langstrath Valley? In short, be flexible; there's much to see, regardless of the weather on the heights.

𝑥 Ascent of Great Gable

(2,949 feet/899 meters)

Distance: 1.5 miles/2.4 kilometers round trip; allow 2 hours
Difficulty: Steep, but broad and clear vertical path
Total Elevation Gain: About 1,000 feet/300 meters
Gear and Maps: As above

From Sty Head, Great Gable, a vast pyramid of black rock, simply invites ascent. A broad path rises westward and upward directly to the summit—a bit of a trudge, but the result at the top is stunning: a finer view of the Lake District and the surrounding region than can be had from virtually any other summit.

On the way up, the grassy slope thins slowly, eventually giving way to scree. On the right, the hillside slopes off into Aaron Slack, a rocky ravine that drops from Windy Gap to Sty Head Tarn. Soon only the dark and weathered volcanic rock remains and the path picks its way through the rubble to the summit, a wide stretch of bare rock capped by a huge cairn built by the Fell and Rock Climbing Club in 1923 in memory of club members who died in World War I. A plaque atop the cairn has a detailed relief map of the entire area, which helps as you swing your eyes around the horizon.

To the north, Borrowdale is visible between nearby peaks and Keswick, backed by Skiddaw (3,054 feet/931 meters) and Blencathra (2,847 feet/868 meters) is just beyond. A little to the east, beyond the Borrowdale Fells, Helvellyn rises to 3,116 feet/950 meters. Due east, Glaramara (2,560 feet/780 meters) guards Seathwaite, and Great End (2,984 feet/910 meters) marks the northernmost edge of the rising ridge atop which Scafell Pike (3,206 feet/977 meters) sits. Between

Sty Tarn, high in the wild volcanic peaks above Seathwaite

them, in the far distance, Windermere can sometimes be seen. For the best view south, walk a hundred yards or so to the southwest to Westmoreland Cairn. Far below, Wasdale stretches southward toward the Irish Sea, with the Isle of Man sometimes visible beyond. Further around to the west, Pillar (2,927 feet/892 meters) looms above the upper reaches of Ennerdale.

The startling thing about this view is not its beauty but its scale—craggy fells, crystal tarns, streams and waterfalls, alpine moorland, pastoral valleys, crowded Windermere, and lonely Wasdale are all gathered together in one tightly crumpled bit of landscape, much of it impenetrable except on foot. To return to the main route of today's walk, simply go back down the slope the way you came.

(**Note:** Experts have an alternative—the challenging and dramatic Gable Traverse, which begins near the Westmoreland Cairn, crosses under the steep south face of Great Gable above Wasdale, and picks its way through the crags past Napes Needle, a huge outcrop of volcanic rock popular with technical climbers, eventually meeting the path up from Wasdale at Sty Head. This is a difficult route; see Ken Wilson and Richard Gilbert's *Classic Walks* (listed in Further Reading) for a detailed route description.)

🏃 Ascent of Scafell Pike

(3,206 feet/977 meters)

Distance: About 4 miles/6.5 kilometers; allow 4 hours
Difficulty: Moderate to difficult; good path
Total Elevation Gain: 1,192 feet/363 meters
Gear and Maps: As above

A side trip to Scafell Pike is included here as much out of respect as affection. As many Lake District writers have noted, the climb to the top of this, the highest of England's peaks, is often crowded—the inevitable price of prominence.

This side trip begins just a few yards east of the Mountain Rescue Box at Sty Head. Put Great Gable at your back and walk **uphill** on the "main street" of the northern fells, the path that connects Sty Head with Esk Hause, high above Langdale. Just after you begin climbing uphill, turn **right** at a point where a path, called the **Corridor Route,** branches off around the foot of Great End. The path drops down the scree from Skew End, on the flank of Great End, and then rises along a kind of grassy ledge or plateau, skirting the edges of Great Gill and Piers Gill, dizzying water-cut ravines that plunge hundreds of feet down toward Wasdale Head. The path skirts the volcanic outcroppings of Round How and then, opposite Lingmell Crag, meets the path up from Wasdale Head and turns **sharply left** for the steep climb to the summit.

Once reached, the summit can be a bit of a disappointment. For one thing, it is a vast field of fractured stone, rather than a narrow peak. Wainwright, dean of the fell walkers, describes the summit as "a barren waste where only mosses and lichens can find sustenance, an inhospitable desert without grace, without charm, and without colour other than the drab grey of volcanic rocks." The views of the area are good, but because Scafell Pike is hemmed in by other quite high peaks, they are not as dramatic as those from Great Gable.

Picking your way through the rocks, head **northeasterly** away from the summit cairn toward Esk Hause. The path descends gently at first, then more steeply, following a **line of cairns** through a rocky landscape. Then it threads between Broad Crag on the left and Ill Crag below on the right, across a gravel plateau and through a boulder field. Continuing its descent, the path cuts across a thin ridge, then a grassy slope, bending to the east to avoid Great End before entering Calf Cove, and finally opening onto the high saddle at Esk Hause. To rejoin the "core" route, turn **left** toward Sty Head a few hundred yards, then **right** at the ravine above Sprinkling Tarn for the descent into **Grains Gill** to Seathwaite.

🏃 Return to Seathwaite via Glaramara

(2,560 feet/780 meters)

Distance: 5.5 miles/8.8 kilometers; allow 2 hours, including the return to Seathwaite
Difficulty: Steep at outset, then easy
Total Elevation Gain: 558 feet/170 meters
Gear and Maps: As above

Not infrequently, Great Gable and Scafell Pike can be shrouded in cloud while Glaramara, towering over Seathwaite but some 400 feet (122 meters) lower than Great Gable, is beneath the cloud line. If the prospect of returning so soon to Seathwaite disappoints you when you reach Sprinkling Tarn on the "core" route, consider Glaramara—a classic ridge walk.

To reach it, continue **east** past Sprinkling Tarn a few hundred yards toward Esk Hause. Directly opposite the return path from Scafell, a path on the **left** climbs steeply up through a fissure in the **Allen Crags.** Atop the crags you will already have reached the highest point of the trip; Glaramara is actually a few feet lower. The path then traverses a long ridge, descending slightly several times into shallow depressions (cols) marked by a string of tiny tarns, before rising to the summit of Glaramara. Sweeping views down into Seathwaite to the west, Borrowdale to the north, and Langstrath to the east are the reward.

Continuing north from the cairn at the summit, the path forks. The **left fork** descends sharply into Seathwaite, following a narrow gill and ending just south of the farm, making a handy, if tricky, shortcut. The **right fork** continues north along the gently descending ridge line, then drops below Capell Crag, edges a mixed hardwood forest, and ends a half-mile or so from Seatoller on the main road through Borrowdale. To return to Seathwaite, turn **left** and then **left** again when you reach the minor road to Seathwaite Farm.

If you choose not to climb either of these peaks, simply head east (**straight ahead** with your back toward Great Gable) out of Sty Head and up the hill toward Esk Hause. This is one of the busiest trails in the fells, and the path is quite literally being "loved to death." To the extent possible, avoid forging your own overland route (it exposes the gravel beneath the turf to erosion); try to stick to the path (unless it's become a stream) or hop from stone to stone.

The path from Sty Head rises through a gap between the back of Seathwaite Fell, on the left, and the towering crags of Great End, on the right. **Sprinkling Tarn,** one of the Lake District's prettiest glacial ponds, is on the **left.** In good weather, its indented shores make a delightful spot to soak one's feet, savor a much-earned lunch, and watch the snowy tips of the cotton grass dance in the wind.

Just beyond Sprinkling Tarn, a clear path branches **left** running parallel to a small stream called Grains Gill. The stream slips through a dramatic 50-foot (15-meter) ravine cut deep into the black volcanic rock along an ancient fissure, eventually emerging at the head of a vast and classic U-shaped glacial valley punctuated with volcanic outcrops and littered with the rubble of centuries of landslides.

The slope is steep and the stream drops quickly, careering around giant boulders and cutting into the softer glacial debris. Occasionally, it lingers briefly in pools so clear that you can only judge their depth by the intensity of the blue-green color of the water. So eroded is the steeply descending footpath in places that to stabilize the surface the Lake District Special Planning Board has put teams of men to work in the fells—the modern equivalent of the last century's itinerant wall builders—to create beautifully executed stone steps running fully half the way down the steep valley.

About three-quarters of the way down the valley, just after the beck plunges through another ravine, the Grains Gill path is joined by the more heavily traveled trail from Sty Head, and together they cross humpbacked Stockley Bridge, a reminder that this was once a pack-horse route.

From here on, it's a gentle downhill coast through the upper walled meadows of the valley, and back through the cobbled farmyard to your car, the Borrowdale bus, or your nearby B&B.

THREE EASY WALKS AROUND BORROWDALE

From the southern end of Borrowdale, dozens of shorter, less strenuous walks are available, from strolls along the leafy banks of the Derwent to hikes on the lower fells. Here are three favorites. (Tony Hopkins's *Walks to Remember* (Polecat Press), available in Keswick and at National Trust centers, and the National Park's brochure *W2: 3 Walks in Borrowdale* are good, detailed companion guides.)

⋌ Easy Walk: Over the Lower Fells to Watendlath

(4.5 miles/7.5 kilometers; allow 4 hours, including lunch)

This walk, just out your back door if you're staying in Stonethwaite, combines a short and somewhat strenuous initial uphill trudge with a fine walk that encompasses the lower fells, a lovely isolated tarn, a

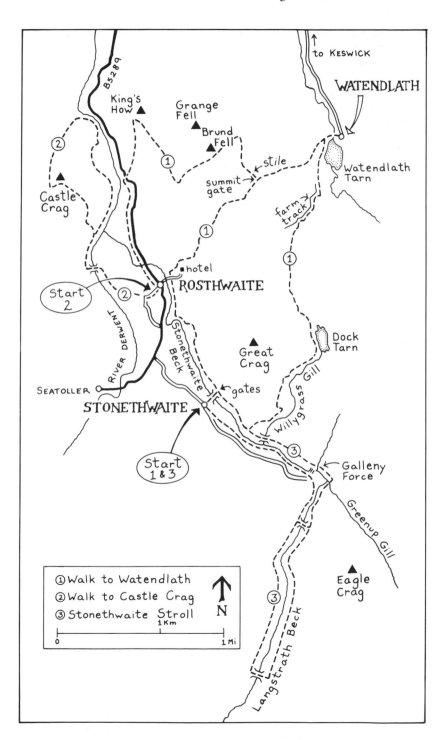

B5289

King's How ▲

Grange Fell ▲

Brund Fell ▲

to KESWICK

WATENDLATH

②

Castle Crag ▲

①

stile

summit gate

Watendlath Tarn

farm track

①

Start 2

②

hotel

ROSTHWAITE

①

Dock Tarn

RIVER DERWENT

Stonethwaite Beck

Great Crag ▲

Willygrass Gill

SEATOLLER

STONETHWAITE

gates

Start 1 & 3

③

Galleny Force

Greenup Gill

Langstrath Beck

③

Eagle Crag ▲

① Walk to Watendlath
② Walk to Castle Crag
③ Stonethwaite Stroll

↑ N

1 Km

0   1 Mi

picture-perfect remote hamlet, exceptional views of Borrowdale from the heights, and a wide variety of flora from ancient pollarded trees to alpine flowers.

To begin, take the wide trail that runs **southward** up the east bank of the Stonethwaite Beck behind Rosthwaite and Stonethwaite, starting at whatever point is closest to where you are staying (parking is available in both settlements). The path threads its way among the cows and sheep grazing in the riverside meadows and sometimes is bounded by high, beautifully crafted stone walls. On the left, the fellside forest is composed predominantly of oak and some tall sentinel pines. Flowering cherry and hazel edge some of the meadows, and just beyond the bridge from Stonethwaite, what appear to be grotesquely deformed ash trees dot the landscape.

Pollarding

Since the Bronze Age, Lakelanders have "farmed" their forests as intensively as their stony meadows, using both the larger trees and the smaller "underwood": flexible birch twigs were used for brooms, lightweight willow for milkmaids' yokes, dense alder for waterproof wooden clogs, tough hazel for thatching spars, strong yew for longbows, and much more. The deformed ash trees along Stonethwaite Beck, with their thick, gnarled trunks sprouting spindly branches, have been pollarded for centuries. By lopping off the tops of the trees, just above grazing height, farmers could ensure a steady supply of fast-growing branches for everything from fuelwood to barrel staves.

Continue up the valley in the direction of Eagle Crag and turn **left,** just after passing through a gate, at a **signpost** pointing up the fellside to **Dock Tarn.** The path through the oak forest, which a century or two ago was used as a source of bark for tanning leather and fuel for making charcoal, rises quickly through 300 feet (90 meters), eventually breaking through the trees and rising more gently through a bracken- and foxglove-filled vale cut by Willygrass Gill. At the felltop, the path turns **left,** skirts a ledge, and then drops into the little depression in which lovely Dock Tarn sits, edged with sedges and cotton grass and rich with bird life. The tarn may take its name from the Old English *docce,* for aquatic plant.

The path follows the western shore of the tarn, passing east of Great Crag, and then drops down a long slope clad in heather and bracken. The path scatters into several ribbons here to avoid a boggy area, coming together again near a ladder stile. Next it follows a farm track along a stream course, goes through a farm gate, and edges the western shore of Watendlath Tarn. The tiny hamlet of Watendlath nestles in a deep glacier-cut bowl beneath the shelter of several old trees, just across the ancient stone bridge.

To return to Borrowdale, you have at least two choices. You can walk **due west** up the broad path to the edge of the fell (with great views of Borrowdale below), then through the summit gate, and down the fellside into Rosthwaite, returning to Stonethwaite by turning **left** on the path along Stonethwaite Beck. Or you can take the same route, but turn **right** (north) at the gate above Watendlath and hike to the top of Brund Fell, then on to King's How and down steeply, following the line of cairns, to the B5289. Then turn **left** for the return to Rosthwaite and Stonethwaite.

Sun and rain compete for center stage among the Borrowdale fells.

🏃 Easy Walk: A Short Scramble to the Top of Castle Crag

(3 miles/5 kilometers; allow 2–3 hours)

The enormous plug of rock that forms the Jaws of Borrowdale is the centerpiece for a short, pastoral, and generally very easy walk accessible to anyone who owns a pair of sneakers and is fit enough to handle a few short steep segments not much more challenging than a few flights of stairs. The payoff—lovely riverbank walks, alpine meadows, and splendid views both north into the fingers of Borrowdale and the summits beyond and south to Derwent Water, Keswick, and Skiddaw—far exceeds the effort.

Begin by taking the narrow lane opposite the Rosthwaite Post Office and store **west,** past Yew Tree Farm, to the River Derwent, crossing by either the ancient steppingstones or the new bridge. Then turn **right** for a few yards, passing through a gate into a meadow on the **left** with a clearly visible path up a long, gentle, bracken-covered slope toward the crag. Further up the hill, you pass over a stile and, a bit further on, through another gate.

As the path steadily rises, pause from time to time to look back at the changing panorama of the valley below: Stonethwaite Beck on the left, meandering through neatly walled meadows to join the fast-flowing Derwent as it races down from Seathwaite and Seatoller; the cozy cluster of Rosthwaite, huddled around Miller How; and Stonethwaite Farm in the distance under the black glare of Eagle Crag.

The path next passes through a gap in a stone wall, enters a forested area, and, still climbing, opens up again at a ladder stile near a fence. Off to the left, a noticeably broad path runs between Honister and the Grange. This path, marked on maps as a bridleway to Seatoller, was originally a packhorse trail from one of the many slate and graphite quarries in the surrounding fells. Borrowdale, in fact, gave pencils to the world, opening the world's first pencil factory in 1566. The graphite ran out in 1880, but the factory remains, using imported "lead." Today, the Cumberland Pencil Company maintains an odd but intriguing "pencil museum" in Keswick.

After the ladder stile, turn **right** past tall pines that grow out of the debris of an old slate quarry, following a line of slate cairns gently curving upward and to the **left** to the bare summit and its panoramic view.

Having taken in the sights, you have two alternatives, both beginning back at the ladder stile at the foot of the slate scree. For the shortest return, go over the stile and retrace your steps. A longer return circles the northern base of Castle Crag. Turn **right** after crossing the ladder stile and walk down to the old packhorse trail, turning **right** again and following Broadslack Gill until it joins the river at a deep sec-

Slatestone cottages near Rosthwaite, Borrowdale, with Castle Crag rising just behind

tion known as Gowder Dub. Turn **right** here, with the Low How Woods on your right, and follow the river south until the path diverges to the right across a grassy slope. The path slips through a gap in a stone wall, traverses the remains of a quarry, passes through another wall gap, and eventually rejoins the river and the new bridge.

🏃 Easy Walk: A Stroll through Two Glacial Valleys

(2.5–6 miles/4–9.5 kilometers, depending on route; allow 2–4 hours)

Here is a fine low-level walk that can be either 2.5 or 6 miles long, depending upon where you turn back. It provides, in a very short distance, a remarkable contrast between the pastoral tranquillity of the tiny hamlet of Stonethwaite and the wild barrens of Langstrath.

Begin at the small parking area near Stonethwaite Farm. Head down the stone-wall-lined farm track toward the river. Cross the iron bridge, go through the gates, and turn **right,** walking upstream along a well-marked path on the east side of the beck. Go past the path that leads to Dock Tarn and continue toward the brooding hulk of Eagle Crag at the head of the valley in the distance. The low island opposite was used by the abbots of Furness, some 400 years ago, as an iron smelter.

At the point where Stonethwaite Beck is formed by the confluence of Greenup Gill and Langstrath Beck, there are several small but beautiful waterfalls, some sheltered from sight by a dense canopy of scrubby oak trees. On hot summer days, with the soaring fells above, a variety of rock ledges upon which to bask, and several small but deep swimming pools, there can hardly be a more perfect, or dramatic, site for swimming and sunbathing in all of England.

A bit farther up the valley, above the confluence, turn right over the footbridge **across Greenup Gill** and follow the path **straight** ahead up into the Langstrath Valley under the gaze of Eagle Crag, named for golden eagles that once patrolled the updrafts above these fells. Langstrath—a long, lonely valley carved into the characteristic glacial U shape—seems deeply isolated. Apart from the clatter of the beck and the wind, there is no sound. Indeed, despite its accessibility, this valley is one of the least visited in the Lake District.

Crossing the first bridge off to the right will return you to Stonethwaite, completing a circular route of about 2.5 miles (4 kilometers). But if the weather is fine, you may want to continue up along the southern side of the valley, past Blackmoss Pot, then return via the crossing farther up. This is a leisurely walk, requiring only lightweight walking shoes or sneakers, yet it is deeply evocative of the Lake District solitude that so moved Wordsworth. (In midsummer there are many places to cross Langstrath Beck by stone hopping.) Returning to the point at which Langstrath Beck meets Greenup Gill, turn **left** over the stiles and carry on through a small campsite to Stonethwaite. Stonethwaite Farm has been the site of a dairy since the thirteenth century—indeed, it was so highly valued that the abbeys at Furness and Fountains squabbled over it for decades, though Fountains eventually won. Today, Victor Brownlee and his daughter Allison still operate a small dairy at the farm, continuing a tradition seven centuries old.

DIVERSIONS

Remember that the lakes didn't fill up by magic. If the weather during the brief period you are in the Lake District is uncooperative, you still have several choices.

🚗 A Circular Car Tour of the Most Pristine Lakeland Lakes

Distance: About 30 miles/48 kilometers
Roads: Mostly 2-lane roads, occasionally narrower
Driving Time: Allow 3–4 hours, not including walk around
    Buttermere
Map: Michelin Map #402

Actually, you needn't wait for bad weather to take this drive. During the long Lakeland summer days (it is still daytime at 10:00 P.M. in

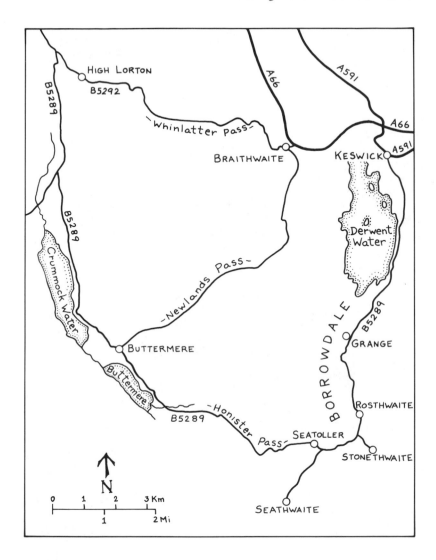

late June and early July) you can spend the day walking, then visit two of the most remote and beautiful lakes in the district—**Buttermere** and **Crummock Water**—by a car tour that is at once hair-raising and breathtaking, and still have time for a late dinner in Keswick.

Begin at **Seatoller,** where the **B5289** climbs steeply up the Honister Pass. A sign at the bottom orders you to get into low gear and means it.

After climbing upward through a leafy glade beside the tumbling

Haus Gill, the road finally breaks out into the treeless, rubble-strewn fells of the pass, rising to the 1,176-foot (358-meter) summit near the Honister Youth Hostel and an old slate quarry. Just beyond the quarry, signs again caution you to get into low gear. Finally, just before the road tips over the edge for the drop down to Buttermere, possibly the sternest road sign in all of Britain admonishes, YOU HAVE BEEN WARNED. Dodging house-sized boulders, the road tumbles alongside the Gatesgarthdale Beck until it deposits you at idyllic, meadow- and tree-rimmed Buttermere, its surface mirroring the scarred peaks and silvery waterfalls of the opposite fells.

The road skirts the northern edge of the lake, passing through the village of Buttermere (where a turn to the **right** will take you over the **Newlands Pass** into Keswick), then carries on around Crummock Water, finally turning right toward High Lorton. Here, take the **B5292** over the **Whinlater Pass** through Thornthwaite Forest to Braithwaite, turning **right** again onto the **A66** for Keswick.

Lakeland Sports Events

There are few experiences more humbling or amazing than watching a good sheepdog and a shepherd work a field of stubborn, skittish sheep. Typically they perform these miracles out of sight on the fells. But if you should happen to be in the vicinity of one of the several Lakeland **sheepdog trials** held each year, don't miss it. Check at any National Park Information Centre to see if any are scheduled during your visit. And while you are at it, check for any of the Lake District's other unique sporting events, including **fell running,** in which men run—that's right, *run*—up the treacherous fells and hurtle back down again, trying not to break limbs in the process; **fellhound races,** in which specially bred, extraordinarily sleek and tough foxhounds follow an aniseed-scent trail over the fells and back again; and **Lakeland wrestling,** a curious hybrid of the sport in which men who appear to be dressed in long underwear and elaborately embroidered overshorts seek a quick throw.

CREATURE COMFORTS

See yesterday's listings.

Enchanting Buttermere and its neighbor, Crummock Water, are among the most unspoiled of the Lakeland lakes.

A Dash to the Scottish Highlands

BORROWDALE ◆ GLASGOW
LOCH LOMOND ◆ GLENCOE

- ◆ A motorway drive across Scotland's western lowlands
- ◆ A scenic ride along the "bonnie banks" of Loch Lomond
- ◆ A dramatic drive through the wilds of Glencoe, the "Weeping Glen"
- ◆ Optional side trips to Glasgow and Inveraray
- ◆ An afternoon walk in the Lost Valley of Glencoe

. . . in Loch Lomond are gathered a million beauties: soft green banks and braes; a whisper of woodland; regal mountains with the ermine of white clouds round their purple shoulders; and always, mile after mile, silver water. . . where islands lie at anchor like a green flotilla.
———H. V. Morton
In Search of Scotland, 1927

Glencoe itself. . . is an awful place. It is shut in on each side by enormous rocks from which great torrents come rushing down in all directions. In amongst these rocks. . . there are scores of glens, high up, which form such haunts as you might imagine yourself wandering in, in the very height and madness of a fever. . . . The very recollection of them makes me shudder.
———Charles Dickens

Scotland is a place of stark contrasts, born of conflict. There can be few places on earth with a history more wracked with strife, both geological and political: first rent by unimaginable tectonic catastrophes, then torn by virtually continuous warfare—between early tribal "kingdoms"; among a succession of Roman, Viking, and Norman invaders; between and among clans; between Hanoverian kings and Stuart "pretenders"; between Presbyterian and Episcopalian believers; and between crofters and generations of callous landowners. The history of Scotland is a tale of heroic struggles on behalf of lost causes in a landscape of epic grandeur.

On a sunny afternoon by the shores of Loch Lomond it is easy to

The Rise and Fall and Rise of the Clans

The word *clan* means children. Clan history really began in the 1100s when Somerled, a Gaelic Irish warrior chieftain, won back part of the southwest Scottish coast and isles from the Norse Vikings. It was his grandson, Donald, who founded the oldest clan, the MacDonalds ("sons of Donald"). By the thirteenth and fourteenth centuries clans had been established throughout the western Highlands and islands, each with its own distinctive *plaid* or tartan. During the mid-1400s, the leader of Clan Donald held dominion over many of them and the title "Lord of the Isles."

Over the centuries, however, clan alliances shifted constantly, often with brutal consequences for those loyal to clan leaders on losing sides. The spectacular failure of Bonnie Prince Charlie in the 1745 Jacobite (from the Latin for James, the former Stuart king) rebellion led to the disarming of the clans, the banning of tartans and bagpipes, and the forfeiture of clan leaders' legal powers.

But ultimately, it was economics, not politics, that doomed the clans. By the early 1800s, the wealthy, Anglicized clan leaders realized that their land could be used more profitably if it was populated by sheep rather than their own clansmen, so the clansmen—their "children"—were simply removed. Many were displaced to tiny, infertile crofts and left to slowly starve. Others were "encouraged" to emigrate to America or Australia—or simply kidnapped and deported. By the end of the century, greedy Scottish landowners had done what the English armies had failed to do for centuries: the glens were empty.

Almost as soon as they disappeared, however, the clans were revived—as romance. Poet and novelist Sir Walter Scott turned Scotland's harsh history into heroic legend and Queen Victoria, from her summer residence at Balmoral, resurrected the tartan as high fashion. The rest is tourism history.

forget all this and to appreciate the affection the Scots have for the loch's "bonnie banks." But the gentle allure is a trap: the farther north you penetrate, the wilder the scene becomes. Soon, the broad island-dotted expanse of shimmering blue water narrows to a leaden sliver, increasingly in shadow as the brooding mountains encroach from both sides. The mood darkens further as you leave the lake behind and wander across the grim wastes of Rannoch Moor, drawn deep into the violent heart of the wild Highland glen Macaulay called the "Valley of the Shadow"—Glencoe. It is a landscape that aches with tragedy.

THE DASH TO THE HIGHLANDS

Distance: About 225 miles/362 kilometers
Driving Time: 5.5–6 hours
Roads: Motorway/divided highway to Glasgow; good major roads
   along Loch Lomond and into Glencoe
Map: Michelin Map #401

Lovers of the poems of Robert Burns will think it a sacrilege, but today's objective is the wild fastness of the Highlands, and bypassing the gentler pleasures of Burns's beloved Lowlands is an unfortunate necessity.

From **Borrowdale,** head for Keswick and follow signs to the **A66** to **Penrith.** At Penrith, join the **M6** heading for Carlisle. Along the way, you may want to stop at the Scottish Tourist Information Centre at the **Southwaite Service Area.**

The M6 becomes the divided **A74** highway just over the Scottish border at **Gretna Green**—where, until 1940, runaway English couples used to go to get married under Scotland's easier marriage laws. A few miles beyond the now tragically famous town of Lockerbie, rounded hills begin to close in on the highway as it enters Annandale and begins to climb into the Southern Uplands. On the other side of the Uplands range, the highway once again changes form and name, becoming the **M74** as it coasts down into Scotland's central industrial plain, with **Glasgow** dead ahead.

As with all major cities, Glasgow traffic can be a bit frantic, but the motorway system is so smooth that you can be out of the city and heading north to the Highlands before you know it. From the **M74,** take the **M75 north** to the next exit, then follow the limited-access **M8 west,** straight through the heart of the city and out the other side, in the direction of Greenock, to **Exit 30.** Then follow signs for the **M898** to **Erskine Bridge.** After you pass through the tollbooth, turn left, following signs for the **A82** toward **Crianlarich.**

(**Note:** Travelers arriving at Scotland's Prestwick International Airport, on the coast roughly 40 miles (65 kilometers) to the southwest of

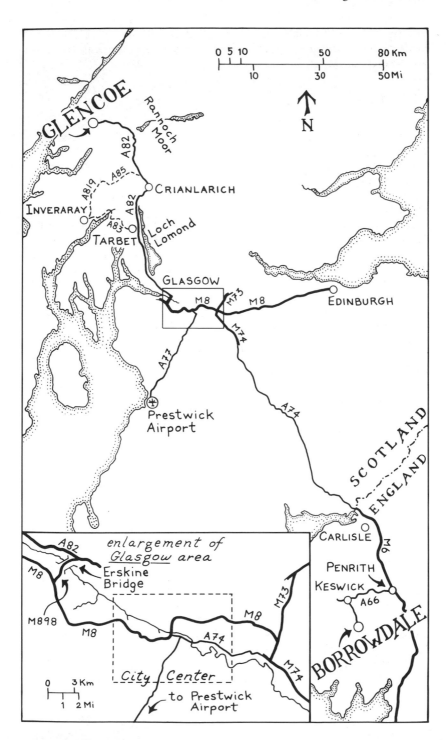

0 5 10   50   80 Km

10   30   50 Mi

N

GLENCOE

Rannoch Moor

A82

A819   A85

INVERARAY

A82

A83

TARBET

CRIANLARICH

Loch Lomond

GLASGOW

M8   M73   M8

EDINBURGH

A77

M74

A74

Prestwick Airport

SCOTLAND

ENGLAND

CARLISLE

M6

PENRITH

KESWICK

A66

BORROWDALE

enlargement of <u>*Glasgow*</u> *area*

A82

Erskine Bridge

M8

M898

M8

M73

M8

A74

M74

City Center

0   3 Km

1   2 Mi

to Prestwick Airport

Glasgow, can join the itinerary at this point by taking the A77 out of Prestwick and following signs for the M8 or City Centre from the outskirts of Glasgow.)

❖ Side Trip: A Quick Visit to Glasgow

Glasgow was, until only a generation or so ago, the British Empire's "Second City" (after London)—producing a third of the world's merchant ships and ocean liners in the sprawling yards along the narrow River Clyde, and half of the world's locomotives as well. Then both industries collapsed, leaving behind soot-covered Victorian merchant buildings, sprawling tenements, and brutal poverty.

Unemployment persists, but in the last few years Glasgow has undergone a renaissance unrivaled anywhere in Europe. The soot is disappearing, revealing architectural jewels. The arts are flourishing as well. Top museums (all free) include the Burrell Collection, the largest private art collection in Britain, in Pollock Country Park (open Monday through Saturday 10:00 A.M. to 5:00 P.M., Sundays 2:00 P.M. to 5:00 P.M.); the Art Gallery and Museum at Kelvingrove Park (same hours as the Burrell); and the Hunterian Art Gallery at Glasgow University (Monday through Friday 10:30 A.M. to 12:30 P.M. and 1:30 P.M. to 5:30 P.M.; and 9:30 A.M. to 1:00 P.M. Saturday).

Should you be in an urban frame of mind, follow signs for "City Centre," then signs for "Tourist Information" to the Scottish Tourist Authority's office on St. Vincent Place, a half-block or so from Great George Square (named after the king who lost the American colonies). Plan on being on the A82, bound directly for Glencoe, by no later than 3:00 P.M. (1:00 P.M. in winter). ❖

As you leave Glasgow and climb out of the valley of the Clyde on the **A82** the landscape returns abruptly to sheep-dotted farmland and soon, ahead and to the right, **Loch Lomond,** long and sinuous, stretches to the horizon.

Loch Lomond is Britain's largest and longest freshwater lake, yet it is very nearly not a lake at all. Though it seems to penetrate deep into the Highlands, it is only a mile and a half from the sea at one point and its surface is only 20 feet (6.1 meters) above sea level.

Beyond the rose-bedecked Victorian village of **Luss,** the loch narrows sharply, and on the shore opposite **Tarbet,** the pyramid of **Ben Lomond** (*ben* or *beinn* means mountain) rises abruptly from near sea level to almost 3,200 feet (975 meters). What you see before you—the sudden narrowing of the loch and its sharp turn to the right, Ben Lomond itself, and the crowded shoulders of Ben Vorlich and several other peaks over 3,000 feet (1,000 meters)—are the camouflaged signs of the **Highland Boundary Fault,** a massive geological rift that divides

Inveraray Castle, ancestral home of the Clan Campbell

Scotland diagonally from southwest to northeast. Some 400 million years ago this landscape was wracked with earthquakes. The urbanized land behind you—the central industrial plain—was created when the land between the Highland Boundary Fault and another fault to the south subsided, so long ago that there was even time for a swamp to flourish and die, creating coal deposits. The Highland Boundary Fault is much more than a geographic feature; it dominates the Scottish psyche. For centuries, Lowlanders considered remote and isolated Highlanders rigid and backward, and Highlanders considered Lowlanders soft and of questionable patriotism. So the mountains themselves account for the some of the divisions in Scotland's soul.

❖ Side Trip: A Circular Detour to Inveraray

Lovers of castles and members of the extended Clan Campbell may want to take the longer route to Glencoe by way of **Inveraray**. (**Note:** You won't have time for this loop if you paused in Glasgow or hope to get in a late afternoon walk in Glencoe. If you have no reservation for accommodations in Glencoe and expect to get there after 5:00 P.M., consider stopping at the tourist information office at Tarbet and having them book ahead for you.)

From **Tarbet**, turn left onto the **A83** and, after skirting the end of Gare Loch, climb steeply up into the Argyll Forest. This is a dramatic ride, with great stone outcroppings looming above the road, edged with purple heather. At the summit—called "Rest and Be Thankful"— the road drops down into Glen Kinglas and, regaining sea level, bends around the eastern end of **Loch Fyne**. A few miles farther on, the A83 bends sharply to the right and the lovely whitewashed Georgian village of **Inveraray** flashes into view across an arm of the loch. A bit to its right are the conical towers of **Inveraray Castle,** ancestral home of the Campbells. Actually, the current castle, more a country house than a castle, dates only from the 1740s, the same time that the third Duke of Argyll relocated and rebuilt the village. It is best known for its weapons collection and surrounding landscape gardens.

Return to the main itinerary by taking the **A819** north out of the village, up through Glen Aray, to **Loch Awe** and the **A85.** Turn right

Even a rainbow cannot soften the fierce beauty of Glencoe.

and drive about 3 miles (5 kilometers) to a **left turn** onto the **B8074,** heading up wild and lonely **Glen Orchy.** At the other end of the glen, turn **left** onto the **A82** toward **Glencoe.** ✥

Those who forsake the detour to Inveraray in order to spend more time in the wilder setting of Glencoe should continue north from Tarbet on the **A82** to **Ardlui.** Here the road climbs steeply through a rocky gorge with the falls of **Glen Falloch,** whisky-tinted from peat, boiling and thundering along the roadside. At Crianlarich, in the shadow of **Ben More,** the A82 turns sharply left, passes through **Tyndrum** (the Tourist Information Centre here offers an accommodation booking service), and turns due north, paralleling the rail line to the Highlands.

Beyond **Bridge of Orchy,** the road skirts the eastern edge of little Loch Tulla, crosses Black Mount Pass, and then begins the traverse of **Rannoch Moor,** an immense and lonely expanse of boulder-strewn peat bog, becks, and tarns more than 50 square miles in area. Huge pinnacles of steel gray rock, the frost-shattered remnants of a vast, long-vanished volcano, rim the ravaged moorland. As the A82 turns to the west, the rail line bends away from the road to the northeast, crossing the watery wastes of the moor on a thick bed of tree branches.

Ahead, guarding the gates of **Glencoe,** the gaunt pyramid of **Bauchaille Etive Mor** ("the Great Shepherd of Etive") towers darkly above a wide glacial valley, devoid of humanity but for the Kingshouse Inn—the oldest inn in Scotland—which huddles in a shallow depression off to your right. (A narrow dead-end minor road on the left makes a memorable detour, a breathtaking 10-mile/16-kilometer run to isolated **Loch Etive.**) Ahead and on the right is the flat-topped mass of **the Study,** a corruption of an old Gaelic name that meant "Anvil of the Mists."

Even in brilliant sun, Glencoe is a stark and humbling place, so untamed it seems frozen at the dawn of creation. But in a summer thunderstorm, with sheets of rain lashing your windshield and lightning suddenly illuminating the dark, hanging glens, it outstrips even the wildest visions of Blake or Dante. Vicious peaks and ridges slash the sky. Here and there a tree crouches, gnarled and bent by the wind. Torrents plunge off cliffs and rage down ragged gullies to join the tumbling River Coe as it chews away at the glaciated valley floor on its way to the sea.

It is a brooding, brutal landscape, as if every rock held within it the memory of that morning on February 12, 1692, when, before daylight and in the teeth of a raging blizzard, 120 soldiers under the Campbell of Glenlyon put some 40 of the MacDonalds of Glencoe to the sword—after the MacDonalds had provided them shelter and hospitality for two weeks. The MacDonalds' sin? Because of bad weather, they were a few days late in swearing allegiance to the new Hanoverian monarchs,

William and Mary. In fact, their tardiness was just a convenient excuse for murder. The English had sought an opportunity to crush the clans, and Under Secretary of State for Scotland Sir John Dalrymple saw an opportunity to bring the Papist and Jacobite clans in line at last. His instructions were clear: "They must all be slaughtered, and the manner of their execution must be sure, secret, and effectual." But the secret did not keep; some MacDonalds escaped and the world soon heard of the massacre. Instead of being weakened, the Highland clans redoubled their efforts to return the Stuarts to the throne, and used Glencoe as a rallying cry through the several Jacobite rebellions that followed.

As if whistling past the graveyard, the A82 hurries through the glen, passing the **National Trust Visitor Centre** at Clachaig before it reaches quiet Glencoe Village near the shores of Loch Leven. Turn **right** here to enter the village and settle your accommodations for the night (see Creature Comforts below).

𝅊 A WALK INTO THE HILLS TO THE "LOST VALLEY"

Distance: 2–3 miles/3.2–5 kilometers, depending upon how far up the valley you walk; allow 2–3 hours
Difficulty: An occasionally steep but dramatic walk
Total Elevation Gain: About 1,000 feet/300 meters
Gear: Sneakers or boots, rain gear
Maps: Ordnance Survey 1:50,000 Landranger Map #41 or 1:63,360
Tourist Map for Ben Nevis and Glencoe

If you have avoided today's earlier side trips and/or have at least two hours of daylight before dinner, head for the hills. However spectacular Glencoe may be from the road, it is nothing compared with the mountains themselves. Glencoe is a walking and climbing mecca (guides are available at the mountaineering store just west of the village for those wishing to stay longer). The peaks, however, while magnificent, can be dangerous in bad weather. This walk, which has both scenic and historical attractions, sticks to lower elevations.

(**Note:** Unlike England, where public footpaths are numerous and marked by signs, Scotland has few marked rights of way. With a different governmental and legal tradition from England's, the Scottish system is less formalized. In a few places, local planning authorities have reached public footpath agreements with local landowners, and help maintain them. But elsewhere, access is with the forbearance of landowners. In open country—moorlands and mountains—there are few restrictions, so long as you follow the Country Code.)

The southern flank of Glencoe is dominated by **Bidean nam Bian,**

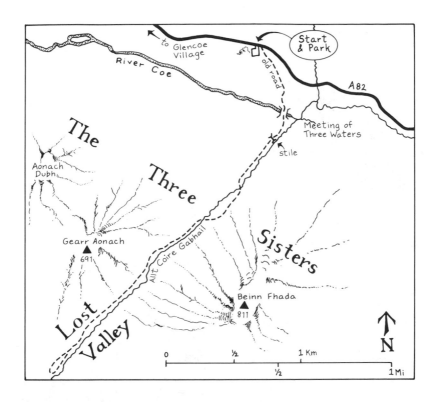

the "Peak of the Peaks," so named because it encompasses some nine distinct summits. Its true summit is blocked from view by the lower but still impressive **Three Sisters,** which rise directly from the river to the sky. In between the Sisters are *corries,* suspended valleys cut thousands of years ago by the great glaciers that spread from Rannoch Moor across the Highlands.

The walk focuses on **Coire Gabhail,** the "corrie of the bounty," also known as the **Lost Valley.** Completely hidden from Glencoe itself, Coire Gabhail possesses a lovely high alpine meadow—used by the MacDonalds of Glencoe to hide stolen cattle. To begin this walk, drive back up Glencoe, a couple of miles past the National Trust Visitor Centre, and park in the gravel area on the right just beyond a big boulder, about 1.5 miles (2.4 kilometers) up the valley from tiny Loch Achtriochtan. From the upper end of the parking area, walk toward the river, following the old military road until a gravel path branches off to the right. The path leads down to a footbridge over the river at a spot known as the "Meeting of Three Waters."

On the other side of the footbridge, the path immediately begins a steep climb into a ravine cut by the rushing water of the Allt (stream)

Coire Gabhail, between two of the Sisters. Beyond the stile, the main path clambers along the bank of the stream as it tumbles over waterfalls and through pools (a minor path branches right up the hillside). Then, after crossing the stream, the path wanders through a maze of huge boulders dumped into the glacial valley bottom by a stupendous landslide long ago, then suddenly breaks out into a long flat meadow—Coire Gabhail, the cattle thieves' sanctuary. Green and strewn with wild thyme and eyebright, it is an oddly pastoral place, wedged in between the dark volcanic peaks. Off on the right, just where you encounter the meadow, are a number of shallow caves.

If time, energy, and skill permit, the climb to the ridge leading to the summit of **Stob Coire non Lochan,** "peak of the corrie with the little loch," offers some splendid views of the area. Cross to the far end of the valley and take the path up the left side of the gorge to the corrie ridge. The summit is a short hike up to the right.

To return, simply retrace your steps.

CREATURE COMFORTS

Daily Bed

Accommodations in and around Glencoe Village range from small and friendly hotels in both **Glencoe** and **Clachaig** (near the visitor center) to a variety of B&Bs. The B&Bs are found within the village proper, along the shoreline, and up the hill on the road to the hospital. More B&Bs can be found on the main road down the loch near Ballachulish. There is also a youth hostel in Glencoe Village. Finally, larger (and fancier) hotels can be found at either end of the Ballachulish bridge at the mouth of Loch Leven, about 2 miles west of Glencoe. Should you find yourself completely without options, there are accommodations galore on the way to Fort William, only a dozen miles or so north of the bridge.

Daily Bread

Dining tends to be informal in Glencoe. There are restaurants at the hotels and a handful of cafés, including a "wholefood" (natural food) restaurant in the village itself. Farther afield, there is a fine pub restaurant overlooking the Loch Leven narrows in the hotel on the other side of the bridge in North Ballachulish, which serves excellent haggis, complete with the "wee dram" of malt whisky that traditionally accompanies it. And finally, there is a formal restaurant in the rather grand Victorian hotel on the south side of the bridge.

Glen Etive, closely guarded by "The Great Shepherd," Bauchaille Etive Mor

Haggis and Other Mysteries of Scottish Cuisine

Menus in Scotland are full of items with names that provide few clues as to their ingredients or gustatory prospects: finnan haddie (smoked haddock), cock-a-leekie (a rich chicken soup), and Forfar bridies (meat and onions in a pastry shell), among others. But of all the mysteries of the Scottish table, none is more mysterious than haggis. Mention it anywhere in Britain and, though they have no idea what it really is, people will scrunch up their faces and make disparaging remarks. An ancient British dish that is extinct except in the Highlands, haggis gets its ambiguous reputation because of its contents: the ground-up bits and pieces of lamb that don't usually make it to the butcher's shelves—heart, liver, lungs, and the like—mixed with onions, oatmeal, spices, and herbs, and then steamed (in a boiled sheep's stomach). Having put that part behind us, here's the secret: the taste can be terrific—spicy, savory, rich, and satisfying. (Of course the malt whisky that comes with it helps.)

Beyond haggis, the abundance of Scotland's oceans and streams, lush grazing lands, and game-filled moors provides plenty of inspiration for chefs in a growing number of remote but remarkable restaurants. The *Taste of Scotland* guidebook, produced by the Scottish Tourist Authority, offers reliable recommendations.

Over the Sea to Skye

GLENCOE ◆ FORT WILLIAM
KYLE OF LOCHALSH ◆ SKYE

- ◆ Three alternate routes through the remotest Highlands, featuring Bonnie Prince Charlie's haunts, Iron Age forts, and the quintessential Highlands castle
- ◆ Ferry trips to Skye, the "Isle of Mists"
- ◆ An afternoon drive through the ancient stronghold of the MacDonalds

. . . in all that wide landscape you might be the sole survivor; silence and immensity fill the soul. . . .
—J. A. MacCulloch
"The Misty Isle of Skye," 1905

Maps of Scotland are oddly unbalanced. In the south and even in the southern Highlands, major and minor roads scurry through valleys and glens, connecting a multitude of small towns and cozy clustered villages. But north of the long diagonal gash of the Great Glen, roads dribble into nothingness and settlements vanish, as if the mapmakers ran out of ink.

That the maps are accurate becomes abundantly clear as soon as you drive west or north from Fort William. Towering mountains spring directly from the floor of the sea and narrow glens lead deep into a wilderness in which red deer and golden eagles hold dominion, not man. There are no cities in the northwest Highlands. There are few roads. The landscape is deserted.

This great emptiness is due, in part, to the natural barrier created by the mountains. But the more compelling cause is economic and environmental, not topographic. After centuries of forest cutting and overgrazing, the thin Highland soil is unproductive. The elements are harsh, leaching nutrients from the earth and testing the limits of human endurance. Even before the Clearances, people who lived in these glens were desperately poor. All that remains of their time on the land is the occasional remote and roofless husk of a crofter's cottage. Surrounding these relics is a vast, untamed wilderness where magnificent peaks march across a changeable sky and a ragged coastline reaches crooked, salty fingers deep into inland glens.

And at the end of one of those very few Highland roads, across a narrow, tide-ripped strait, is an island only 50 miles (80 kilometers) long but with more than a thousand miles of coastline, perhaps the most ferocious mountains in Britain, bizarre landscapes of cliffs and pinnacles, brilliant sunshine and breath-snatching gales, and, arguably, the finest malt whisky in Scotland: the Isle of Skye.

🚗 ROADS TO THE ISLES

Distance: 90 miles/145 kilometers to Kyle of Lochalsh
Roads: Breathtaking 2-lane primary roads
Driving Time: Allow 4–5 hours with stops
Map: Michelin Map #401

Technically, there are at least three "roads to the isles," and you'll have an opportunity today to choose among them to suit your schedule and sense of adventure. Each has its attractions: one passes sites that marked the beginning and end of Bonnie Prince Charlie's quest for the Crown and ends with a delightful sea voyage; another follows a spectacular mountain road and ends with two Iron Age fortresses; and the third is a wildly scenic ride through the Highlands with a picture-postcard castle near the end. But first, let's leave melancholy Glencoe behind.

From **Glencoe Village,** make the short run to the mouth of Loch Leven and follow the **A82** over the bridge to North Ballachulish and up Loch Linnhe to **Fort William,** a remarkably unattractive market town founded and garrisoned by the English in the mid-1600s to keep the clans in line.

Looming above Fort William to a height of **4,406 feet (1,343 meters)** is **Ben Nevis,** the highest mountain in Britain. A huge hunk of volcanic rock, Ben Nevis hunches like a slumbering bull, softly rounded but no less menacing, just east of the town. But it lacks the theatricality of Bauchaille Etive Mor in Glencoe or the ferocity of the Black Cuillins you will encounter on Skye this afternoon, and its name in Gaelic, which means "mountain with its head in the clouds," provides a clue to what greets most climbers when they complete the long but relatively easy trudge to the summit.

Fort William, with its hordes of milling, invariably damp holiday-makers, would be best avoided were it not for two attractions. First, it is virtually the only opportunity you'll have to stock a picnic lunch before plunging into the fastness of the northwest Highlands. And second, it has two excellent information resources at the upper end of town, near the waterfront: a first-class **Travel Information Centre** with excellent displays and information materials, and the **Nevisport Bookstore,** with perhaps the finest stock of travel and outdoor guidebooks in Scotland. In addition, if you have decided to take the short route to Skye via the 30-minute ferry trip from Mallaig (see route below), you should arrange reservations with the ferry company, Caledonian MacBrayne (telephone 0687-2403 in Mallaig, or their headquarters in Gourock, near Glasgow, 0475-33755) before you leave Fort William. Without a reservation, you may well find yourself stranded at Mallaig overnight (a disruptive but delightful experience).

Whichever route you choose to Skye, begin by heading north again on the **A82** in the direction of **Spean Bridge.**

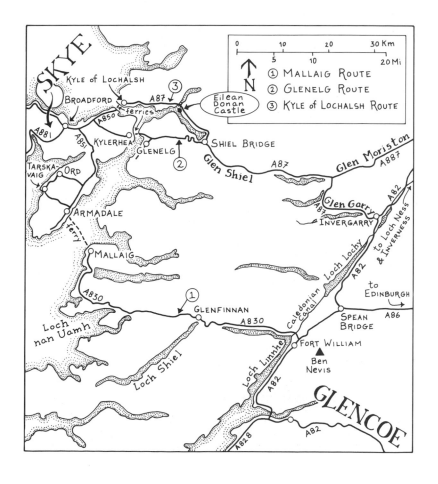

To Skye via Ferry from Mallaig

The shortest route to Skye is the **A830** to the picturesque fishing port of **Mallaig,** some 50 miles (80 kilometers) to the west. This superbly scenic ride begins just north of Fort William, where you turn **left** onto the A830. After about 15 miles (24 kilometers), you pass the **Glenfinnan Monument,** where young and charismatic Charles Edward Louis Phillip Casimir Stuart—"Bonnie Prince Charlie"—first raised his standard and set off to restore the British Crown to the Stuart line. He almost succeeded. With an army of 5,000 Highlanders, Roman Catholics, and Episcopalians, Prince Charlie reached as far as Derby, in the English Midlands, before winter and disappointment at the lack of English support caused the army to hesitate. The English, led by Prince Charlie's own cousin, the Duke of Cumberland, seized the initiative and hounded the Jacobites all the way back to Inverness, finally crushing them at Culloden Moor.

Beyond the monument, as the road runs along the southern flank of the Morar peninsula, it twists and turns to follow the shoreline, first of Loch Eilt, then Loch Ailort, and then the island-dotted **Loch nan Uamh,** the site (marked with a plaque) where the prince first came ashore to begin his quest and where, a little over a year later, after months as a fugitive, he departed in defeat for France. At **Arisaig,** the A830 curves sharply to the right, running along the seacoast with the

This page, grounds-keepers take a break at the golf course outside Mallaig; opposite page, *the picturesque Highland fishing village of Mallaig, one of three ferry ports to Skye.*

humps of the island of **Rhum** and the headland of little **Eigg** in the distance. On the right, the road passes **Loch Morar,** cut by a glacier to a depth of 1,017 feet (310 meters), the deepest in Britain. A few miles later, the road ends at Mallaig, a busy fishing port that rings with the cries of gulls, the creak of winches, and the chugging diesel engines of scores of brightly painted commercial fishing boats.

To get to the queue for the ferry, follow signs directing you around to the left of the fish warehouse and onto the quay. The ferry is a large ship and the process of loading cars, buses, and trucks aboard, via hydraulic lifts and revolving turntables, is almost as entertaining as the trip itself, which is long enough (30 minutes) to seem like a voyage and short enough to preclude seasickness.

The two other routes to Skye are longer but have the benefit of ferries that require no reservations. To reach either of them, head **north** out of Fort William on the **A82** up the Great Glen in the direction of Spean Bridge and Inverness. The road cuts across the edge of Leanachan Forest and then, beyond **Spean Bridge,** drops down to Loch Lochy, the first freshwater lake in the glen.
(**Note:** If you spent longer in Yorkshire and the Lake District than this itinerary plans and you are unable to visit Skye and Torridon, Spean Bridge is a good place to change course for Edinburgh. Take the A86 east through Glen Spean to Laggan. Then turn right onto the A889 and, about 10 miles later, pick up the southbound A9 into Glen Garry to Perth. Outside Perth, follow signs for the M90 and Edinburgh.)

Ben Nevis, Great Glen, and the rest of the mountains in the northwest Highlands are, despite their grandeur, merely the worn-down nubs of a mountain range created some 400 to 500 million years ago during what geologists call the **Caledonian Mountain Building Episode.** In an epic geologic fender bender, two vast chunks of the earth's crust—the North American and European plates—collided as they cruised the primordial globe. On impact, the landscape scrunched together like a crumpled piece of sheet metal, reaching heights that rivaled the Himalayas. The two plates ultimately disengaged, and part of the Highlands coast headed west to what today is the northern New England and Canadian coast. The massive Great Glen fault is dramatic testimony to these events: its northern side slipped some 65 miles (105 kilometers) southwest, while its southern side stayed put. Earthquakes and volcanoes followed, shattering the folded stone and injecting it with molten lava. Erosion ate away at these towering peaks slowly until, 2 million years ago, the first of some twenty ice ages began. When the last of the glaciers receded some 10,000 years ago, filling the hollows with meltwater, what you see today was all that remained. And what splendid remnants they are, furred with heather and bracken and draped with silvery waterfalls.

Beyond Spean Bridge, the A82 runs along the eastern shore of Loch Lochy, then crosses to the west side of Loch Oich, passing over Thomas Telford's "folly," the **Caledonian Canal.** Running 60 miles (97 kilometers) and connecting the three lochs from Inverness to Fort William, the canal was completed in 1834 and was a white elephant from the day it opened. In the years from inception to completion, steamships too big to fit through the canal's twenty-nine locks replaced sailing vessels and railroads replaced canals as fast, cheap forms of transport. It limped along through World War II, serving small fishing boats until the recreational boating industry gave it new life.

At **Invergarry,** you finally leave the A82—the road you've been on since Glasgow—to follow the **A87** along Loch Garry, up and over the birch- and conifer-forested pass to Loch Loyne, and then west along the north shore of Loch Cluanie. Here the road begins to climb higher to the head of **Glen Shiel.** As it tips over the top you have the sensation of reaching the summit of a roller coaster and the long ride through the **Pass of Stachel** does nothing to dispel that feeling. Down the narrow gorge the road plummets, clinging to the rumpled skirts of the **Five Sisters,** the mountains rising on the right. Golden eagles and even peregrine falcons patrol the ragged heights and wild goats and red deer haunt the lower elevations.

Eilean Donan Castle, near Kyle of Lochalsh, may be the most romantically—and strategically—sited castle in Scotland.

The A87 reaches sea level again at **Shiel Bridge,** at the head of **Loch Duich,** the point at which you have to make your choice of routes to Skye. The main road continues to **Kyle of Lochalsh,** but a minor road to the left leads to a privately operated ferry at **Glenelg,** which runs only during the summer and never on Sunday. (In midsummer, this alternate route generally has much shorter waiting lines than the main ferry at Kyle.)

To Skye via Ferry from Glenelg

The Glenelg route is the old cattle-drove road from the days when Skye cattle were forced to swim the narrows between Kylerhea and Glenelg on their way to market. Coming out of Shiel Bridge the road swings round the end of the loch and then begins a series of hairpin switchbacks as it climbs steeply up to the pass of **Mam Rattagan,** over 1,000 feet (300 meters) high. There are terrific views back into Glen Shiel.

Next, the road turns downhill along isolated **Glen More,** eventually reaching a Y-junction. The ferry is about 2 miles (3.2 kilometers) to the right, but detour to the left first through a forested area to visit two *brochs*—Iron Age fortifications built by the Picts, the early tribes who re- sisted the Celtic settlers from Ireland known as the *Scoti* before finally being united with them by Kenneth MacAlpine, the first king of Scot- land, in A.D. 843. The brochs, **Dun Telve** and **Dun Trodden,** are squat, cylindrical fortresses with walls 13 feet thick at the base and rising some 30 feet high, and are believed to have been built to protect the Picts from the marauding Norse. Inside these brochs, the finest on the mainland, there were interior walls and galleries and a central court- yard. After exploring the brochs, take the ferry from Glenelg across the strait to Skye.

To Skye via Ferry from Kyle to Lochalsh

The main itinerary, meanwhile, follows the **A87** west from Shiel Bridge along the north shore of Loch Duich eventually revealing per- haps the most romantically sited castle in all of Scotland, **Eilean Donan,** rising from the rocks of an islet at the mouth of Loch Duich and connected to the mainland by an arched causeway (open April through September, Monday through Saturday 10:00 A.M. to 6:00 P.M., Sunday 1:00 P.M. to 6:00 P.M.).

Beyond the castle, the A87 crosses a bridge over the outflow of Loch Long and travels overland for the final 5 miles (8 kilometers) to the **Kyle of Lochalsh** and the ferry to Skye, a simple roll on–roll off af- fair that crosses the strait to **Kyleakin** in five minutes. In midsummer, when the lines can be long, you can use the time to visit the **Tourist In- formation Centre** in the village and stock up on brochures for Skye.

🚗 OVER THE SEA TO SKYE

Skye gives special meaning to the phrase "So near and yet so far." Separated from the mainland at Kyle by the slimmest of straits—just a few hundred yards wide—there is nevertheless an otherworldliness about Skye, as if it were caught somewhere between reality and myth.

The narrow strait between the island and the mainland, dug by a passing glacier, is extremely deep and has a fearsome tidal rip. As it leaves Kyle, the ferry first is swept downstream, then labors sideways, crablike, to the opposite shore, fighting the current. On a rough day, with the wind out of the east, disembarking on the other side can be a bit of an adventure as you try to time your exit with the rise and fall of the ferry on the surf along the concrete ramp on the foreshore. **Kyleakin** (pronounced "ky-lakkon" and named after the Norse King Hakkon, who sailed through here after his defeat by the Scots at the battle of Largs) is guarded by the haunting shell of **Moil Castle,** once ruled by a legendary chatelaine called "Saucy Mary," part Viking princess and part MacKinnon, who strung a chain across the strait to exact tolls from passing ships.

Skye owes its name to the Vikings, who called it *Skuyo,* the Cloud Island: Not for nothing is this known as the "Misty Isle." Exposed to the North Atlantic gales, Skye has a classic maritime climate. You will most certainly get wet during your visit, but you are just as likely to see brilliant sunshine (especially in May and June), sun-dappled moorlands and mountains, unearthly shafts of light piercing the clouds and playing like searchlights across dark lochs and bays, and brilliant sunsets beyond the outer isles. Weather changes constantly and differs dramatically from place to place on the island, and the visual experience is so-varied that time seems to expand. At the end of a day in Skye you'll have the odd sensation of having experienced several days in one.

Whether you took the longer ferry from Mallaig or either of the shorter ferries, you arrived, probably by midafternoon, on **Sleat** (pronounced "slate"), the southernmost of Skye's five main peninsulas. The other four are **Trotternish, Waternish,** and **Duirinish** on the northern end of the island, and **Minginish** on the west. Ahead to the west, the jagged peaks of the **Cuillins** (pronounced "coolins"), crowned in mist and wrapped in an eerie majesty, dominate the horizon.

If you came by either of the short ferries, follow the **A850** around the southeastern coast, with the small islands of **Pabay** and **Scalpay** off on the right and the **Applecross** peaks behind them on the mainland, to the town of **Broadford.** The only town of any size in the southern half of the island, Broadford straggles along the coast rather unattractively, a poor introduction to Skye. But it has two important resources worth your time. The first is the **Isle of Skye Field Centre,** on your right as you enter town, with its small but helpful museum and Environmental

Resource Centre, run by Paul and Grace Yoxon. The nonprofit field center has a wealth of information on the natural history of Skye, conducts biological and geological research for government agencies, offers a full program of natural history tours and walks, and is a great source of advice for walkers and those interested in Skye flora and fauna. (For details of special programs, write Isle of Skye Field Centre, Broadford, Skye IV49 9AQ.)

The second worthwhile stop is the **Tourist Information Centre,** on the right at the center of town. Stop here to get your bearings, make arrangements for accommodations if you're uneasy about taking pot-luck, and collect brochures, maps, and booklets on Skye's history and attractions. A color booklet called "Isle of Skye & South West Ross: Where to Stay" provides detailed listings of hotels, guesthouses, and many (though not all) B&Bs throughout the island.

Thus informed and equipped, you're free to explore. The chances are good that the day has dwindled down and you have too little time to explore the central and northern extremities of the island or begin a hike. Instead, consider turning around and heading south a few miles farther into Sleat.

(**Note:** Those who arrived late in **Armadale** by the longer ferry from Mallaig should consider this option as well.) There are two excellent reasons for taking this course. The first is the opportunity to visit the award-winning Clan Donald Centre, whose audiovisual program and exhibits provide a sweeping overview of Skye's turbulent clan history and help make sense of the sights you'll take in tomorrow. (The center is open April through October, Monday through Saturday, 10:00 A.M. to 5:30 P.M.; also Sunday 1:00 P.M. to 5:30 P.M. June through August only.)

The second is a minor road that loops over to two small settlements on the **west coast** of Sleat. Missed by virtually all who visit Skye, this drive affords some of the finest views of the magnificent Cuillins available anywhere on the island. Watching the sun set behind them, changing the peaks from plum to gold, then magenta, and finally deep lavender blue, is one of the finest bits of open-air theater in Britain.

To explore Sleat, take the A850 back beyond the east end of Broadford and turn **right** onto the **A851.** The road wanders across a boggy landscape dotted with small, silvery lochans and abloom in spring and summer with wildflowers and heathers.

Sleat is known as "the garden of Skye," but the phrase makes sense only by comparison with the starkness of the rest of Skye. There *are* scattered bosky remnants of ancient forests near the shore. But along Sleat's spine, surrounded for miles in every direction by rough moor-

The ragged ruins of Moil Castle stand guard over the busy ferry port of Kyleakin, Skye.

land suitable only for the hardiest sheep, the characterization seems hyperbolic in the extreme.

Farther on, perhaps 10 miles (16 kilometers) from the fork outside of Broadford, a road branching to the left drops down to the coastal settlement of **Isleornsay,** a handsome old crofting community. Bypass the turn and continue straight ahead for roughly another 10 miles (16 kilometers), ignoring both side roads to the right. The Clan Donald Centre is in a wooded arboretum on the right (left if coming from Armadale Pier) and is well marked.

When you are ready to leave the Clan Donald Centre, turn **left** and take the first side road to the **left,** toward **Tarskavaig,** one of dozens of places in Skye that still retain their Norse names. The single-lane road climbs steeply and the coastal forest immediately disappears, replaced by a lumpy moorland covered with heather and bracken. The road, such as it is, scurries up hill and down dale through a scrubby landscape, past a pretty freshwater loch, before reaching the sea at the southern end of **Tarskavaig Bay.** Here the road clambers up and over the top of a bluff high above the bay and runs along above Tarskavaig, Sleat's largest cluster of crofts, sheltered from the sea in a shallow swale. The views from this bluff are magnificent, with **Eigg** to the south across Cuillin Sound, **Rhum** to the right of Eigg, little **Canna** hiding just beyond Rhum's right shoulder, and far off across the Sea of the Hebrides, the low profile of **South Uist.** Nearer and to the right, the **Strathaird** peninsula shelters the hamlet of **Elgol;** behind it tower the savage peaks of the Black Cuillins, lords of all they survey.

After another mile or so the road dips down to the red sandstone shores of a bay called Ob Gauscavaig. On a bluff at the right-hand entrance to this bay, growing from the very rocks themselves, is the ruined hulk of **Dunscaith** (originally Dun Sgathaich) **Castle.** This strategic site, with its natural moat bridged by a stone arch, was the stronghold of the MacDonalds of Sleat in the fifteenth century. If time permits, walk out along the shingle beach, explore the ruins, and drink in the spectacular surroundings.

From the beach, the road scrambles up through a gnarled wood of oak and birch, one of the few remnants of Skye's original forests. Then it tumbles downhill again to the tiny settlement of **Ord** before crossing the peninsula again and joining the A851.

CREATURE COMFORTS

All of Skye is a tourism destination, however remote, and accommodations and restaurants are scattered throughout the island. Many cluster in and around **Portree,** the island's only major town, situated on a small bay on the east coast, at the base of the Trotternish peninsula. It is a friendly, bustling little town (except on Sundays, when the influence of the strict Church of Scotland shuts down almost everything in Skye) and has an excellent Tourist Information Centre, but it would be a shame to hole up there given the more spectacular opportunities elsewhere on the island. If you haven't found a place to stay yet, the "Where to Stay" booklet and a pocket full of 10p coins for the public phone can save you from wandering far out some peninsula only to find all the rooms booked.

(**Note:** Remember that B&Bs, guesthouses, and hotels in remote settlements often list themselves under the name of the nearest large village or town. A B&B in Elgol at the end of the Strathaird peninsula, for example, might list itself under Broadford. So read the fine print in the addresses listed to find the remote and scenic places you seek.)

Daily Bed

Assuming that you've chosen to spend this afternoon in Sleat, you'll find accommodations clustered in a few places en route. There are two small hotels in **Isleornsay** (and a superb country house hotel at **Kinloch,** between Broadford and Isleornsay). There are also several hotels scattered along the east coast all the way to **Ardvasar,** beyond the Clan Donald Centre. On the west coast, there are a handful of remote but beautifully sited B&Bs in **Tarskavaig** and **Ord** (along with a small hotel at Ord).

Somewhat farther afield, but still in the south, there are many B&Bs and hotels in **Broadford** and **Kyleakin,** as well as several B&Bs on the **Strathaird** peninsula road stretching south from Broadford to Elgol. Finally, there are youth hostels at Broadford and at remote but magnificent **Glen Brittle,** on the north side of the Cuillin range near the coast, beyond Broadford and on a minor road off the A863.

Daily Bread

Many B&Bs in Skye offer dinner to guests, often at excellent prices, and the quality of the cuisine at some B&Bs can be quite high (especially those run by newcomers from England). If you arrive late and unannounced, however, your chances of taking advantage of this opportunity are slim.

In addition, although pubs in the English manner don't exist in Skye, the saloon bars of most hotels operate like pubs and often have good, if basic, menus. More formal hotel restaurants (one or two in the first-class category) also serve nonresidents. The best way to sort out the options is to ask the people where you are staying for suggestions; some B&B owners keep a selection of menus from local hotels and restaurants. Expect to do a bit of driving to reach dinner; despite the island's small size, places to eat can be pretty widely spread out.

Exploring the Misty Isle

◆ Two walks into the heart of the Black Cuillins
◆ A side trip to the Talisker Distillery
◆ A driving tour of Skye passing the ancestral strongholds of the MacLeods and MacDonalds
◆ A climb into the fractured pinnacles of the Quiraing

From the lone shieling of the misty island
Mountains divide us and the waste of the seas—
Yet still the blood is strong, the heart is Highland,
And we in dreams behold the Hebrides.

When the bold kindred, in time long vanish'd
Conquered the soil and fortified the keep—
No seer foretold the children would be banish'd,
That a degenerate lord might boast his sheep.
—Anonymous exiled Highlander, 1829

If Skye's tumultuous and ultimately tragic clan history is responsible for its mystique, then its tumultuous geologic history is responsible for its spectacular scenery. There are ancient rock formations in Skye as old as any in Britain, but most of what you see today is young, at least in geological terms.

Some 60 million years ago, Skye was not the place to come for a quiet holiday by the sea. The island was wracked by volcanic activity more violent and more extensive than anywhere else in Britain. First, stupendous explosions threw clouds of ash and rock into the air. Then the countryside split open and molten lava flowed out of huge fissures and across the surface for miles, covering virtually all of the northern two-thirds of today's Skye. Again and again the lava coated the ravaged surface of the island, building layer upon layer of rapidly cooling new rock to a thickness of nearly 4,000 feet (1,200 meters) in some places. As the violence gradually subsided, just beneath the surface of the earth a massive magma chamber—the source of much of the lava—was cool-

No matter where you are on Skye, the serrated summits of the Black Cuillins are always on the horizon.

ing, slowly changing from liquid to solid. Tens of thousands of years later, after successive ice ages shaved off the softer surface rock, this vast plug of hardened lava was revealed and exposed to the elements. When marauding Norse seamen first arrived on Skye, more than a thousand years ago, they called the jagged tops of this formation *Kjollen*, or "keel-shaped ridges." Today, in the native Gaelic that still survives here and in the Outer Hebrides, they are called the **Cuillins.** Savage and majestic, they are omnipresent—always lurking off on the horizon, distant and mysterious when wreathed in mist, awe-inspiring when they glitter in the sun.

Along with the sea, which is never more than five miles away, the Cuillins define the Skye landscape. Penetrating them is this morning's objective. Later today, you'll explore the lava plateaus of the north of Skye and walk along the fractured escarpment on Trotternish called the Quiraing.

TWO ROUTES INTO THE CUILLINS

On Skye, more so than anywhere else on this trip, let the changeable weather organize the day's activities. There are several ways of enjoying Skye's most exciting outdoor attractions, depending upon weather conditions, and there are indoor attractions as well. What's more, nothing is much more than an hour from anything else.

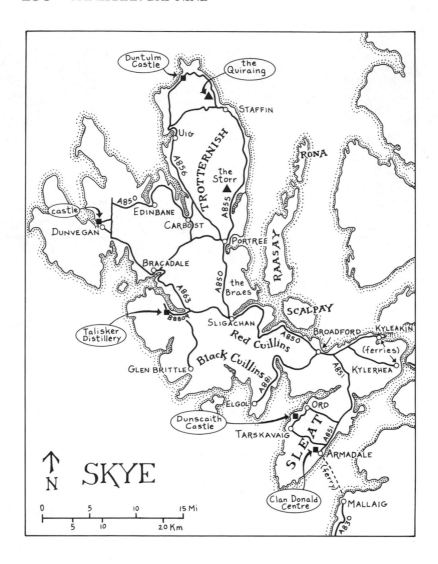

If you spent last night somewhere on the Sleat peninsula, begin this morning by returning to Broadford. From here you have several choices. If the weather is good and you fancy a half-day excursion that includes a boat ride into the very heart of the Cuillin range, turn left at the northern end of town onto the A881 for the scenic 14-mile (22-kilometer) ride to Elgol. If the weather is uncertain, a splendid 3-hour walk up into the Cuillins from the beach at Glen Brittle, not far from Broadford, is a good way to spend the morning. If the weather is hopeless, head for the west side of Skye to visit either the Talisker Distillery (a fascinating experience even if you don't take a "wee dram" of this matchless malt whisky) or Dunvegan Castle—still occupied today by the chief of the Clan MacLeod.

𝕜 The Cuillins via Boat from Elgol

The A881 branches off to the left at the end of town near the inn where Bonnie Prince Charlie mixed whisky, honey, and other ingredients to produce *dram buidheach*—the liqueur now called Drambuie. The road runs up the valley cut by the Broadford River, then bends around the flanks of Beinn na Caillich (2,400 feet/732 meters), one of the Red Cuillins, to the right. Beyond the village of **Torrin,** the road curves around the head of Loch Slapin with the first of the Black Cuillins, **Bla-Bhienn** (or "Blaven") towering to 3,045 feet (928 meters) straight ahead across the loch.

From this spot it becomes clear that the Cuillins are, in fact, two distinct sets of mountains, both in shape and color. The **Red Cuillins,** on your right, are made of granite with a faintly pink or rusty color, depending on the light. Softly rounded because the granite erodes relatively easily, the Red Cuillins have a benign character. The jagged **Black**

The gentle swell of the eroded Red Cuillins, near Elgol, Skye

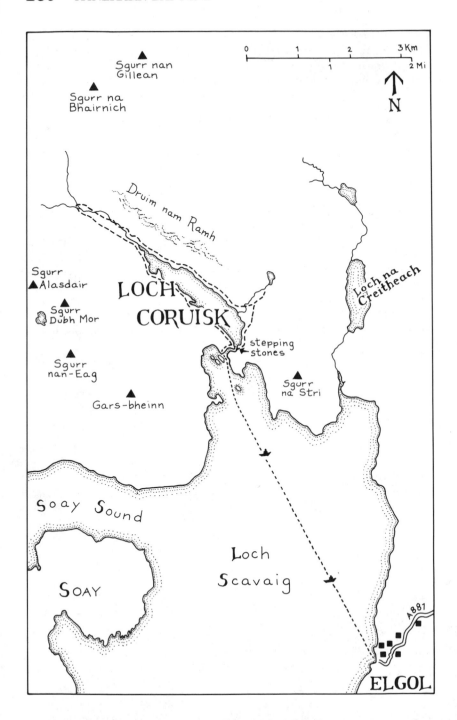

Sgurr nan
Gillean

Sgurr na
Bhairnich

0   1   2   3 Km

1

2 Mi

N

Druim nam Ramh

Sgurr
Alasdair

Sgurr
Dubh Mor

LOCH

CORUISK

Sgurr
nan-Eag

Gars-bheinn

Loch na
Creitheach

stepping
stones

Sgurr
na Stri

Soay Sound

Loch
Scavaig

SOAY

A881

ELGOL

Cuillins, across the loch on your left; most assuredly do not. They are made of a hard, dark volcanic rock called *gabbro.* Sliced by nearly vertical cracks, called *dykes,* once filled with softer granite but now eroded away, the ragged spiked summits of the Black Cuillins—more than a dozen of them over 3,000 feet (1,000 meters)—offer some of the finest climbs and ridge walks in Britain.

The A881 now runs south along the western shore of Loch Slapin, before cutting across the southern tip of the Strathaird peninsula to **Elgol,** a small village perched on a cliff overlooking **Loch Scavaig.** In the summer, boats make the 5-mile (8-kilometer) trip to the head of Loch Scavaig for the short overland walk to freshwater **Loch Coruisk** (from the Gaelic *Coire Uisg,* or "corrie of water").

Loch Coruisk, a favorite subject of nineteenth-century landscape painters like Turner, hangs suspended some 26 feet (8 meters) above sea level and cuts nearly 2 miles (3 kilometers) into the heart of the Cuillins, whose gnarled volcanic flanks soar to the sky on three sides.

A popular path runs deep into the valley, returning along the opposite shore. (**Note:** After the boat returns you to Elgol, drive back to Broadford, skip the outings described below, and drive north on the **A850** past Portree, and rejoin the itinerary as it runs up the west side of Trotternish on the **A856.**)

The route north from **Broadford,** the **A850,** skirts the eastern edge of the Red Cuillins and parallels Skye's eastern coast, providing sweeping views across the Inner Sound toward the mainland's Applecross peninsula and the nearer islands of Scalpay and Raasay. Roughly 14 miles (22 kilometers) north of Broadford, the road turns sharply west and runs up the treeless shore of **Loch Ainort** with the Black Cuillins straight ahead. (Bypass the thatched "Old Skye Crofter's House" museum at Luib; a better example is available at the northern end of Trotternish.) At the head of the loch, the road climbs overland through a high glacial valley at the base of 2,543-foot (775-meter) **Glamaig,** which sweeps up to the left. At the other end of the valley the road descends to the sea again east of the village of **Sconser.** Ahead, across the mouth of **Loch Sligachan** and to the right of **Ben Lee,** is a series of coastal hamlets known collectively as the **Braes.** It was here, in 1882, that the long and brutal exploitation of Highland tenant farmers by their landlords began to be broken.

For more than a century, Skye's major landowners—principally the chiefs of the clans MacDonald and MacLeod—had been summarily evicting their tenants (and former clansmen) from the land they occupied as tenants to make way for large sheep operations. When a plot by the clan leaders to kidnap tenants and ship them overseas was exposed, the landlords responded to the public outrage by the simple expedient of relocating the tenants to small, infertile plots of land (*crofts*) along the coast—like the settlements at the Braes. When Lord Mac-Donald subsequently barred them from their only common grazing area, the men of the Braes voted to refuse to pay their rents and repelled a force of fifty policemen sent by MacDonald to arrest them. Other rebellions followed elsewhere on Skye, but it was not until after World War I that crofters were finally given full tenure of their land. Today, crofting is growing again in Skye. Typically, it involves some sheep grazing, some fishing, and either a cash-income-producing craft or a job off the croft. It is still a difficult way to earn a living, but it preserves the independence the people of Skye struggled so long to achieve. It all began at the Braes.

The **A850** reaches the head of Loch Sligachan and crosses a small bridge by the Sligachan Hotel, a climbers' headquarters for more than a century. West of the hotel, broad and bleak **Glen Sligachan** stretches through the mountains to the southwest and **Sgurr nan Gillean** (3,167

The fifteenth-century fortress of the Clan Donald, Dunscaith, seems to grow directly from the rocks near Ord on the Sleat peninsula, Skye.

feet/965 meters) claws at the sky, with the rest of the saw-toothed Black Cuillins in close rank behind.

Turn **left** at the hotel onto the **A863,** winding through narrow, heather-clad Glen Drynoch toward Loch Harport and Dunvegan. (Those who spent the morning at Loch Coruisk, however, should stay on the A850 to the Trotternish peninsula.)

"Corduroys of Conifers"

The flanks of Glen Drynoch—and a great deal of Scotland's moorlands—have a curiously corrugated surface, thanks to the Forestry Commission's reforestation program. Digging miles of deep, parallel drainage ditches and planting acres of tiny evergreens, they aim to return the barren hillsides to forest cover and generate economic activity. But it is a mixed blessing at best. The huge, regimented plantations of Sitka spruce and lodgepole pine—noted British naturalist and author John Hillaby calls them "corduroys of conifers"—are unnatural, visually jarring, and virtually lifeless. The forest floor is dark and dank. With no sunlight or underbrush, the lower orders of the food chain perish and larger animals and plants never take up residence. There are few birds and the woods have an eerie silence. Naturalists and planners have begun to make some headway in persuading the Forestry Commission to plant mixed hardwood and softwood forests more like those that covered Scotland centuries ago, but it is an uphill battle, one made more difficult by the government grants and income tax credits given to private landowners, until recently, to encourage them to rip up the moors and plant trees— even where the moorlands were too infertile to support tree growth.

At the foot of **Glen Drynoch,** with the shores of **Loch Harport** stretching out ahead, dotted with whitewashed crofters' cottages, there is another choice to be made. Following the **A863** will take you north toward **Dunvegan** and eventually around to the dramatic **Trotternish** peninsula. But a left turn onto to the **B8009** above Loch Harport will quickly bring you to two very different attractions: a relatively short but spectacular walk into the Black Cuillins, and a visit to Skye's Talisker Distillery to learn how Scotland's most famous export—*uisge beatha,* the "water of life"—is made.

(**Note:** If the weather rules out a walk this morning, an easy but spectacular afternoon walk through the bizarre formations of the Quiraing on Trotternish is later in today's itinerary.)

🏃 The Cuillins via Hike from Glen Brittle

Distance: About 6 miles/9.7 kilometers; allow 3–3.5 hours
Difficulty: Steady uphill walk on clear path with a bit of a scramble at
  the top
Total Elevation Gain: 1,845 feet/562 meters
Gear: Good walking shoes (sneakers in dry weather), rain gear
Maps: Ordnance Survey 1:50,000 Map #32 "South Skye," or the
  excellent brochure "Walks From Glen Brittle," available at campsite
  shop

About a mile from where you turned onto the **B8009,** turn very
sharply left onto a minor road signposted for **Glen Brittle.** The road
climbs the right flank of a narrow glen, eventually entering a section of
the Glen Brittle Forest. On the other side of the forest there is a sweeping panorama of many of the highest Black Cuillins, their serrated summits reaching well above 3,000 feet (1,000 meters).

The road now bends right, traveling down the valley cut by the
meandering River Brittle on its way to the sea. Several waterfalls lace
the rugged hillsides on the left as you approach the small settlement of
Glen Brittle. There is a youth hostel here and, at a modern bungalow
called "Stac Lee," Skye's only outdoor guide service, run by the leader
of the Mountain Rescue Squad. The road now turns right (bypassing a
twin-pillared driveway), and heads for the parking area near the campsite along the beach.

The most rewarding walk from Glen Brittle is the one to **Corie
Lagan** (Route 5 in the brochure sold in the campsite shop), a sparkling
mountain tarn cupped in a magnificent volcanic amphitheater, with
views across the Sea of the Hebrides to the outer islands. The path begins, conveniently, behind the campsite's public toilet building, and
climbs straight up the rumpled, heather-clad hillside. Ignore paths
branching off to the right and stay to the left of the little stream, crossing it farther uphill, after about 20 minutes. This part of the walk,
frankly, is a bit of a slog, but stop often to catch your breath and take in
the surroundings: the pink and magenta blossoms of the many different
heathers that carpet the peaty ground, the sweep of the layered lava
cliffs above Loch Brittle (with the shelf of an ancient beach formed
when the ocean level was much higher), the hazy island of Rhum rising
from the sea beyond, and the silence.

After perhaps an hour and a half of steady climbing, the occasionally
boggy path arrives at the foot of a stony scree slope. Below on the left,
Loch an Fhir-bhallaich glitters on the lower slopes. Ahead, a waterfall
tumbles over the edge of a vast bowl, cut by a glacier, suspended between two vicious peaks. Across the outer lip of the bowl, a huge

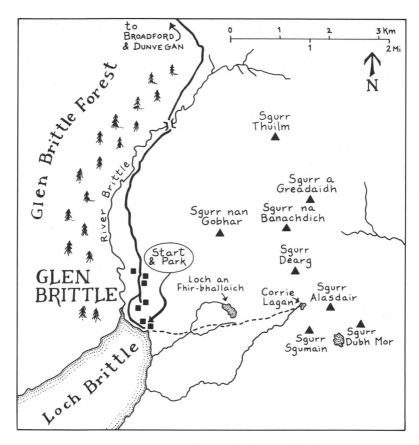

mound of rock—a lava flow frozen in its tracks—lays smooth and rounded like some great sleeping beast.

Stay to the left of this narrowing area of scree, following a path marked by cairns. After a minor scramble up the left side of the lava barrier, you reach the bottom of the corrie itself, and there, cupped within soaring walls of black volcanic peaks, as majestic as the legendary "Hall of the Mountain Kings," is a cold, crystal-clear lochan. Looming above and reflected in its still dark surface are Sgurr Dearg (3,235 feet/986 meters) on the left and Sgurr Alasdair (3,258 feet/993 meters) on the right, the highest of the Black Cuillins, and its buttress Sgurr Sgumain. Connecting them is the knife-edged ridge of Sgurr Mhic Choinnich. (**Note:** Experienced climbers, for whom ascending the Cuillins is the real purpose of any visit to Skye, can reach the ridge by way of the Great Stone Shoot, the scree-filled gully on the left at the back of the corrie.)

Amid the volcanic formations girding Corrie Laggan, in the Black Cuillins above Glen Brittle, Skye

The return to Glen Brittle is by the same route. You'll find the downhill walk easier if you use the rocks embedded in the peat as stepping stones. Their rough volcanic surfaces provide surer footing than the wet peat.

🚗 ACROSS LAVA PLATEAUS TO SKYE'S NORTHERN PENINSULAS

The walk completed, head north again toward Dunvegan by backtracking up Glen Brittle and turning **right** onto the **B8009** for about a mile, then left onto the **A863**—unless, of course, you choose to take in the **Talisker Distillery,** which produces one of the most distinctive of the over 100 malt whiskies distilled in the Highlands and the only one made on Skye. The classic pagoda-roofed distillery, about a mile west of the point where the Glen Brittle road joins the B8009, offers tours Monday through Friday, 10:00 A.M. to 12:00 noon and 2:00 P.M. to 4:00 P.M.

"The Water of Life"

Malt whisky is to Scotch what Cognac is to cooking brandy—complex and as aromatic as perfume. (Scotch, in fact, is a blend of malt whisky and cheaper grain alcohol.) First produced by monks in the fifteenth century (which must certainly have sped the adoption of Christianity by the locals), malt whisky distilling begins with barley that is soaked and spread in a "malting house" to increase its sugar content, then dried over peat fires in kilns with pointed spires. Next it is ground and mixed several times with fresh hot water. Yeast is added to ferment this sweet liquid ("wort"), and the result ("wash") is then cooked in large copper-topped stills. The clear alcohol produced is then diluted with fresh water and stored in old oak sherry casks (from which it takes its color) for eight to twelve years or more. The precise details of each step are closely guarded secrets and enormous attention is given to assuring that the distinctive taste of each brand is maintained. When the mainland Macallan distillery added new stills to increase production several years ago, for example, each one was carefully dented to match the originals.

As you continue along the **A863,** the jagged peaks of the south give way to broad, stepped plateaus—the remains of those lava flows that covered the land millions of years ago. The A863 runs north along the edge of one such ledge, high above Loch Harport, then loops into the little village of **Bracadale.**

(**Note:** If you are running short of time and plan to walk into the Quiraing, take the minor road to the **right** here, crossing the moors toward Portree. After perhaps 9 miles (14.5 kilometers), take the only **left** turn you encounter north to Carbost. Turn **left** and drive a few hundred yards on the **A850,** then **right** onto the **B8036** joining the **A856** north into **Trotternish.** Then consult the itinerary below.)

The A863 continues northwest above island-dotted Loch Bracadale, and near Dunvegan you'll see Skye's westernmost peninsula, **Duirinish,** crowned by two flat-topped mountains called **MacLeod's Tables,** pointing north toward **North Uist,** across the Little Minch sound.

Dunvegan's claim to fame is its castle, the seat of the Chief of the Clan MacLeod. An architectural hodgepodge, it sits upon a rock outcropping above Loch Dunvegan and claims to be the oldest continuously inhabited castle in Scotland (open daily May through September from 10:30 A.M. to 5:00 P.M.; and, from Easter to mid-May and during October, Monday through Saturday from 2:00 P.M. to 5:00 P.M.).

Unless you are a MacLeod or hopelessly attracted to castles, you would probably be better advised at this point to turn **east** toward Portree and **Trotternish,** the largest and most varied of Skye's northern peninsulas. Take the **A850,** cutting across the base of **Waternish,** Skye's middle peninsula, past **Edinbane** (which has a nice pottery), then **left** after **Skeabost** onto the **B8036,** eventually joining the **A856** as it runs north up the western coast of Trotternish.

Along the A856 there are magnificent views across **Loch Snizort** to the high volcanic cliffs of Waternish and across the Minch to the Outer Hebridean **Isle of Harris** (where Harris Tweed comes from). After roughly 15 miles (24 kilometers), the road bends sharply to the right and picks its way down the edge of a steep cliff into the port of **Uig,** from which Caledonian MacBrayne ferries sail to the Outer Hebrides. After passing the Ferry Inn, **bear right** at the fork onto the **A855** (the left fork goes to the ferry pier). The A855 climbs up along the steep hillside above the port, switches back on itself as it climbs higher, then bends left again to run north along a high lava plateau toward **Kilmuir.** (**Note:** Another shortcut opportunity presents itself at the top of the hill above Uig, where a minor road to the right climbs over the top of Trotternish to the east. Five or six miles later, just above a hairpin curve, this road reaches the edge of the Trotternish escarpment. Ahead and slightly to the left is the **Quiraing;** parking is on the right. The road continues down to the coast to Staffin Bay.)

After two or three miles, the ruins of **Monkstadt House** appear on

"Black houses" preserved at the Skye Cottage Museum near Kilmuir at the tip of the Trotternish peninsula

a bluff above the sea off on the left. It was to this spot, in June of 1746, that twenty-three-year-old Flora MacDonald brought the fleeing Bonnie Prince Charlie (disguised as her maid) on his final voyage to the mainland to rendezvous with a French ship and a life in exile.

At Kilmuir, near the tip of Trotternish, consider visiting both the **Skye Cottage Museum** for a sense of the harsh realities of crofting a century or two ago, and the wildly romantic, crumbling ruins of **Duntulm Castle,** for centuries the seat of the MacDonalds.

Beyond Duntulm, the A850 curves around the coast to the east and turns south. There are great views of the **Torridon** peaks across the sound on the mainland and, on the right, the high basaltic escarpment that runs all the way to Portree. About three miles beyond the village of **Flodigarry,** a minor road branches **right** toward Uig. Even if you don't plan to take the walk into the **Quiraing,** detour a couple of miles to the top of the hairpin turn just above the escarpment for one of the finest views in all of Skye.

🚶 A WALK INTO "THE PILLARED STRONGHOLD"

Distance: About 3 miles/4.8 kilometers; allow 2 hours
Difficulty: Easy, with panoramic views; moderate climb to The Table
Total Elevation Gain: Roughly 650 feet/200 meters
Gear: Comfortable walking shoes or sneakers, rain gear
Map: Ordnance Survey 1:50,000 Landranger #23 "North Skye"
(though path is clear and no map is really necessary)

The walk into the remarkable **Quiraing** (pronounced "coo-rang") begins across the road from the parking area at the top of the pass. The path crosses a short boggy area and then runs east along the eroded flanks of the escarpment. The lumpy hillside is coated in emerald grass and kept closely cropped by sheep and also by rabbits, which find shelter among the rocks that have fallen from the fractured cliff above. In places, the path hugs the base of the dark cliff and crosses a succession of tiny waterfalls and burns. In these sheltered places, alpine wildflowers thrive—purple saxifrage and alpine lady's mantle, among others.

Away to the south, the weirdly tilted landscape, caused by massive subsidence and landslides (the largest in Britain), looks a bit like the shattered pieces of a huge table smashed by an angry giant. Directly below, in the boggy areas between several small lochs, neat stacks of drying peat clods stand in rows above large peat beds, their newly cut black edges shining in the sun.

Ahead is the Quiraing itself, a maze of towering pinnacles that takes its name from the Gaelic *Cuith Raing* or "pillared stronghold." On the

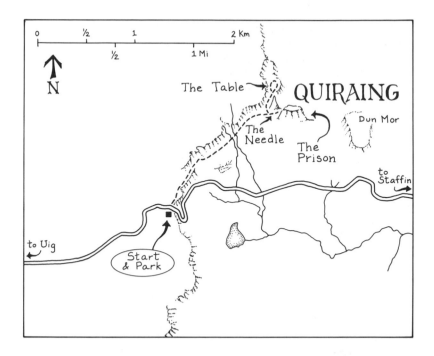

left, The Needle rises a sheer 120 feet (37 meters) above the scree slope filled with giant boulders. High above, golden eagles and buzzards are common (Skye has the largest population of golden eagles in Britain), floating soundlessly on updrafts rising from the columned basaltic cliffs.

At the top of the saddle, the path appears to continue straight ahead around the base of the cliffs. Instead, however, directly opposite The Prison, turn left and climb the steep slope, following a zigzagging "staircase" worn into the hard earth, keeping to the left of the narrow spire of The Needle. The path then cuts right, into a narrow gully and then up through a cleft in the rock. Beyond the cleft, the path rises still higher, to the left and left again, eventually reaching The Table—a huge platform, as flat and green as a giant billiard table and hemmed in on all sides by monolithic pinnacles and the face of the cliff itself. It is an eerie, magical place, where fairies might frolic on still moonlit nights. Since The Table is completely invisible even from the path below, it is said that as many as 4,000 stolen cattle could be hidden here, though how they might have been persuaded to climb up the slope is anybody's guess. It is a magnificent, memorable spot. Return by the same route.

"The Needle," one of many bizarre formations in the Quiraing, on the
Trotternish peninsula

Portree, Skye's principal market town

If you have already made arrangements for the night on the west side of Trotternish (see Creature Comforts), you can get there by continuing on the minor road across the top of the plateau to Uig. Otherwise, backtrack to the **A855** and continue **south** in the direction of **Staffin** and **Portree.**

The A855 stays close to the coast and presents a succession of superb seascapes with wave-cut natural arches and gull-wreathed basalt towers rising from the frothy water. About two miles south of Staffin, near the waterfall at the road edge below **Loch Mealt,** a parking area leads to a path to **Kilt Rock,** so named because the pattern caused by the vertical columns of basalt as they join horizontal beds of sedimentary rock at the water's edge looks like the pleats of a plaid kilt.

Finally, 6 or 7 miles (10–11 kilometers) north of Portree, the escarpment that forms Trotternish's backbone begins to break up in another strange formation called **The Storr.** The largest of nearly a dozen pinnacles here is "The Old Man Of Storr," a massive column of volcanic rock some 160 feet (50 meters) high that dominates the skyline for miles around. (A path from a parking area in another of Skye's ubiquitous conifer plantations leads directly to the foot of this formation.)

DIVERSIONS

Although craftwork has traditionally been a component of crofting, the steady increase in tourism in the Hebrides has both attracted fine craftspeople and spurred those already here. Small shops are tucked away in dozens of remote locations. There are silversmiths who produce jewelry and other decorative items in traditional Celtic motifs, weavers of traditional Highland fabrics, knitters who use wools with the subtle heather tones common to Harris Tweeds to produce sweaters the equal of those from Aran, potters of all kinds, and excellent galleries representing a variety of painters and other artists. To find them, stop at the tourist information centers in Broadford and Portree, or just keep your eyes peeled for modest roadside signs.

Four annual events are worth special attention: the Skye Provincial Gaelic Mod (song festival), held in June; the Skye Agricultural Show, held in late July; the Skye Highland Games (traditional sports, piping, and dancing), held late in August; and the Silver Chanter Piping Competition, held at Dunvegan Castle in August. For details in advance, write to the main Tourist Information Centre, Meall House, Portree, Isle of Skye IV51 5VZ.

CREATURE COMFORTS

The truth is, Skye is small enough that you can stay almost anywhere and eat almost anywhere on the island if you don't mind driving an hour or so from wherever you are. If you particularly liked where you stayed last night, you could conceivably do today's tour of the north and then simply shoot back south for the evening. After all, you'll have to go that way in the morning to catch the ferry anyway. On the other hand, there is far more choice in the north than in the south of Skye, including some splendid B&Bs and at least one superb, if remote, restaurant.

Daily Bed

In addition to a range of hotels, there are excellent B&Bs (clockwise around Trotternish) at **Kensaleyre, Linicro,** and **Kilmuir** on the west coast, in **Staffin** on the east coast, and, of course, in **Portree** itself. Secure a room by late afternoon, even if you plan to continue touring around the area, and always inquire about the evening meal if you check in early enough. There is a youth hostel in **Uig.** If you have trouble, call the Tourist Information Centre in Portree (0478-2137) for recommendations.

Daily Bread

As elsewhere in the more remote parts of Scotland, dinner is most easily found in hotels—informal meals in their pubs, formal meals in their restaurants. While some freestanding restaurants exist in Portree, the finest in the island is somewhat remote—in the tiny settlement of **Colbost** on Duirinish, not far from Dunvegan (it also operates one of the few good "off-licence" wine shops in Skye).

Into the Ancient Hills of Torridon

SKYE ♦ KYLE OF LOCHALSH ♦ PLOCKTON
APPLECROSS ♦ TORRIDON

♦ Back to the Scottish mainland via palm-lined Plockton
♦ Over the "Pass of the Cattle" to the remote Applecross peninsula
♦ Around Loch Torridon to some of the oldest mountains in the world
♦ An afternoon walk into the wilderness of the National Trust's Torridon Estate

Glen Torridon, its loch and the mountains to either side exhibit more mountain beauty than any other district in Scotland. . . .

—W. H. Murray
Highland Landscape, 1962

The Beinn Eighe National Nature Reserve, in the heart of the Torridon Range on the mainland coast north of Lochalsh, is barely 20 miles (32 kilometers) from the Isle of Skye as the eagle flies. But it is a measure of the extraordinary variety of the Highland landscape that the two pieces of land are separated by more than a *billion* years of geologic history. Skye's ravaged volcanic landscape is so new that it has yet to weather appreciably. In contrast, the round-shouldered red sandstone Torridon mountains, whose peaks contain fossils of some of the earliest forms of life, sit on a base of rock formed 2.5 billion years ago, making them more than half as old as the earth itself. They are among the oldest mountains anywhere in the world and give new meaning to the phrase "as old as the hills."

Torridon's human history seems to have eroded too. Empty and

Abhainn Coire Mhic Nobuil tumbles out of the ancient Torridon hills to isolated Loch Torridon.

wind-swept, the ancient hills seem simply not to have bothered to keep track of the fleeting movements of man. This much is known: in A.D. 673, long before the Norse Vikings arrived, the area around Torridon housed an Irish Christian monastic community second only to the monastery on Iona. A thousand years later, after the clans drove the Vikings out of the western Highlands, the Clan MacKenzie rose to dominate much of this coastal region. But their support of the Stuart cause cost them dearly, both politically and economically; in only 100 years, Torridon and its surrounding communities went from one of the richest areas in the Highlands to one of the poorest. By the mid-1800s, the lands were sold to absentee English landlords as hunting preserves and the remaining residents were evicted.

Ironically, only a generation or two later, the rich Victorian land-owners were forced to abandon the land themselves because of con-fiscatory estate taxes. Their mock-Gothic mansions and hunting lodges today are country-house hotels that cater to those who have come to visit the wilderness that has reclaimed the area once again. The land it-self is controlled by two conservation organizations: the National Trust for Scotland and the Nature Conservancy Council.

Torridon is today's objective. But along the way you'll experience a range of visual contrasts—majestic seascapes, one of the highest passes in Britain, and a serene coastal village with, of all things, a palm-lined shorefront.

🚗 TO THE SEA LOCHS AND SAND-STONE SUMMITS OF WESTER ROSS

Distance: About 75 miles/121 kilometers from Kyle of Lochalsh to
   Glen Torridon via Applecross
Roads: Twisting, sometimes breathtaking 1- and 2-lane minor roads
Driving Time: Allow 3–4 hours, with stops
Map: Michelin Map #401

From wherever you spent last night, head south along Skye's east coast to the Kyleakin–Kyle of Lochalsh ferry. As you drive off the ferry onto the mainland again, watch for a minor road branching to the left and signposted for **Plockton.**

(**Note:** If your own itinerary is running a bit behind, or you've been caught in one of those endless mid-Atlantic low pressure troughs and are thoroughly sick of dripping-wet Highland scenery, this is your chance to cut across to the east coast and Edinburgh. From Kyle, go back up the A87 through Glen Shiel, and turn south on the A82 at In-vergarry and then east on the A86 at Spean Bridge. At the eastern end of Glen Spean follow signs for the A889 to the A9 south through Pit-

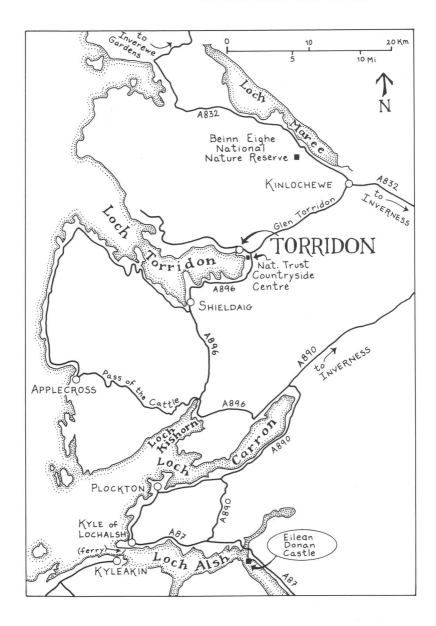

lochry to Edinburgh. Consider spending the night in Pitlochry—it's less expensive then Edinburgh—and then making the run to Edinburgh in the morning.)

The little road out of Kyle clambers over the lumpy backbone of the

Loch Alsh peninsula and, after a few more turns and a short ride through an evergreen forest, deposits you on the main street of tiny, postcard-scenic Plockton. The left side of the narrow street is lined with brightly painted nineteenth-century stone fishermen's cottages that look out upon a sheltered harbor much favored by British yachtsmen. Tucked safely in the lee of the peninsula, the little harbor is often mirror-smooth, reflecting the islets that dot beautiful Loch Carron and the crenelated towers of Duncraig Castle, built in the last century and now a residential girls' school. So mild is the mini-climate in this protected spot that palm trees grow in places along the seawall.

Leave Plockton the same way you entered, but turn **left** at the first opportunity and drive through the conifer- and rhododendron-clad hills past the school in the direction of **Achmore** and **Stromeferry** (where there is no longer a ferry). Here, turn left again onto the **A890** north above the shores of Loch Carron. At the head of the sea loch, the road traverses a broad, flat valley at Strathcarron (*strath* means a wide valley, as distinct from a narrow *glen*) and then crosses the meandering river from which the loch takes its name—Carron, or "winding stream." Turn left at the T-junction onto the **A896,** go through the village of Lochcarron, and continue over the hills to **Tornapress** on shallow Loch Kishorn. At Tornapress, the A896 forks right to Shieldaig and a **minor road** forks **left.**

Take the minor road, signposted APPLECROSS SCENIC ROAD. This is the *Bealach na Ba*—the "Pass of the Cattle"—a breathtaking climb from sea level to more than 2,000 feet (600 meters) in the span of perhaps 5 miles (8 kilometers). The road, paved but rugged, turns away from the loch and climbs a narrow ledge high above the bottom of a rubble-

The quartzite-tipped summits of Beinn Eighe, in the heart of the Torridon Estate

strewn glacial corrie hanging below the cliffs of Meall Gorm (2,330 feet/710 meters). At the end of the corrie, the road zigzags wildly and steeply, finally struggling up over the lip of the high plateau, revealing a vast moonscape of bare ground and car-sized boulders. Across the shattered landscape to the right is the naked summit of Beinn Bhan (2,940 feet/896 meters). Far off to the left, across the Inner Sound and gleaming in the sun under a ragged sky, are the peaks of Skye's Red and Black Cuillins.

At the western end of the pass, the road begins a more gentle descent to lovely Applecross Bay (from *Aber Crossan*, "mouth of the river Crossan"), with the estate of Applecross House in the tree-filled strath to the right. It was here in Applecross that St. Maelrubha (Irish Celtic for "red-haired") built his monastery in the late A.D. 600s. Even after the Vikings destroyed the church some three hundred years later, the pastoral area within the strath was a religious sanctuary for fugitives of all kinds. No sign of the church or St. Mealrubha's grave remain; they were all destroyed by fervent Protestants during the Reformation.

From Applecross, the road runs high along the cliffs and bays above the Inner Sound with the low profile of rocky Raasay and Rona in the foreground and the escarpment of Trotternish in the background. On almost any summer day, this view can be a contradictory canvas of weather patterns—brilliant patches of sun over the Quiraing on the north end of Skye, dark clouds enshrouding the summits of the Cuillins to the south, and slanting shafts of light moving across the sound like ghosts in a darkened room, leaving only ephemeral silvery footprints on the rippled surface of the sea.

Rounding the northern tip of the roughly triangular peninsula, the road snakes through several lovely fishing hamlets along the southern shore of outer Loch Torridon, before reaching the **A896** and the village of **Shieldaig,** nestled in a protected arm of upper Loch Torridon. The name comes from the Norse *Sild-vik*, or "herring bay," and fishing was the principal economic activity in the Loch Torridon area for centuries. The recently rerouted A896 runs along the northern flanks of Beinn Damh (2,956 feet/901 meters), high above the beautifully wooded and deeply indented shoreline, to **Annat,** providing spectacular views across the wide loch to the towering red sandstone peaks of Torridon.

Just beyond Annat, the road swings out across the flat delta of the River Torridon where it flows out of Glen Torridon, away to the north on the right. Ahead on the left, where a minor road leads off along the northern shore of Loch Torridon, is the **National Trust Countryside Centre** (open June through September). Stop here briefly to take in the audiovisual program and other exhibits on Torridon and pick up a copy of the National Trust booklet "Torridon: A Guide to the Hills," with maps and route descriptions for six walks into the surrounding mountains. (**Note:** Ralph Storer's *100 Best Routes on Scottish Mountains,* listed in Further Reading, provides detailed routes for Torridon's most challenging climbs.)

For those who intend to spend the afternoon walking in these ancient hills or climbing the ring of peaks, now would be a good time to settle the issue of where you intend to spend the night (see Creature Comforts). If a walk is not in your plans, see Diversions below.

🚶 A WALK INTO THE WORLD'S OLDEST MOUNTAINS

Distance: About 4–5 miles (6.5–8 kilometers); allow 2–3 hours
Difficulty: Relatively gentle uphill walk
Total Elevation Gain: About 1,000 feet/300 meters
Gear: Walking shoes (sneakers in dry weather), rain gear
Maps: Ordnance Survey 1:50,000 Map #24, or National Trust's *Guide to the Hills*

The best way to appreciate the vast panorama of the Torridon Estate is on foot, and this 2- to 3-hour walk provides a splendid introduction to some of the more remote parts of the range. Moreover, it serves as the foundation of several longer, more difficult climbs to the Torridon peaks for experienced climbers.

To begin, drive along the **minor road west** from the Countryside Centre, along the northern shore of Loch Torridon. Beyond **Torridon village,** the road leaves the shoreline and climbs up the side of the hill into a mixed forest. Just beyond Torridon House, over a handsome **stone bridge,** there is a small parking area for walkers. Park here, cross back over the bridge, and follow the obvious path up the right side of the gorge.

Just at the point where you enter the forest of Scotch pine, birch, and rhododendron, the burn—the **Abhainn Coire Mhic Nobuil** (the "River of MacNoble's Corrie")—tumbles over a series of ledges deep within the gorge, culminating in the beautiful waterfall just above the stone bridge. In the shade afforded by the trees—a remnant of the original Caledonian forest—a variety of moisture-loving ferns and wildflowers thrives in the mist from the waterfall. Higher up, heather and bayberry flourish along sandstone ledges.

The wood ends quite suddenly, opening up to a wide valley of heather, heath, bracken, and scrubby clumps of birch, with the stream crashing through the gorge on the left. Ignore the wooden footbridge on the left which leads across the moorland to the southern arm of the huge horseshoe of **Beinn Alligin,** the "jeweled mountain" (3,231 feet/985 meters). Composed of layer upon layer of red horizontal sand-

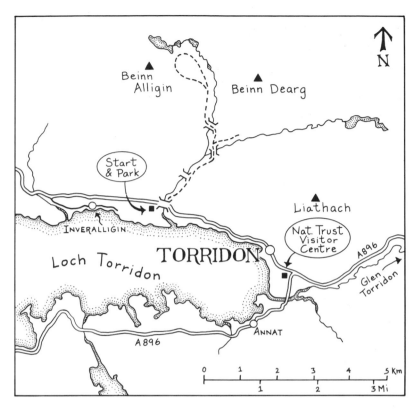

stone beds deposited by primeval rivers in some young ocean at the dawn of time, Beinn Alligin's face is creased by long vertical clefts, the most dramatic of which is **Eag Dhuign,** the "black notch," a massive gash that plunges 1,800 feet (550 meters) from just below the summit to the scree slopes at the mountain's base. A circular walk up and around Beinn Alligin's narrow ridge is a breathtaking 6-mile (9.5-kilometer), 6.5-hour climb for experienced climbers.

Continue uphill on the right side of the stream. Ahead, the looming bulk of **Beinn Dearg** (3,000 feet/914 meters) splits the valley in two. To its right, **Coire Mhic Nobuil** stretches across rubbly moorland toward quartzite-topped **Beinn Eighe** (with seven summits), eventually curving around to the right to join the road through Glen Torridon. To the left, another corrie leads up to **Bealach a'Chomhla,** the "pass of the gate." At this point, above yet another waterfall, a new stream—the **Allt a'Bhealaich** ("river of the pass")—joins the main stream from the left. Just above the junction there is a second footbridge. Turn **left** over this footbridge and follow the right bank of the new stream.

The Allt a'Bhealaich at this point is an almost continuous series of waterfalls, as the stream cuts through fissures in the bedrock and tumbles from ledge to ledge. Cross the **third footbridge** to the left of the stream and follow the path along the left flank of the valley. Two choices are presented here. One path carries on through the valley, roughly paralleling the stream, though at a higher elevation, eventually reaching the "pass of the gate." Another, less obvious path branches left to a steep grass slope rising to **Na Rathanan** ("the horns") and eventually to **Sgurr Mor** (the "big peak"), the highest point of Beinn Alligin.

Unless you are an experienced climber, stay on the lower path. The reward is magnificent Highland scenery: behind you, back across the valley, is the long ridge of **Liathach** which, like Beinn Eighe, has seven summits, four of them topped with glittering quartzite, as if they were perpetually snowcapped. All around you, cathedral walls of purplish-brown sandstone climb to the sky, huge deltas of scree fan out at the foot of long crevasses, buzzards and golden eagles soar on the updrafts, and shadow and light dance on the cliff faces as clouds race across the sky. Between huge glacial boulders, masses of ling heather carpet the valley bottom with magenta flowers in late summer, turning a rich sienna when fall approaches. In boggier spots, the fluffy white flags of cotton grass wiggle in the wind. If you are exceptionally lucky, you may catch a glimpse of red deer patrolling the high flanks of Beinn Dearg late in the afternoon. There are pine martens and wildcats as well, but they are nocturnal and seldom seen.

The return is by the same route, with superb views of Loch Torridon in the afternoon light.

Time permitting, drive back in the direction of Torridon village, and take the minor road from the stone-bridge car park westwards along Loch Torridon for a delightfully scenic 10-mile (16-kilometer) ride. The little road zigzags through the woods for a while before clearing the trees above the tiny village of **Inveralligin.** Then it begins an arduous climb up over **Bealach Na Gaoithe,** the aptly named "pass of the winds," before descending to the pier at the end-of-the-road fishing hamlet of **Daibaig.** The summit of this climb provides the finest views of the southern region of the Torridon Estate—a top-of-the-world sweep of weathered mountains and whitecapped seascapes.

DIVERSIONS
Inverewe Gardens

If you've decided to pass up the walk into the Torridon mountains, a splendid diversion awaits: **Inverewe Gardens**—a subtropical landscape garden that is farther north than Moscow! Take the **A896** north through Glen Torridon to **Kinlochewe** (you would have come this way tomorrow morning anyway) and turn left onto the **A832** for the 10-mile (16-kilometer) run along the shore of Loch Maree to **Gairloch.** Five or 6 miles (8–10 kilometers) farther, just beyond the village of **Poolewe,** is Inverewe Gardens, a National Trust property.

Begun in 1865 by Osgood Hanbury MacKenzie, Inverewe is able to support subtropical species, lush traditional perennial border plantings, a terraced vegetable garden, and acres of landscape plantings, because an arm of the Gulf Stream brings warm sea currents into the loch. There is also a National Trust Gift Shop with an excellent stock of English gardening books.

CREATURE COMFORTS

Daily Bed

As lonely as the Torridon Estate seems to be, there are accommodations tucked away quietly throughout the area, ranging from plush Victorian hunting lodges to a youth hostel. On the southern side of the Torridon region, there are small hotels and scattered B&Bs in **Shieldaig, Annat,** and **Torridon.** To the west, out the minor road to Daibaig, there are two or three beautifully situated B&Bs in **Inveralligin.** In addition, there is a youth hostel in Torridon village, close to the National Trust Countryside Centre.

On the northern side of Torridon, below the Beinn Eighe National Nature Reserve, there are hotel and B&B accommodations available in the hiking center of **Kinlochewe.** A bit farther afield (though not if you take the diversion to Inverewe) there are excellent B&Bs and several hotels around Gairloch and on the southern side of Loch Gairloch at **Badachro** (a quaint little fishing harbor) and **Shieldaig** (not to be confused with the Shieldaig on Loch Torridon). There is also a youth hostel in Gairloch, as well as a Tourist Information Centre.

Daily Bread

Dining options are limited to the hotels in **Shieldaig, Annat,** and **Torridon** on the south, and **Kinlochewe** and the **Gairloch** area on the north, though between their bar meals and dining rooms, the cuisine ranges from pub food to imaginative fine dining. Check at the visitor center for recommendations, or ask your B&B host; phone ahead for reservations at the more formal of the hotel dining rooms.

East and South through the Grampians to Victorian Pitlochry

TORRIDON ◆ INVERNESS
CAIRNGORM MOUNTAINS ◆ PITLOCHRY

- ◆ **Across Scotland from west to east**
- ◆ **An optional side trip to Loch Ness and Castle Urquhart**
- ◆ **A stop at Culloden Battlefield**
- ◆ **A drive through Scotland's highest mountains**
- ◆ **An optional tour of the "Whisky Trail"**
- ◆ **South to Victorian Pitlochry and its discount woolens shops**

Urquhart Castle, above Loch Ness near Drumnadrochit

*T*his is a day devoted principally to driving, but the drive is also full of surprises and dramatic changes of scene, from the remote glens of the northwest Highlands to the pastoral farmlands bordering the Moray Firth near Inverness, the conifer-clad slopes and naked summits of Britain's highest mountains, the Cairngorms, and the deep green valleys of the rivers Spey, Garry, and Tummel.

Along the way, there are several seductive attractions: hoping for a glimpse of Loch Ness's legendary sea monster from the evocative ruins of Castle Urquhart; lingering to ponder "what if . . ." at Culloden, where the dreams of Bonnie Prince Charlie's Highlanders died; wandering the "Whisky Trail" through the hidden glens of Speyside; exploring the Glen More Forest Park and the wind-swept rockscapes of Cairn Gorm; and shopping for discount woolens among the fanciful Victorian storefronts of Pitlochry.

🚗 FROM TORRIDON TO TUMMEL: A DRIVE THROUGH SCOTLAND'S HEARTLAND

Distance: About 150 miles/240 kilometers (Kinlochewe to Pitlochry)
Roads: Major 2- and 4-lane primary roads
Driving Time: 4–5 hours with stops; longer with side trips
Map: Michelin Map #401

The road east out of Torridon, the **A832,** eases you gently out of the dramatic scenery of the northwest Highlands. From Kinlochewe, the A832 rises through **Glen Docherty,** its steep walls rising a thousand feet to sandstone crags, before it opens to a long, wide valley floor covered in bracken and heather. By the time you reach **Loch a'Chroisg** ("lake of the crossing") you have reached, at least in one respect, "the East"—from here on, all streams flow eastward to the North Sea. Beyond **Achnasheen** ("field of storms"), you enter Strath Bran, a wide forest-edged valley cut by a meandering river.

At **Garve,** where you turn right onto the **A835** for **Inverness,** the landscape softens further and soon you are driving through a pastoral scene with billowing fields of blue-green barley and wheat (called "corn" in Britain). At the village of **Contin** you must make the morning's first decision. If you cannot conceive of being in this part of Scotland without visiting **Loch Ness,** follow the side trip directions below. Otherwise, stay on the **A835** through **Maryburgh,** join the **A9** in the middle of **Black Isle** (which is neither black nor an island, but a fertile farming region), and head **south.**

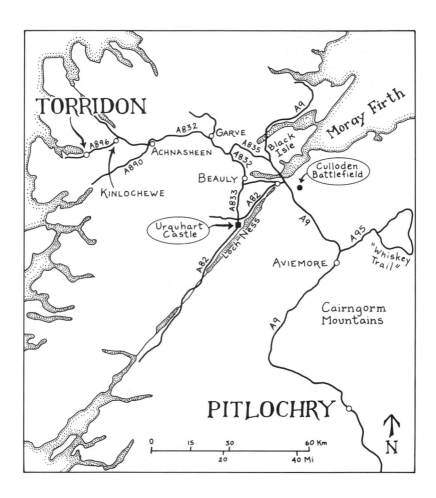

✤ Side Trip: Loch Ness and Urquhart Castle

At **Contin,** turn **right** onto the **A832** toward **Muir of Ord.** After passing the malt whisky distillery at Ord, you turn right onto the **A862** toward **Beauly.** Beauly itself is a handsome village with a wide, tree-lined main street and a venerable old fabric and clothing store that carries the largest range of tartan cloth in Scotland.

South of the village, take the **right** turn onto the **A833.** After a lovely 12-mile (19-kilometer) run through Glen Convinth, the **A833 dead-ends** just west of **Drumnadrochit**—a name you cannot help but roll off your tongue with a Highland burr. Turn **left** and then, a few hundred yards later, turn **right** onto the **A82** west in the direction of

Fort William. Ignore the "Nessie" commercialism and follow the road along an arm of Loch Ness to **Urquhart Castle,** which fell into ruin after the last Jacobite rebellion. From Urquhart (open Monday through Friday 9:30 A.M. to 7:00 P.M., Saturday and Sunday 2:00 P.M. to 7:00 P.M.) the view of Loch Ness, narrow and serene, is superb.

To rejoin the itinerary, take the **A82 east** to **Inverness,** following signs first to the **City Centre** and then for **Perth** and the **A9 south.** ✤

Inverness ("mouth of the Ness") itself, though beautifully situated on the banks of the river, has little to offer, so give it a pass and drive south on the **A9,** Scotland's main north-south artery.

✤ Side Trip: Culloden

To visit the site of the battle that finally brought the Scottish-English tug-of-war to an end, watch for the **B9006** just south of Inverness and follow the signs for **Culloden,** some 5 miles (8 kilometers) to the east. The bloody encounter on Culloden Moor occurred on April 16, 1746. Bonnie Prince Charlie's ragtag Highland army had been in retreat for weeks. An attempt to surprise the English army during the night had failed. By noon, both armies were arrayed across the barren moor—the nine thousand superbly equipped English soldiers (supported by the Clan Campbell) on one side, and the half-starved, poorly ırmed supporters of the Young Pretender on the other. After a perfunctory artillery battle, the Highlanders mounted a charge so ferocious it broke through the English army's first line. But then the immutable statistics of warfare took over: with greater numbers and superior firepower, the English forces mowed the Highlanders down. Only forty minutes later, the battle was over. Some twelve hundred Highlanders died on Culloden Moor that afternoon; the English lost only forty-six men. It was the end of the dream of a Stuart king, of an independent Scotland, and of the clans. It was the end of an era as well. The American and French revolutions were brewing, the empire was growing, and science and technology would soon transform traditional patterns of life. The National Trust Visitor Centre is open daily June through August from 9:30 A.M. to 8:00 P.M., and in April, May September, and October from 10:00 A.M. to 7:00 P.M. ✤

South of Inverness, the A9 climbs steadily for at least 10 miles (16 kilometers) to high moorlands, reaching a summit beyond **Tomatin.** Ahead, the **Cairngorms,** Britain's highest mountains, with six summits over 4,000 feet (1,220 meters), rise to the clouds above the Spey River Valley.

Situated in the heart of the **Grampian Range,** the Cairngorms were formed 400 million years ago from crystallized volcanic magma, uplifted some 50 million years ago, and then shaved smooth by successive ice ages. Some 100 square miles (160 square kilometers) of this area make up the **Cairngorms National Nature Reserve,** established in the 1950s and 1960s.

A minor road to the left just beyond the Tourist Information Centre at the southern end of **Aviemore** runs deep into the **Glen More Forest Park** before climbing nearly to the top of one of the region's highest mountains, **Cairn Gorm** (4,085 feet/1,245 meters). A ski lift takes you to within a hundred yards of the summit. The subarctic landscape above the tree line, constantly buffetted by high winds and shattered by the elements, is inexpressibly bleak. On a good day, the views across the **Spey River Valley** are lovely, but despite its great height, Cairn Gorm leaves something to be desired. In fact, while this entire region is noted for its wildlife and mountain scenery, the truth is that it lacks the drama of the northwest Highlands. It has neither the theatricality of Glencoe and Skye's Cuillins nor the grandeur of Torridon. Consequently, this itinerary suggests you pass up the Cairngorms and press on toward the south—unless, of course, you respond to the siren song of the "Whisky Trail."

✤ Side Trip: The Whisky Glens of Speyside

The Spey River Valley is famous for two things: trout and whisky. Its remote glens and villages have names with recognition far out of proportion to their tiny size: Glenlivet, Glenfiddich, Knockandhu, Tomintoul, Dufftown, and Grantown, among others.

If you didn't have an opportunity to visit Skye's distillery, you may wish to follow the **"Whisky Trail"** to one of the distilleries that offer tours (get a brochure at the Aviemore Tourist Information Centre). Later, take the A9 to Pitlochry, 56 miles (90 kilometers) to the south. ✤

South of Aviemore, the A9 speeds through the upper reaches of the Spey valley, passing **Kincraig** and **Kingussie.** A mile or two to the east, between these two towns, is **Insh Marshes,** the most important wildfowl breeding and wintering habitat in Britain and home to a large population of whooper swans. The Royal Society for the Protection of Birds operates an information center (open Wednesdays and Sundays, April through June, and Wednesdays only in July and August) just east of Kingussie on the **B970.** The route also passes the ruins of **Ruthven Barracks,** where the Highland chiefs waited in vain for new orders from Prince Charlie after Culloden.

Beyond **Newtonmore,** the A9 leaves the valley of the Spey and climbs up bleak **Glen Truim** to the **Pass of Drumochter,** then descends through the **Forest of Atholl** via **Glen Garry.** Near the south-

The classic pagoda-roofed profile of a Highland's whisky distillery, high in the Grampians

ern end of the glen, the highway passes the brilliant white towers of **Blair Castle,** a classic Scottish baronial pile begun in the 1200s but substantially redesigned in the 1860s.

After it crosses the **River Garry,** the A9 squeezes through the **Pass of Killiecrankie,** site of a major battle during an early Jacobite uprising in 1689. At this point, take the **exit** from the A9 signposted for **Pitlochry.**

Pitlochry, nestled in a densely wooded valley cut by the **River Tummel,** sits roughly at the geographical center of Scotland. It owes its existence to the purported healing powers of the waters of a local stream, and to "Tartanitis"—the Victorian-era craze for all things Scottish that was created by Queen Victoria's love of the Scottish countryside. This irresistible combination led to a late-1800s construction boom in the typically jumbled architectural styles of the Victorian period: miniature baronial castles with tall windows and ceilings, conical turrets and pyrimidal towers, intricate iron fretwork and wooden gingerbread trim, and formal gardens.

When the lure of "taking the waters" faded, the town fathers responded with a summerlong theater festival that flourishes today. Shopping was always important to the spa goers, and over the years the town has become a regional center for woolen-mill outlet stores, so bargain hunters throng the main street.

If you roll into Pitlochry on a rainy afternoon, all that gray granite can look a bit dreary, despite the fanciful trimmings. Stop anyway, this is a hospitable place and—since it's only two hours from Edinburgh—a good base for the night.

(**Note:** If, by some miracle, it is still early and you want to press ahead toward Edinburgh, by all means do. If you haven't reserved a room in advance, see directions to the city's Tourist Information Centre in tomorrow's itinerary.)

CREATURE COMFORTS

Daily Bed

Pitlochry may have more places to stay than anywhere else you've been on this trip, so finding a nice room for the night should pose few difficulties. As always, B&Bs will tend to be off the main streets up along the hillside, while larger guesthouses and hotels will be closer to the center of things.

Daily Bread

No problem here either; there is a wide range of restaurants, cafés, and pubs in Pitlochry from which to make a choice for dinner. Remember too that you're in the heart of salmon country, so consider it and other local game specialties.

A Walk through Old Edinburgh

PITLOCHRY ◆ EDINBURGH
THE TWEED RIVER VALLEY

- ◆ A quick drive south into Edinburgh
- ◆ A driving tour of the New Town
- ◆ An afternoon walk through the streets, closes, and wynds of the Old Town
- ◆ Visits to a castle and a palace
- ◆ A drive into the pastoral Tweed Valley

This profusion of eccentricities, this dream of masonry and living rock...
——Robert Louis Stevenson, writing of his hometown

*E*dinburgh is a city with a split personality, one boisterous and emotional, the other coolly intellectual. The two halves of the city keep their distance, confronting each other across a green ravine, once a swampy loch and today a splendid garden. On one side is the New Town, a place of straight streets, sharp right angles, and perfect circles, trimmed out in the orderly classical proportions of Palladio. Austere Georgian facades are ranked along the curbsides, aloof and elegant, with the studied serenity of aristocrats waiting for a carriage. New Town is a city with high cheekbones.

On the other side of the ravine, perched high on the black basaltic ramparts of an ancient volcanic ridge, is the Old Town, a hopeless jumble of narrow alleys, cobblestone courtyards, steep stone stairs, and towering medieval tenements squeezed so tightly together that it seems all their mass has been pushed upward. They lean against each other like amiable drunkards, giving the impression that if one were removed all the rest would tumble to the ground in a heap. It is a bustling, energetic place, a city with the ruddy red cheeks that come from hard work and even harder play.

Edinburgh's reputation as the "Athens of the North" is built in large part upon the classical foundations and precise proportions of its Georgian New Town. But the city's heart beats in the Old Town. Its main artery is the "Royal Mile": a straggle of streets—Castle Hill, Lawnmarket, High Street, Canongate, Abbey Strand—that merge into each other in a roughly straight line running down the hill from the castle to the Palace of Holyrood House. It is a superb urban environment today, lovingly restored and lined with delightful small shops and little gemlike museums.

🚗 EXPERIENCING THE BEST OF EDINBURGH

Distance: About 70 miles/113 kilometers
Roads: High-speed highway and motorway
Driving Time: About 2 hours
Map: Michelin Map #401

If you stayed in Pitlochry last night, you have an easy and fast run into Edinburgh this morning. Be off by 9:00 A.M. and you'll be in the center of the city by 11:00 A.M. If you stayed somewhere else, just head for the **A9** south toward **Perth.** The highway continues down the valley of the River Tummel through Dunkeld and Birnam (yes, this is the Birnam wood of *Macbeth,* though it's a long haul to Dunsinane). As the A9 reaches the bypass around the west side of Perth, follow signs for the **M90,** which cuts across the Fife peninsula through Kinross and Dunfermline (once Scotland's capital), finally crossing the Firth of Forth by bridge. On the other side of the bridge follow signs for the **A90** east to Edinburgh's **City Centre.** The A90 becomes the **Queensferry Road,** which takes you directly to the west end of the New Town.

The one-way traffic pattern gets a little frantic at this point, and there are two ways you can handle it. First, you can simply follow the blue-and-white "i" signs to the Tourist Information Centre above the **Waverley Centre** (on the corner of Princes Street and Waverley Bridge), or you can slow down and enjoy the Georgian architecture of the New Town, since you'll have to drive through it anyway. The truth is that much of what the New Town has to offer—the elegant facades, the handsome squares and circuses—is best experienced from the car. The interiors, for the most part, have been converted to offices, banks, insurance companies, and the like; the gracious homes have mostly disappeared.

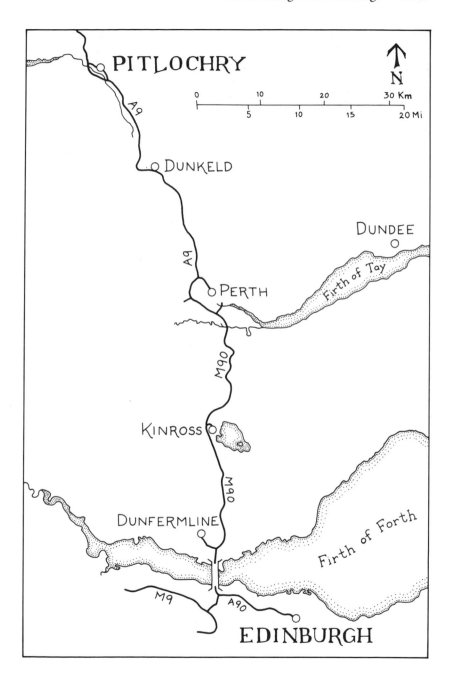

🚗 A Quick Cruise through New Town

Your short driving tour of New Town begins where the Queensferry Road is diverted away from **Princes Street** (the main retail street) and around exquisitely Georgian **Charlotte Square,** in a clockwise direction. Then, three-quarters of the way around the square, you turn left onto **George Street,** New Town's main axis (Sir Walter Scott lived at number 108 after his marriage). Princes Street runs parallel to George two blocks to your right; **Queen Street** does the same two blocks to your left. In between are two narrow one-way alleys. Of these, **Rose Street** (between George and Princes) is the most famous—for its pubs (at one time it had more than twenty). You can't help but marvel at the irony of the naming of these streets after the English Hanoverian king and his family a scant thirty years or so after Bonnie Prince Charlie's rebellion failed.

Take a few minutes to zigzag through these streets. Then, when you've had your fill of their orderly classicism, simply go straight down George Street to **St. Andrew Square** (Charlotte's mirror image),

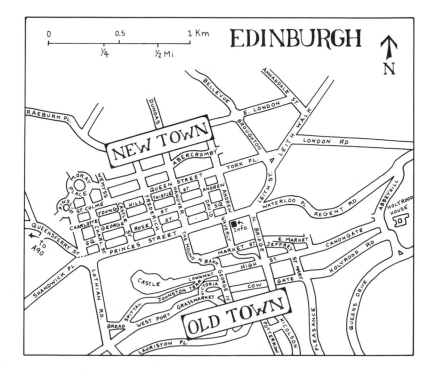

around it clockwise, and out to Princes Street. Stay to the right and turn **right** onto Princes Street, but cut all the way to the left immediately to turn **left** at the light onto **Waverley Bridge Road.** The Tourist Information Centre is on the corner on your immediate left above the new Waverley Centre shopping mall; if you reach the train station you've gone too far.

If you have someone with you, pull over and stop here and send them into the information center. Otherwise there is underground parking beneath the center.

There isn't a better information center in all of Britain than Edinburgh's. It's open during normal business hours all year, but in the summer, through the end of August, it stays open until 9:00 P.M. daily (phone 031-557-2727). If you plan to spend the night in the city (this itinerary doesn't), you can use the accommodation booking service to find a room in whatever price range or geographical area you prefer. Otherwise, consult Creature Comforts below for some suggestions.

John Knox's house, High Street, Old Town Edinburgh

While you visit the center, however, be sure to pick up the following: either "Edinburgh: A Guide to the Royal Mile and Old Town" or "Walk the Royal Mile," a foldout, plastic-coated, illustrated walking map published by Bartholomew, the map people. Either one is an excellent companion guide and each costs about a pound. For a more detailed description of the entire city and its environs (and a nice souvenir) consider the *Edinburgh City Guide* published by the Ordnance Survey and the Automobile Association. While you are at the center, be sure also to pick up the Scottish Tourist Board's *Scottish Borders: Where to Stay Holiday Guide,* for a terrific listing of B&Bs, guesthouses, and hotels in the Tweed River Valley, where you'll be heading later this afternoon.

Princes Street, in front of the information center, was once Edinburgh's grand promenade, edged by elegant shops on one side and the city gardens—as well as the extraordinarily ugly memorial to Sir Walter Scott—on the other. The gardens are still lovely (and the memorial is still ugly), but the shops now are mostly national chains.

Next, perhaps the most valuable piece of information in this entire book: **where to park conveniently in Edinburgh Old Town!** From the information center, continue across Waverley Bridge toward the Old Town, dead ahead on the hill. Just beyond the railroad station, turn **left** (you can't go straight anyway). Pass under North Bridge and bear **right** onto **Jeffrey Street,** curving up the side of the hill. At the top, turn **left** onto **Canongate** and go to the intersection outside the gates of **Holyroodhouse.** Turn **right,** and follow your nose around to the left to the large parking lot. Then walk through the side gates to Holyroodhouse and the **Royal Mile.**

🏃 The Royal Mile: a Walk Through Scottish History

Edinburgh's Old Town occupies one of the most dramatic physical sites in Europe. It is perched high on the dark basaltic core of an extinct volcano exposed by erosion and the work of a passing glacier. As it rode over the hard core, the glacier left behind a long tapered ridge of rubble, and it is on this ridge that the city grew. Given its strategic position, Edinburgh may have been one of the earliest settlements in Scotland, but its recorded history dates from the sixth century, when the Anglian King Edwin swept north through the Borders from Northumberland and rebuilt an earlier Celtic fortress called *Dun Eadain* ("fortress on the slope"). Inevitably, the old name intertwined with the king's name; *Dun Eadain* and "Edwin's Burgh" became *Edinburgh.* In

A few of the dozens of architectural details along Edinburgh's "Royal Mile"

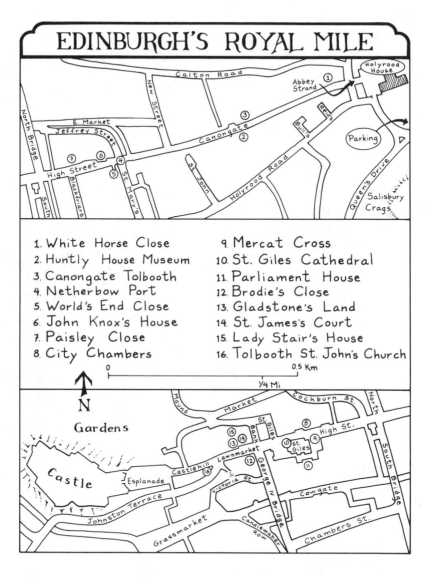

EDINBURGH'S ROYAL MILE

1. White Horse Close
2. Huntly House Museum
3. Canongate Tolbooth
4. Netherbow Port
5. World's End Close
6. John Knox's House
7. Paisley Close
8. City Chambers
9. Mercat Cross
10. St. Giles Cathedral
11. Parliament House
12. Brodie's Close
13. Gladstone's Land
14. St. James's Court
15. Lady Stair's House
16. Tolbooth St. John's Church

the eleventh century, the Scots King Malcolm Cranmore and his consort Margaret lived in the castle, and some years later their son David I founded an abbey at the foot of the hill, calling it Holyrood.

The defeat of the Scots by the English at Flodden Field in 1513 spurred the city to build a new wall, and for the next 250 years all growth was contained within its confines, forcing the city up instead of out.

Shop fronts and building facades have changed, of course, but as you walk along the Royal Mile (actually only eight-tenths of a mile) you see the city largely as it was when Bonnie Prince Charlie seized it in the mid-1700s. Today's walk begins at the bottom of the long, sloping ridge of which the Royal Mile is the spine, at the Palace of Holyroodhouse.

PALACE OF HOLYROODHOUSE. Holyrood began life in 1128 as an Augustinian abbey founded by Malcolm and Margaret's son, the devout King David. The abbey prospered and later a guesthouse was built—the first "Holyroodhouse." In 1528, James V built the northwest tower (on the left as you face the main entrance) and Mary, Queen of Scots, lived in the palace from 1561 through 1567. But if you tour Holyroodhouse, most of what you'll see was rebuilt during the reign of Charles II (the ruins of the abbey remain). Holyroodhouse is full of intrigue and surprises and is an excellent example of late-sixteenth-century royal taste, but if you want to experience the real Edinburgh, go out through **Abbey Strand** and begin the gentle uphill stroll along **Canongate** (named after the canons of the abbey).

CANONGATE. Branching left and right off the Royal Mile are dozens of narrow **closes** (pronounced as in "close call") that lead into the residential courtyards of the Old City. Wonderfully atmospheric today, they teemed with humanity in the eighteenth century, when twenty times as many people lived in Old Town as do today. One of the loveliest closes, on the right as you begin this walk, is **White Horse Close,** named after the old White Horse Inn, from which the London stagecoach once departed.

Uphill and across the street is **Huntly House,** a free museum of Old Town history set in a fine sixteenth-century mansion, complete with projecting upper stories, gabled roof, and the first of what will be many beautiful overhanging signs.

Across the street, **Canongate Tolbooth,** with its gigantic Victorian clock, is a reminder that until as recently as 1856 Canongate was a town quite separate from Edinburgh, with its own town council—and tollbooth. Nearby, the letter *S* cut into the road marks the old sanctuary line of Holyrood Abbey.

HIGH STREET. Several blocks farther uphill, at the point where Jeffrey Street enters from the right (becoming St. Mary's Street on the other side), several bronze studs set into the road indicate where **Netherbow Port,** the gate to Edinburgh proper, once stood. At this point the Royal Mile gets its second name change, becoming **High Street.** Immediately on the left is **World's End Close,** an eloquent comment on the risks once associated with leaving the protective confines of the old city walls.

Ahead on the right, beyond the Netherbow Arts Centre and projecting slightly out into the street, is **John Knox's House,** a marvelous confection of stone and wood, curves and angles, overhanging stories, gables, exterior stairs, odd little windows, and intriguing architectural details.

Uphill a few steps at the entrance to **Paisley Close,** an earnest young face is carved in gray limestone beneath a scroll with the legend HEAVE AWA' LADS I'M NO DEID YET, commemorating a survivor of the collapse in 1863 of one of the towering tenements that lined these alleys. Poorly built, roofed with thatch, and with open fireplaces throughout, the structures were constantly threatened by fire and collapse. Indoor plumbing did not exist and water was carried home as needed from ten wellheads scattered around the town.

The next segment of the Royal Mile has a distinctly official flavor, including the **City Chambers,** the **Mercat Cross** (from which royal proclamations were made), **St. Giles Cathedral,** and **Parliament House** (now Scotland's law courts).

LAWNMARKET. At the intersection with **Bank Street** and **George IV Bridge,** High Street becomes **Lawnmarket.** The first close on the left, appropriately dark and sinister, is **Brodie's Close,** where Deacon Brodie—the basis for Stevenson's *Dr. Jekyll and Mr. Hyde*—lived before he was apprehended and executed.

Across the street is **Gladstone's Land,** an almost perfectly preserved version of the hundreds of "lands" or apartment buildings that lined the streets and alleys of seventeenth-century Old Town, complete with its worn outside stone staircase, a remnant of its arcaded front, and a splendid set of furnished rooms with richly painted ceilings.

Behind Gladstone's Land, through **Lady Stair's Close,** is **James's Court,** an airy courtyard that was an early-eighteenth-century improvement on the dark, dank medieval closes. **Lady Stair's House,** nearby, has lovely interiors and an exhibit of Scott, Stevenson, and Burns documents.

CASTLEHILL. The tall spire of **Tolbooth St. John's Church,** which offers services in Gaelic, splits the upper end of Lawnmarket. Ahead, built on a landfill made from the rubble of old houses along the Royal Mile, is the **Esplanade,** the approach to **Edinburgh Castle** itself. Frankly, the castle is a lot better to look at than to visit. Torn down and rebuilt several times, the complex now boasts only one truly ancient part, eleventh-century **St. Margaret's Chapel.** But do walk around the grounds; the views are spectacular on a good day.

As you leave the Esplanade, heading back down the Royal Mile, cross **Johnston Terrace** on the right and take the narrow alley and stairs downhill to **Victoria Street,** a splendid curving street of quaint shop fronts, including an entire store devoted only to brushes, from the smallest and finest to brushes for sweeping the inside of chimneys. Victoria Terrace ends at **Grassmarket,** the site of cattle, sheep, and horse auctions and, until 1785, public hangings. Then walk up **Cowgate,** parallel to the Royal Mile, and return to your car either by this route or by returning to the Royal Mile and its many shops.

Edinburgh Castle, on Castle Mount, is more interesting to look at than to visit.

🚗 ON TO THE VALLEY OF THE RIVER TWEED

Distance: 30 miles/48 kilometers to Innerleithen
Roads: Excellent primary roads along pastoral river valley
Driving Time: 1 hour
Map: Michelin Map #401

Unless you're in town for the **International Festival** (see Diversions) or feel the need for a more extensive urban experience after more than a week in the countryside, leave Edinburgh at the conclusion of your walk along the Royal Mile and head south for **Peebles** and the valley of the **River Tweed.**

If you've given yourself time to explore and shop in Old Town, it will probably be middle to late afternoon when you reach your car again. Dig out your road map and the *Scottish Borders: Where to Stay Holiday Guide* you picked up at the information center (or return there to get one), and then take **Princes Street** west to the end of the park and turn **left** onto **Lothian Road.** From there, just follow signs for the **A702** and Peebles.

As you approach the suburban village of **Loanhead,** bear **left** onto the **A701.** Nine miles (14.5 kilometers) later, at **Leadburn,** do the same thing, bearing **left** onto the **A703** and following signs for Peebles.

Peebles (from the old English *Pebyll,* "a settlement of skin tents") is a handsome town that has escaped most of the architectural depredations of the twentieth century. Unless you have done so already, this is a good place to phone ahead to one of the hotels, guesthouses, or B&Bs in the *Where to Stay Holiday Guide* to settle tonight's accommodations. Any town, village, or farm between Peebles and Galashiels is fine (see Creature Comforts). If you need help, there is a Tourist Information Centre in Peebles. Time permitting, detour a couple of miles to the west on the **A72** to see **Neidpath Castle,** perhaps the finest example of a fourteenth-century "tower house" in Scotland, situated on a steep slope above a wooded curve in the Tweed. Then, return to Peebles.

The stretch of road and river between Peebles and **Galashiels** illuminates the gentle side of the Scottish landscape. The Tweed Valley is soft and still, the river silky and sinuous, almost indolent compared with the furious torrents of the north. Above the rich green meadows, the hills are rounded and rolling, cloaked in patches of mixed hardwoods and orderly fir plantations.

From the center of Peebles, take the leisurely **B7062** (or the **A72,** if you're in a hurry) to **Innerleithen,** a good base for the night. The narrow minor road follows the twists and bends of the Tweed, passing **Kailzie Gardens** and **Traquair House,** one of the oldest continuously inhabited houses in Scotland (see Diversions). Past the entrance to Tra-

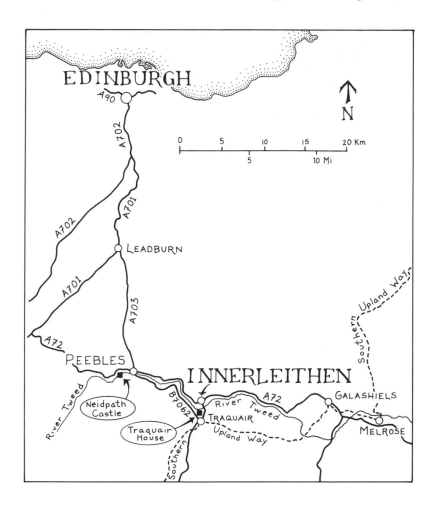

quair, the road crosses a small bridge and dead-ends at **Traquair** village. In addition to Traquair House, the village is one of the few places where the Southern Upland Way long-distance path leaves the hilltops and encounters civilization. Lovely forest walks are good summer-evening options in either direction (see Diversions). To reach Innerleithen and the A72, turn **left** at the T-junction in Traquair and, after a few hundred yards, **left** again, over the Tweed and into the town. Innerleithen is a modest milling village, but its central location in the valley and the attractions of Traquair House and the Southern Upland Way make it a good place to stop.

DIVERSIONS

What with walking around Edinburgh's Old Town and making the short drive south to the Tweed, this is a full day for anyone, but three diversions are worth considering.

Edinburgh's International Festival

Each August, Edinburgh hosts its **International Festival,** one of the world's premier performing arts events. Together with its larger and less formal **Fringe Festival,** the event attracts over a quarter-million visitors. Tickets for performances in the main festival are almost impossible to acquire on short notice, but unsold tickets for a given day's performances are sold from a booth on the Mound (in the middle of the gardens next to Princes Street) between 1:00 P.M. and 5:00 P.M. Tickets for Fringe events (which range from marvelously inventive to inexpressibly bad) are more readily available. (Fringe Festival office, 170 High Street; International Festival office, 21 Market Street; information and tickets can be obtained in advance from Edwards and Edwards, 1 Times Square Plaza, New York, NY 10036, 212-944-0290.)

A Visit to Traquair House

Traquair House is one of the finest examples of the Lowlands' "tower houses," designed to lift their occupants out of harm's way. Behind its harled (stuccoed) walls, Traquair harbors nearly 1,000 years of history and has sheltered twenty-seven English and Scottish monarchs and one would-be king, Bonnie Prince Charlie. In addition to the handsomely furnished rooms, there are craft, antique, and art galleries and a small 200-year-old brewhouse which still produces and bottles its own Traquair Strong Ale. (Open during May and June and September 15 to 30 between 1:00 P.M. and 5:30 P.M., July through September 14 10:30 A.M. to 5:30 P.M.)

Walks along the Southern Upland Way

The **Southern Upland Way** is Britain's first coast-to-coast long-distance path, stretching 212 miles (342 kilometers) from Portpatrick in the southwest (near Stranraer, the ferry port to Northern Ireland) to Cockburnspath in the northeast (east of Edinburgh). From the hamlet of Traquair, where the way crosses the B709, easy forest walks can be taken in either direction. In the center of the hamlet, directly opposite the point where the B7062 dead-ends into the A709, the way climbs up

Street scene, Old Town Edinburgh

a lane and then follows a path (marked with the thistle symbol of the Countryside Commission of Scotland) uphill and eastward through the Elibank and Traquair forests, eventually reaching a ridge that offers sweeping views across the Tweed Valley to the Lammermuir Hills in the northeast. It is a lovely walk to take on a long summer evening before dinner. The official walking guide (two volumes) by Ken Andrew is available in local bookstores or from Her Majesty's Stationer's Office, 71 Lothian Road, Edinburgh EH3 9AZ, and in all likelihood is on the coffee table of your hotel or B&B.

CREATURE COMFORTS

This itinerary does not call for your spending the night in Edinburgh, for two reasons. First, having had a quick review of New Town and a long walking tour of Old Town, you will have experienced many of the most interesting things about Edinburgh. Second, accommodations in Edinburgh tend to fall into one of two categories: very expensive or dingy. Staying out in the country is a more economical and much more attractive proposition.

Nevertheless, for those who wish to spend more time in the city, or who plan to take in some of the International or Fringe festivals in August, suggestions are provided below, along with how to find the best accommodations along the Tweed Valley.

Daily Bed

In addition to using the booking service of the Tourist Information Centre, you can try to find something on your own, either by using the *Edinburgh Tourist Accommodation Register* available from the tourist center, or by driving to the area south of the city center where many of the B&B guesthouses cluster. From the parking lot at Holyroodhouse, take **Holyrood Road** (which becomes **Cowgate**) west and turn left onto **Pleasance Street.** After a name change or two it becomes **Dalkeith Road.** Off to the left beyond the turnoff for **Commonwealth Pool** and on the right between **Dalkeith Road** and **Minto Street** (which runs parallel to Dalkeith) are any number of leafy side streets full of B&Bs. You can expect warm hospitality and a good breakfast, but the rooms will tend to be a bit cramped and the facilities something less than luxe. Do a bit of inspecting until you find one that suits you.

For those who press on to the Tweed Valley, the prospects are much brighter. Armed with your *Where to Stay Holiday Guide* and a pocket full of 10p coins, you can either phone ahead to one of the hotels or B&Bs pictured in the listings or, if it's not too late, wander though the villages along the Tweed Valley until you find someplace that captures your fancy. There are quite a number of small hotels and guesthouses beautifully sited above the river along the A72 between Peebles and Galashiels. B&B's tend to cluster in Victorian houses in the villages and towns proper. But for the most pastoral accommodations, you'll find one or two quite handsome farmhouse B&Bs along the B7062 between Peebles and Innerleithen, including one right next door to Traquair House and within a few hundred yards of the Southern Upland Way.

Daily Bread

During your walk along the Royal Mile today, you'll have no difficulty finding pubs that serve excellent lunches to their largely business crowd. For dinner, should you stay the night in Edinburgh, check the dining guides available at the bookstore in the information center, ask around, or simply take potluck; the choices are wide.

In the Tweed Valley, choices are more limited, but no less attractive. As always, ask for suggestions where you're staying (unless they have their own restaurant!). Here as elsewhere in Scotland, restaurants tend to be in hotels, rather than freestanding, except in larger towns where cafés and even an occasional small first-class restaurant can be found. Close to home, the pub in the hotel near the bridge on the Innerleithen-Traquair road has an exceptional menu and carries the ale brewed at Traquair House.

Over the Border and Back through Time

GALASHIELS ◆ MELROSE AND JEDBURGH
CARTER BAR ◆ HADRIAN'S WALL

- ◆ A visit to the Borders Woolen Centre
- ◆ The Borders' great ruined abbeys
- ◆ Sir Walter Scott's Abbotsford and "Scott's View"
- ◆ A drive back into England through Northumberland National Park
- ◆ A walk through Roman England along Hadrian's Wall

The Border—that No Man's Land between England and Scotland—is a wide and persistent wilderness. . . . This side of the Wall was never tamed.
—H. V. Morton
In Search of Scotland, 1927

*T*here is about the territory along the England-Scotland border a disquieting emptiness, an unnerving loneliness that seems to seep from the bare ledges that run along the tilted ridge tops like the breaking crests of ocean swells. There are no friendly villages. As far as the eye can see, no farmhouse domesticates the wildness. There are the ever-present stone walls, but it is as if their builders had lost heart and simply vanished. The border is enfolded in stillness—the edgy stillness that haunts a lull in a battle whose combatants are temporarily exhausted.

Even before the political border was established, the power-hungry and the plunder-hungry surged back and forth across these bleak moor-

Looking across the Tweed Valley to the Eildon Hills—Sir Walter Scott's favorite view—near Abbotsford

210 ITINERARY: DAY THIRTEEN

lands. The ancient Britons and Scottish Picts raided each other's territory repeatedly. The Romans felt compelled to build the astonishing Hadrian's Wall to defend the civilized world from the barbarians. The Vikings swarmed over the rocky hills and the Normans struggled for centuries to gain dominion over the Scots. The coastal town of Berwick-upon-Tweed changed hands thirteen times before finally succumbing to English control in 1482. To this day, for a score or more miles on either side of the border, there are no towns of consequence and few villages. It is as if the natives are still not sure of the peace.

🚗 FABRIC, FICTION, AND FIGHTING: THE SCOTTISH BORDERS

Distance: 72 miles/116 kilometers to Once Brewed
Roads: Mostly "A" roads, some "B" roads, all scenic
Driving Time: 3–4 hours, with stops
Map: Michelin Map #401

Driving east on the **A72** through the Tweed Valley reveals no evidence of the region's tumultuous history. There is only the langorously meandering river, hills cloaked in soft green velvet and trimmed in deep green fir, and fluffy Cheviot (pronounced "chee-vee-ut") sheep. This is wool country; stone and brick wool mills sit at the heart of nearly every village and town.

There are plenty of wool outlet stores along the way, well marked for travelers, but to really appreciate the story of wool, stop at the **Borders Wool Centre** on Wheatlands Road in **Galashiels** (watch for the sign on the left as you approach the town). Galashiels is the major weaving and knitting center in the Borders (and the home of the Scottish College of Textiles), and the town's Wool Centre offers an excellent free exhibition of wool sorting, hand spinning, weaving, piles of raw wool from a wide variety of sheep breeds, and several sheep still on the hoof in an outside pen. A limited but excellent selection of garments knit or woven in the area is on display and for sale at the center. The Borders Wool Centre is open Monday to Friday 9:00 A.M. to 5:00 P.M. year-round and Saturdays from Easter through mid-October.

As you head **east** on the **A72** out of Galashiels toward **Melrose**, you soon come to a roundabout. Around to the right, the **B6360** branches off toward **Abbotsford**, Sir Walter Scott's home, described by his contemporary, the art critic John Ruskin, as "the most incongruous pile that gentlemanly modernism ever devised." Certainly it is, like his romantic novels, wildly overwrought—a melange of turrets and chimneys dripping with mock-baronial grandiosity and filled with Scott's obsessive collections (Rob Roy's sword, a lock of Prince Charlie's hair,

"Tweed": Profiting from a Misprint

After whisky, tweed—subtly colored and virtually indestructible—is Scotland's most famous product. And while the weaving of wool has been a mainstay of the Borders for centuries (it was brought here from Flanders by the monks who founded the great Borders abbeys in the twelfth and thirteenth centuries), the production of tweed is a recent development—one which owes its name to bad handwriting, poor eyesight, or both. In the mid-1800s, when the big mills grew along Borders rivers that provided abundant water for both power and wool washing ("fulling"), a mill in nearby **Hawick** (pronounced "hoik") twisted three different-colored strands of wool together and had the subtle yarn woven into the tough, diagonal-weave cloth called "tweel" or "twill," often used for military uniforms. A London retailer misread the manufacturer's handwriting, assumed he was trying to cash in on the name recognition of the river Sir Walter Scott had made so famous, and sold it as "tweed." Introduced just as Victorian England was becoming infatuated with all things Scottish, "tweed" was an instant success. Initially, the fabric took its colors from the landscape, literally: dark greens from heather, yellow from rhubarb and bracken root, violet from watercress, browns from yellow lichen and water lilies, red from rock lichen, magenta from dandelion, and so forth. Somewhat more prosaically, the dyes were set with sheep urine. Today, the dyes are all artificial, if more sanitary.

the door from Edinburgh's Tolbooth prison, and much more). It has been left just as he left it, as if he'd just stepped out for a walk to clear his head—as well he might, for at the height of his incredibly productive career, Scott was faced with a stupendous task. In 1826, when he was fifty-five, his partners in a publishing venture failed, leaving him liable for a debt of £117,000—a staggering sum in those days. Viewing the debt as a matter of personal honor, Scott pledged to repay it in full. Already prodigiously prolific, he wrote even more furiously. Only six years later he had repaid some £80,000—and written himself into the grave.

When he needed a respite, Scott would drive his carraige to a high point nearby overlooking the three-peaked Eildon Hills, above a bend in the River Tweed known today as **Scott's View.** And you may wish to do the same. From the roundabout, follow signs for **Melrose** and the

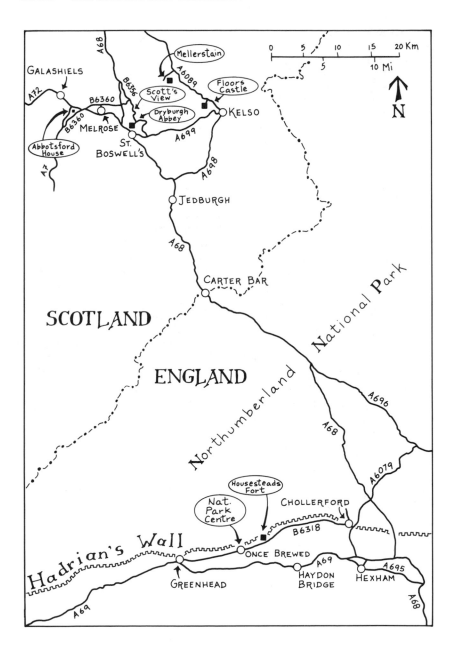

A6091. Take the **A6374** into Melrose proper and consider visiting **Melrose Abbey,** one of three Roman Catholic abbeys founded by King David I in the 1100s (see Diversions).

A minor road signposted for **Newstead** and for Scott's View skirts the abbey, runs along the banks of the Tweed for a short distance, and then ends at a new section of the **A68.** Turn **left** onto the A68 and cross over the river, take the next **right,** and then, at the junction with the **B6360,** turn **left** again. Go uphill to the crossroads, turn **right,** and from here follow signs for **Dryburgh Abbey, Bemersyde,** and **Scott's View.** When you finally reach the view so beloved by Scott, a rolling pastoral landscape opens out to your right. Below, the Tweed twists through fields of wheat, barley, and hay divided by hedges and neat stone walls. Sheep and cows graze meadows that stretch up to the feet of the three peaks of the **Eildon Hills,** site of an Iron Age fort, a lookout post for the Romans and, according to legend, the site beneath which the knights of King Arthur's Round Table lie in perpetual sleep.

From Scott's View the road winds down a long hill, dead-ending in the **B5356.** Here you may wish to detour to the **right** to visit **Dryburgh Abbey,** beautifully situated on the banks of the Tweed (see Diversions). Otherwise, turn **left** and pass through the red standstone village of **Clintmains** until the road dead-ends at the **B6404,** where you turn **right.**

At **St. Boswell's,** turn **left** onto the **A68** and head for the border. Along the way, you'll pass through **Jedburgh,** home of yet another ruined Borders abbey (see Diversions).

Coming out of Jedburgh, the A68 begins to climb out of the lush river valley and up into wind-swept moorland. The England-Scotland border is marked at **Carter Bar** by a stone marker. To the south, and stretching for miles both east and west across the soggy moors, is **Northumberland National Park.** Established in 1956, the nearly 400-square-mile (more than 1,000 square kilometers) park is the least visited in Britain. It is high, wild, and windy, much of it open moorland.

As you drive through the park, the landscape seems oddly askew: the hills all slope gently upward from south to north and then shelve off sharply along their northern edges, creating long east-west escarpments. This tipsy topography owes its existence to the uplifting of ancient sedimentary rock layers and the intrusion, later, of molten magma along the planes of the old sedimentary beds. Erosion and glaciation eventually revealed the harder, uptilted layers and removed the intervening softer rocks and clays. The result is a series of giant's steps, running north to south. Indeed, it was along the most pronounced of these cliffs—the **Great Whin Sill**—that the Romans built a major section of their famous wall, nearly 2,000 years ago.

HADRIAN'S WALL: LAST BASTION OF ROMAN CIVILIZATION

At the southern boundary of Northumberland National Park the road forks. Stay to the right, on the **A68,** avoiding the A696 (which looks like the main road). About 15 miles (24 kilometers) beyond this fork, turn right onto the **A6079,** signposted for **Hexham** and **Chollerford.**

Roman Emperor Hadrian's Wall still striding across the windswept Northumberland hills after nearly 2,000 years

Here the landscape quickly softens. The red sandstone villages of the Scottish side of the border have given way to pale gray sandstone and lichen-covered villages that blend naturally with their surroundings. There are lovely views of the River Choller and, here and there, clusters of forest and farms tucked into the sheltered folds of the hills.

Near **Chollerford,** turn right onto the **B6318** over the lovely old arched bridge, then turn **left** at the roundabout by the riverside pub and continue **east** on the **B6318,** paralleling the remains of **Hadrian's Wall,** with its defensive ditches alternately on your left and right. Bypass **Chesters Fort,** the first major Roman site in the neighborhood, and continue east in the direction of **Housesteads Fort,** some 8 miles (13 kilometers) ahead.

The Emperor Hadrian's Wall, begun in A.D. 121 and completed in A.D. 129, must certainly be one of the world's most emphatic statements of military and social territoriality. It served as a barrier and outpost of the empire for two and a half centuries. That so much of it remains today, after centuries of warfare and vandalizing (it was an irresistible source of precut stone) is testimony both to the quality of its engineering and to the administrative sophistication with which it was built. Replacing an informal frontier that was little more than a road with occasional timber forts, the wall stretched 80 Roman miles (73.5 miles/119 kilometers) across the neck of Britain, from Wallsend on the River Tyne on the east to Bowness-on-Solway on the west. Some 16,000 laborers quarried, carted, and finished 1 million cubic yards of stone and immeasurable quantities of earth to fashion not just the wall (as much as 15 feet high and 10 feet wide, or 5 by 3 meters) but also lookout turrets, milecastles, forts, and civilian settlements.

Of all the temples, villas, and forts along the wall, **Housesteads Fort,** a five-acre complex that accommodated some 1,000 soldiers in the second century A.D., is the best preserved and presented. Here you'll need to make a choice. Depending upon how many border abbeys, stately homes, or woolen mills you visited this morning, it should be early afternoon when you reach the wall. The best way to explore the wall, Housesteads Fort, and the nearby civilian settlement of Vindolanda is by taking a 6- to 7-mile (10- to 12-kilometer) walk centered on the **National Park Information Centre** a mile or two east of Housesteads at the delightfully named crossroads of **Once Brewed.**

But if time is short, or the weather is inhospitable, and especially if you plan to press farther south today, turn into the car park here at Housesteads (which the Romans called *Vircovicium*) and make this your Hadrian's Wall experience. Visit the excellent museum exhibits first, then wander through the gateways into the complex of granaries, barracks, headquarters, bakery, hospital, latrines, baths, and other outbuildings to the wall itself, perched high above the surrounding landscape atop the Whin Sill crags.

🏃 A Walk in the Footsteps of Hadrian's Legionaries

Distance: 7.5 miles/12 kilometers for long route, 4.5 miles (7.3 kilometers) round trip just along the wall; allow 3–4 hours

Difficulty: Some steep sections of wall, mostly easy

Total Elevation Gain: A few hundred feet at most

Gear and Map: Comfortable shoes/sneakers, rain gear; walking map from National Park Centre

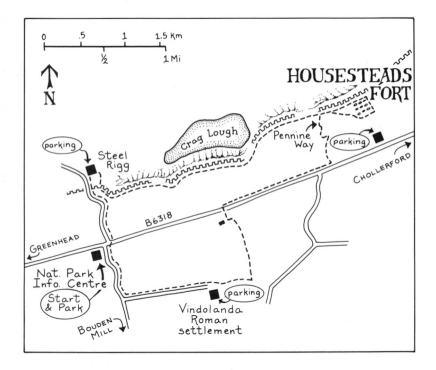

On a good day this is one of those wonderful soul-expanding walks, with sweeping views across miles of open countryside, hawks coasting on updrafts, and fields dotted with bits of woolly fluff and the black-and-white abstract forms of grazing Frisian cows. The ground around Housesteads rolls away like a great green sea, with shafts of sun slashing through the wide sky as puffy clouds tear across the landscape. From the walk's highest point, at 1,050 feet (320 meters) above sea level, it becomes only too clear why the Romans were so successful for so long: with 360-degree visibility for miles, this is a superb strategic position.

Some of the excavated remains of the Roman fort at Housesteads, Northumberland

Indeed, from this point you'll be able to see virtually your entire walking route.

Begin by visiting the National Park Information Centre, which has an excellent exhibit on local history before, during, and long after the Roman occupation. Then walk **north** across the B6318 and up the lane signposted for **Steel Rigg,** with the best section of the wall dead ahead on the ridge line. Turn right into the Steel Rigg car park, then go through the gate in the southwest corner of the lot and follow the obvious path uphill along the wall. After a few hundred yards, the path leaves the wall and cuts **left,** rejoining it shortly to ascend the first crag. From here on, the path generally stays close to the wall, departing only to trace an easier route around particularly steep climbs. Along the way, you'll pass the remains of the 20-foot-square watch **turrets** that housed 4-man patrols between the **milecastles,** which housed 50 soldiers each. The soldiers, incidentally, were not for the most part Romans at all, but a combination of locally recruited Britons and recruits from elsewhere in northern Europe—both well suited to the non-Italian weather. At peak strength, there were 5,500 cavalry and 13,000 infantrymen stationed along the wall.

At a point high above the eastern edge of the lake at **Crag Lough,** the path jogs **right** over a cattle grid and stile and then **left** over another stile further on, regaining the wall near lonely **Hotbank Farm.** The path undulates gently from here, then rises to the top of **Cuddy's Crags,** passing the marker for the **Pennine Way** before reaching another milecastle. From here it's a short stroll through the woods to Housesteads Fort.

Once you've visited the museum and explored the fort you have a choice. In summer, minibuses operate between Housesteads and Steel Rig, offering a shortcut back to the car. For a longer walk taking in another major attraction, however, backtrack to the Pennine Way marker and turn **left,** following the way downhill (past a Roman lime kiln) to the B6318. Turn **right** and follow the road for perhaps a mile and then take the footpath to the **left** (near the second building you encounter on your left) pointing to **Vindolanda,** the site (still being excavated) of what 1,800 years ago was a busy civilian community housing the soldiers' families, artisans, and other support services. There is a complete reconstruction of the wall, a wide area of excavated buildings and community infrastructure, and an excellent museum.

From Vindolanda, head **west** through the car park and down the lane—actually a section of the *Stanegate,* a Roman frontier even older than the wall—to the T-junction. Turn **right,** and in a half-mile or so you'll be back at the National Park Information Centre where you began.

DIVERSIONS

Depending upon whether your interests run to the sacred or the secular, there are two kinds of diversions worth considering today, both in the Scottish Borders.

Borders Stately Homes

The Borders counties are full of stately homes—vast piles of stone set in grand formal landscape gardens. Two near the route of your itinerary today are Mellerstain and Floors Castle, both on the **A6089** near **Kelso. Mellerstain House** (open Sunday through Friday from May through September from 12:30 P.M. to 5:00 P.M.) was begun by architect William Adam in 1725 and completed by his son Robert in 1778, and is one of the finest Georgian mansions in Britain. **Floors Castle** (open Sunday through Thursday from May through September from 10:30 A.M. to 5:30 P.M., as well as Fridays in July and August) is a vast forest of crenelations and turrets. Begun by William Adam in 1721 and expanded by William Playfair, it is the largest inhabited home in Scotland.

Borders Abbeys

Four great abbeys were established in the Borders in the early 1100s—Melrose, Jedburgh, Kelso, and Dryburgh. The sheep-raising abbots prospered and their abbeys grew to be among the most beautiful—and vulnerable—in Britain. Sacked and plundered during the Wars of Independence in the 1300s, and rebuilt in even greater glory, the abbeys were laid waste again and for good, on orders from Henry VIII, when the Scots refused to permit their infant Queen Mary to be betrothed to Henry's son Edward—a rampage that came to be known as the "rough wooing." All four of these magnificent, melancholy ruins are open April through September from 9:30 A.M. to 7:00 P.M., Sundays 2:00 P.M. to 7:00 P.M.; and in the winter until 4:00 P.M.

CREATURE COMFORTS

As your trip dwindles down to its last few days, where you spend the night will be determined by how far south you want to be the next day. If you rented your car in York, rather than at one of the London airports, there is no reason why you could not be back in York tonight, even with extended visits at one or two of the major Borders attractions and at Housesteads Fort. From Housesteads, simply backtrack to the east and rejoin the **A68** heading south, joining the **M1(A1)** south near **Darlington**. From there it's only a short drive to York. But be sure you have a reservation for the night (see the information in Day Two's itinerary for York), for you'll arrive around suppertime. Then return the car in the morning and use your return train ticket to London. You'll have a day and a half to sightsee and shop before you leave for home.

If you flew into Scotland's Prestwick Airport instead of London, follow the directions to York and then go to the beginning chapters until the itinerary brings you back to Glasgow.

If you rented your car in London, however, a full day awaits you tomorrow (capped by a lovely afternoon river walk in Dovedale). If you take the walk along Hadrian's Wall, you should plan on spending the evening nearby (suggestions below). If you choose only to visit Housesteads Fort, you might consider spending the night in the Yorkshire Dales, just an hour or two to the south, or pushing all the way south to Dovedale (roughly four hours). If you choose Dovedale, see tomorrow's Creature Comforts for accommodation details.

Daily Bed

Though from the top of Hotbank Crags the countryside around Hadrian's Wall seems remote and barren, civilization—in the form of cozy accommodations and warm English pubs—is quite nearby. You will have passed a couple of handsome B&Bs on the B6318 between Chollerford and Once Brewed, and there are more B&Bs, as well as inns and hotels, in the area bounded by Chollerford, Once Brewed, Haydon Bridge, and Hexham. Although they don't run an accommodation service at the National Park Centre, they're nevertheless accommodating: ask them for suggestions and they're likely to have a few neighbors they can recommend. In addition, there is a youth hostel next door to the park center at Once Brewed.

Daily Bread

One of the benefits of crossing the border back into England is the joy of rediscovering English pubs, and there are several outstanding ones in this area, from the big inn on the river at Chollerford to a small pub/restaurant a few miles west of Once Brewed at (what else?) Twice Brewed, which features game pies, venison sausage, and other local specialties. Remember too that you are close to Newcastle, the source of Newcastle Brown Ale, a mild, dark ale that is in a class all its own.
(**Note:** This evening, or first thing tomorrow morning, call your airline and confirm your return flight. If you fail to do so the airline can cancel your reservation and give your seats to someone else. Should you be traveling on a restricted ticket, this can be an expensive, not just inconvenient problem. In addition, since you'll have no forwarding phone in the next couple of days, check in again later to be sure the flight hasn't changed.)

♦DAY FOURTEEN

South to Secluded Dovedale

HADRIAN'S WALL ♦ A1(M1) SOUTH
DOVEDALE (OR LONDON)

♦ **A morning on the motorway**
♦ **An afternoon walk through Izaak Walton's Dovedale**
♦ **An optional side trip to Cambridge**

*I*f you've been looking anxiously at your road map and the calendar wondering how you're ever going to get to London in time for your plane, relax. This is where you come to appreciate just how small Britain really is. If you wanted to, for example, you could leave Hadrian's Wall after breakfast this morning and be in London by midafternoon, with plenty of time to drop off your car, get settled in your hotel, take an evening stroll, and have a leisurely dinner.

But as we noted at the outset, this is a guide to Britain's countryside, not a guide to London, so the route south today stops at the southern edge of England's remarkable **Peak District**—a national park alternately wild and pastoral, wedged in between the nation's major industrial centers.

Dovedale, barely 2 miles (3 kilometers) long, is the Peak District's most secluded and romantic gem, a winding wooded gorge lined with towering cliffs and skyscraper limestone spires and pinnacles—with names like Lovers Leap, Jacob's Ladder, and the Twelve Apostles—all cut by the River Dove, perhaps the prettiest trout stream in England (and the inspiration for Izaak Walton's *Compleat Angler*). You can drive to it, but not through it. For that you have to walk, and there may be no prettier or more visually varied riverside walk in the country. The countryside around Dovedale is dotted with clustered stone villages and especially well-kept B&B farms. All in all, it's a lovely place to bring your tour to a gentle close.

🚗 THE MORNING RUN SOUTH TO DERBYSHIRE

Distance: 220 miles/355 kilometers
Roads: Primary roads or motorways until Dovedale
Driving Time: About 3 hours
Map: Michelin Map #402

From wherever you spent the night near Hadrian's Wall, head east this morning, either by the **B6318** through Chollerford or the **A69** through Haydon Bridge, to the **A68.** Turn **right** and follow the **A68** south to the A1(M) just outside of **Darlington.** Take the **A1(M)** south and soon you'll be on familiar ground again, heading south on the same section of the A1 below York that you drove north on two weeks ago. Below **Doncaster,** take the **M18** south and then the **M1** south past Sheffield. At **Exit 28** leave the M1 and take the **A38** toward **Derby** (pronounced "darby"), but follow signs to the A610 and then the A6 south, before turning west on the **A517** to **Ashbourne.**

Fooled by the disguise, a Dovedale cow ignores a handout.

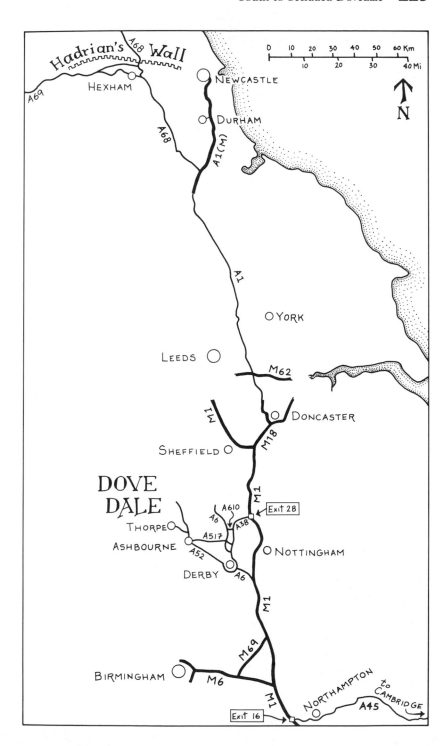

A handsome small town with a thirteenth- to fourteenth-century church the novelist George Eliot called "the finest mere parish church in England," Ashbourne also has some nice shops and is a good place to put together a picnic lunch (or dinner). Then simply follow the road signs along mostly minor roads for **Dovedale** and **Ilam.**

Along the way, you twist through the pretty village of **Thorpe,** which has a good selection of first-class B&Bs. If you plan to stay in the Dovedale area tonight, now would be a good time to make arrangements (see Creature Comforts). Outside of Thorpe, the road climbs up and over a hill and down into a lovely valley at the confluence of the Rivers Dove and Manifold, with the distinctive cone-shaped hill called **Thorpe Cloud** on your right. The parking lot for the popular walk in Dovedale is a hundred yards or so up the lane on your right just beyond the Izaak Walton Hotel, but instead of turning here continue straight ahead into the little planned community of Ilam, and drive to **Ilam Hall.** Once a stately home, Ilam Hall is now a youth hostel, but it also houses a National Trust shop with an excellent exhibit on the Peak District and a three-dimensional model of Dovedale and its surroundings. While you're in the shop, you may want to pick up the *Dovedale Guide,* published by Derbyshire Countryside Ltd., to accompany your walk.

🏃 A WALK THROUGH DOVEDALE'S GORGEOUS GORGE

Distance: 8 miles/13 kilometers or 4.5 miles/7.25 kilometers for river walk only; allow 3.5 hours for longer walk
Difficulty: River walk is on a broad, well-maintained, level path; longer walk has some moderate hills
Total Elevation Gain: Negligible on river walk, a few hundred feet on longer walk
Map: *Dovedale Guide,* Derbyshire Countryside Ltd.

Dovedale provokes hyperbole. It is full of fantastically eroded limestone crags, caves, and pinnacles, all crammed into two miles of impossibly pastoral gorge, and its compact beauty has a magical effect. In a mist, Dovedale is a breeding ground for fairy tales; you have no trouble believing in water sprites and elves. In bright sun, a walk through Dovedale is a continuous series of surprise views. There are wildflowers everywhere, on the sunny slopes and in the wooded glades. The silence is broken only by the soothing mumble of water slipping over tiny trout weirs and by the songs of birds so used to human company that they're nearly tame. Dippers race along the limpid surface of the Dove, competing with the trout for insects. Light and shadow flirt with each other under the branches of the ash and alder trees that line

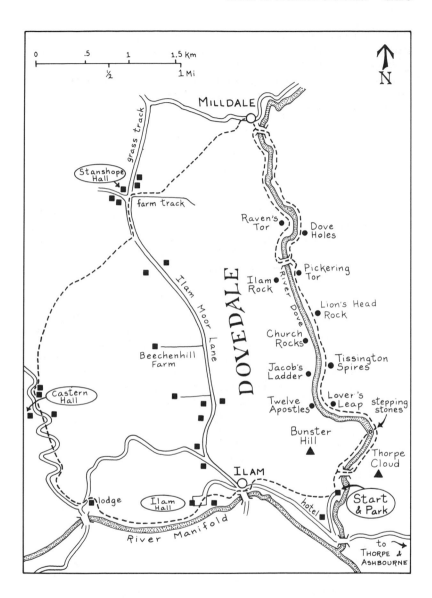

the rocky slopes, in places reaching to touch each other where the gorge narrows. It is a place where lovers stroll, in fact a place where couples who hardly speak to each other anymore cannot help but hold hands.

The walk begins at the car park where a weathered, bewhiskered, ageless character with a shepherd's crook and a change purse (who looks fearsome, but in fact is delightful) sells parking tickets, rain or shine. Don't worry about the crowds; 95 percent of the folks who park here go only as far as the picturesque steppingstones a hundred yards upstream, take pictures, and then return.

The gate to Dovedale is guarded by the imposing bulk of **Thorpe Cloud**—fenced off these days to repair erosion caused by the busy feet of thousands of schoolchildren unable to resist the lure of "king of the hill." Follow the broad main path along the left side of the river and then cross—from Staffordshire to Derbyshire, as it happens—to the other bank by the steppingstones. Both the river and the path now bend sharply left and the valley begins to narrow as it passes **Dovedale Castle,** the first of many limestone outcroppings, on the left. The river bends again, this time to the right, and the path climbs up to a point between **Lovers Leap** and the multiple spires of the **Twelve Apostles** on the opposite bank. It runs above the river now, through a wood that is reputed to be one of the few virgin forests left in Britain. Ahead on the left, **Jacob's Ladder** and **Church Rocks** poke above the treetops. On the right, up a steep path and through a natural arch, is **Reynard's Cave.**

Beyond the path to the arch, the main path drops down to the edge of the river and squeezes into **The Straits,** the narrowest segment of the gorge, passing under the projecting nose of **Lions Head Rock.** This is the most secluded part of Dovedale. Heavily wooded and offering only a sliver of sky, it has a curious otherworldliness, even on a sunny afternoon. Upstream, the towering white monolith of **Ilam Rock** stares across the stream to equally imposing **Pickering Tor.** Ignore the wooden footbridge here and stay on the right bank, following the main path as it clambers up over a rocky ledge and down to **Dove Holes,** two large but shallow caves carved out by the river before it cut down through the limestone to its present bed.

At this point, the gorge softens and the slopes lean back more gently. The river is edged with reeds and flag iris below Raven's Tor, and, a bit farther upstream, the landscape becomes gentler still. The path edges a grassy slope and then crosses a lovely humpbacked pedestrian bridge over the river and into the peaceful hamlet of **Milldale.** Here you have a choice: you can return downriver following the other bank as far as the wooden footbridge and then retrace your steps (a round trip of perhaps 4.5 miles/7.3 kilometers), or you can climb up and over the hills to the Manifold River Valley and Ilam Hall (making a round trip of perhaps 8 miles/13 kilometers).

To follow the longer route, turn **right** on the other side of the bridge, go past the little village store, and then turn **left** up the road. On the **left** as you begin to run out of buildings, an obvious footpath climbs uphill and to the right through a shallow ravine. When it finally

Tranquil Dovedale, inspiration for Isaac Walton's The Compleat Angler

attains high ground, the footpath crosses several stone-walled meadows populated by ruminating cows. Continue through one stile or gate after another until you reach a **farm track** bounded by a high stone wall. Turn **right,** follow the lane downhill to a small village, and turn **left.** At **Stanshope Hall** (a particularly elegant country-house B&B catering to walkers), bear **left** again and follow the road uphill a few hundred yards until you encounter a public-footpath sign on the right. Turn **right** onto the footpath, which offers sweeping views across billowing hills and pastures, and follow it down to **Castern Hall** (a private residence), below which it reaches the **River Manifold.**

Walk past the bridge over the river, staying on the **left** bank and following a broad track to the left of an old white cottage (marked by a box on a post requesting, inappropriately, a donation for passage). The banks of the Manifold are broader than those of the Dove and lined with magenta foxglove, red campion, and Queen Anne's lace, among other wildflowers. Eventually, the path becomes less overgrown and begins to take on a more formal appearance—a sure sign that you are approaching **Ilam Hall.** Beyond a mossy grotto, the hall appears on rising ground to the left, its broad park stretching out ahead. Cross the grounds, following the path around the **left** of the **chapel** and into the village, with its odd mock–Swiss chalet houses. Then turn **right** onto the road and at the fork, bear **left.** Immediately afterward, go over the stile in the wall on your **left** and follow the obvious path that slants to the **right** across the sloping pasture, carries you over the hill past the rear of the Izaak Walton Hotel, and finally returns you to the car park— a walk that combines bizarre limestone spires, wind-swept rolling meadows, and a stately home.

At this point, you can retire to a steaming tub wherever you've settled for the night and await dinner or, if you chose the shorter walk and have some three hours of driving energy still in you, you can drive south toward London, via Derby and the M1 (see tomorrow morning's directions for details).

DIVERSIONS

Cambridge

With so many miles to cover today, there isn't a lot of time for detours, but one diversion—actually an **alternative to Dovedale**—is worth considering.

If no trip through Britain would be complete for you without a visit to one of its two great universities, **Cambridge** is only about 50 miles (80 kilometers) east of the M1 as it hurtles south to London. Cambridge is a symphony of towers, quadrangles, leaded windows, and lush gardens, and every nook and cranny is haunted by the centuries of scientists, writers, painters, philosophers, politicians, and lesser luminaries who have passed through its Gothic portals. Unlike Oxford, which is integrated into a large town, Cambridge is fairly self-contained, cradled by the banks of the curving **River Cam** and the leafy parkland of **The Backs** (in *back* of the colleges) and **Jesus Green.**

To get to Cambridge, take **Exit 16** off the M1 at **Northampton** (south of the turnoff for Dovedale) and follow the **A45** as it bypasses Northampton and then heads west across the flat countryside of Cambridgeshire. Approaching Cambridge, just follow signs to **City Centre** and park in the huge lot at the **Lion's Yard Shopping Centre,** steps away from the **Tourist Information Centre** on **Wheeler Street**.

The best way to see Cambridge efficiently is to take one of the **two-hour guided tours** this afternoon (at 1:00 P.M., 2:00 P.M., and 3:00 P.M. in summer, 2:00 P.M. in winter) that leave from the Tourist Information Centre. Call ahead for reservations (0223-322640). Be sure your guide has a blue badge or you won't get into the colleges. (Also be advised that many colleges and their grounds are closed during end-of-year examinations, May through mid-June.) If you want to explore independently, pick up the Ordnance Survey/Automobile Association *Cambridge City Guide,* available at the information centre or bookstores. After your tour, you can either head south for London or spend the night in Cambridge (best B&Bs are on or near **Jesus Lane,** opposite Jesus Gardens). As usual, the Tourist Information Centre can help.

CREATURE COMFORTS

Daily Bed

The nonprofit **Peak and Moorlands Farm Holiday Association** was one of the first groups formed by farm wives offering B&B accommodations in the countryside. And many of the nicest places to stay in the Dovedale area are farms that are part of this group. You can find details in *The Official Guide of the Farm Holiday Bureau U.K.* (see Further Reading) or by writing the local association directly at The Hall, Great Hucklow, Tideswell, Buxton SK17 8RG.

Alternatively, you can simply look around locally before taking this afternoon's walk. There are lovely B&Bs (as well as several larger country hotels) in the tiny village of **Thorpe** and along the road that runs beyond Ilam to the north. For the latter, follow the road uphill past Ilam Hall and take the right fork (**Ilam Moor Lane**) towards **Stanshope**. There are two or three excellent B&Bs along the way. If they're booked, stop in at **Beechenhill Farm** (on Ilam Moor Lane) and ask Sue Prince, who is a member of the Peak and Moorlands Associa-

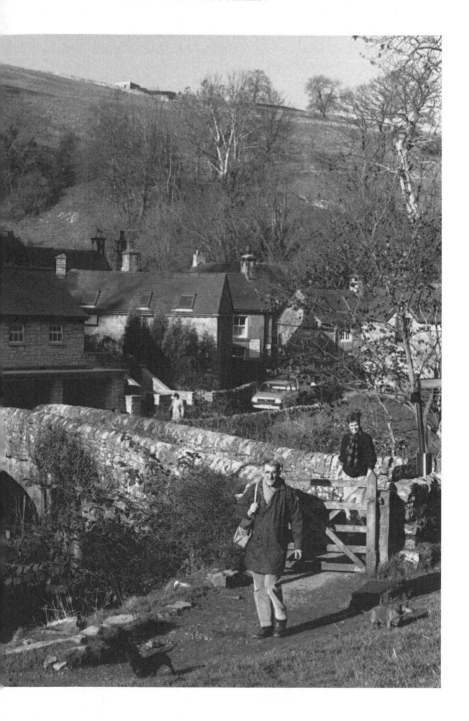

tion, to recommend one of her other nearby association members. There's also the youth hostel at Ilam Hall. Should all else fail, you can always backtrack to Ashbourne.

If you decide to press ahead toward London, you'll need reservations somewhere; it will be too late to go searching once you get there tonight. See Creature Comforts in tomorrow's itinerary for ideas.

Daily Bread

Fortunately (since this may be your last night in the countryside), the villages around Dovedale offer an abundance of cozy pubs for dinner, and there are enough larger hotels (and a few town restaurants) for more lavish menus. But owners and chefs do change; ask where you're staying for some recommendations and poke around a little to find something that suits you.

As an alternative, if the weather is clear and you happen to be traveling in the summer when English evenings are long and golden, consider a picnic dinner above the stream at Dovedale. This afternoon, before your walk, drive into Ashbourne and stock up; there are cheese shops and butchers with lovely pâtés, bakeries for bread and pastries, greengrocers for a bit of tomato or cucumber, and one major supermarket for anything else you'll need, including a nice bottle of wine to celebrate the last two weeks.

The tiny hamlet of Milldale, turning point in the Dovedale walk

A Taste of London

DOVEDALE ◆ DERBY ◆ M1 SOUTH ◆ LONDON

- ◆ **How to get there**
- ◆ **What to do there**
- ◆ **How to get out when you're ready to leave**
- ◆ **Plus a car tour of the Thames Valley**

When a man is tired of London, he is tired of life; for there is in London all that life can afford.
                    —Dr. Samuel Johnson, 1777

The operative word here, of course, is *afford*. London hotels and restaurants are no bargain. That's the bad news. The good news is that most of London's best attractions—its wonderful neighborhoods, the streets with their richly painted Victorian shop fronts, the museums and galleries, many of the monuments and all of the parks, and the incredible passing parade—are free. And many more of the things that are quintessentially London—the theater, the pubs, the Tube, the red double-decker buses, and more—are quite inexpensive. So you can splurge on special purchases or an elegant dinner and still afford "all that life can afford."

That having been said, you won't have much time to splurge unless you extend the sixteen-day itinerary that forms the core of this guidebook. What follows, then, are some tips on getting into, around in, and out of London. For more details, take along one of the London guidebooks recommended in Further Reading.

🚗 HOW TO GET TO LONDON

Distance: About 150 miles/240 kilometers from Dovedale, 75 miles/120 kilometers from Cambridge

Driving Time: 2–2.5 hours from Dovedale (assuming no M1 "tailbacks"), 1.5–2 hours from Cambridge

Roads: Motorway most of the way

Map: Michelin Map #404

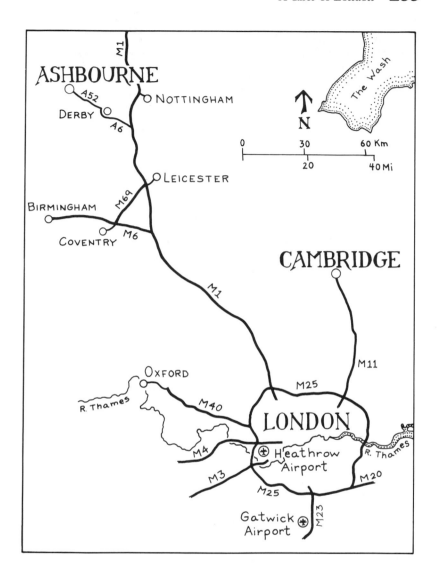

This morning's itinerary depends on a number of things: where you begin; whether you plan to get into the city proper by car or train, if London is your destination (an alternative is provided); and where you plan to spend the night (in the city or near the airports). The permutations are many, so hold on to your hat, here we go.

From **Dovedale,** backtrack to **Ashbourne** and take the **A52** east toward **Derby** (where Rolls-Royces are made). Begin early, by 9:00 A.M.

at the latest. As you approach Derby, you'll begin to see signs for the **M1 south.** Follow them and you'll be guided around the southern edge of town, through more than half a dozen roundabouts, to the **A6** leading to the M1 south. Take the **M1 south** toward London.

From **Cambridge,** it couldn't be simpler: just take the **M11** from the outskirts of the city south to the **M25.**

At **Exit 6A** if you're on the **M1,** or **Exit 6** if you're on the **M11,** you encounter the **M25**—the motorway ring road around the outer London metropolitan area. If you plan to drop your car off at the airport this morning, take the **M25 west** and then **south.** For **Heathrow,** take the exit for the **M4 eastbound** and follow clear signs to the airport and your car rental agency. For **Gatwick,** stay on the M25 halfway around the metropolitan area and take the **M23 south** to **Exit 9.** Again, follow signs for the airport and the instructions from your car rental agency. Then, take mass transit into the city—the Underground ("Tube") from Heathrow, and the BritRail express from Gatwick to Victoria Station (see Day One).

If you (1) plan to drop your car off at an in-town rental office, or (2) will be staying in the city or at an inner suburb B&B (see Creature Comforts) and want to keep the car until tomorrow morning, or (3) want to drive into the city today and drive out to stay somewhere near an airport tonight, and (4) have no fear of driving in the city or already know it well enough not to get flustered in the traffic, then ignore the M25 and continue straight into the city on the M1 (from Dovedale) or M11 (from Cambridge). The **M1** eventually peters out near the suburban town of Hendon, and you follow the **A5** right into central London and **Hyde Park.** The **M11** joins the **A11** farther east near Wanstead, leading you into London's **East End.**

In both cases, the secret to getting where you want to go in London—apart from having extraordinary patience with its narrow, twisty streets and dense traffic—is understanding that the route signs you begin to encounter as you enter the city proper are designed to direct you to the city's neighborhoods (e.g., South Kensington, Chelsea, Paddington). If you know which neighborhood your destination (hotel, B&B, car rental agency) is in and roughly what part of town that is, you're as good as there—just follow the signs. Then use a street map to find the specific location. The same applies if you're just in town for an afternoon of sightseeing and plan to drive out of town this evening. Figure out which neighborhood you want to park in and follow the signs. If you suddenly find yourself going in a direction apparently away from your target, don't panic, and keep following the signs. They're designed to steer you away from chronically congested areas between you and your destination and to help you avoid one-way street traps, and sometimes the result is indirect. As for parking, look for garages or, if you won't be all day, metered spaces. Some in-town residential areas have free on-street parking for those with eagle eyes and good luck. Under no circumstances park next to a double yellow line.

RESOURCES: Both to get *into* London and to get *around* in it, you'll need only the **British Tourist Authority's Official London Map.** Accept no substitutes; send away for it in advance, buy a copy at the information desk when you arrive at the airport (see Day One), or head for one of the BTA's offices in London: at 12 Regents Street, below Piccadilly Circus, open Monday through Saturday 9:00 A.M. to 6:30 P.M., Sunday 10:00 A.M. to 4:00 P.M.; at Victoria Station (similar hours); and at Harrods (Kensington) and Selfridges (Oxford Street) department stores, during normal store hours. In addition, you may want to pick up the BTA's *Quick Guide to London,* a slim brochure with descriptions, locations, times, and phone numbers for every major attraction in the city.

HOW TO GET AROUND TOWN

More a collection of quirky little villages than a city, London is best experienced on foot. But with little more than half a day by this itinerary, you won't have that luxury.

CABS. If you're traveling with several people, take cabs. They're roomy, and the drivers are unfailingly friendly, helpful, and polite (always say "please" when giving directions). They spend up to two years, full time, pedaling around London by bicycle or on mopeds to learn "The Knowledge" and obtain a license, so you can trust your driver to know precisely how to get where you want to go by the quickest route, no matter how roundabout it may seem. The fare, when split among three or four riders, will be competitive with the Tube, except over very long distances. Look for one with its roof light on and wave it down. Tip 10 to 15 percent.

TUBE. There's almost nowhere in London that isn't a few blocks from a Tube station (look for the red circle bisected by a horizontal blue line that says UNDERGROUND). The route map is in your BTA London map (and on the wall in each station). Each line has its own name and color code. You buy your ticket from an agent in the station (or automatic machines) and *keep it* to hand to another agent (or run through an exit machine) at the other end. In stations where two or more lines intersect, just follow signs on the wall. Many platforms have electric signs that tell you how soon the next train will come and, if the line splits somewhere, which branch the next train will take. You can zoom across town quickly (in most cases faster than by cab) and the fares are relatively cheap. If you're planning on doing a lot of "Tubing," buy a one-day pass, valid after 9:30 A.M. (This is a particularly good idea if you've left your car at Heathrow; you'll save a small fortune.) Three-day cards are also available, for those staying longer. The Tube is open Monday through Saturday, 5:30 A.M. to midnight, Sunday 7:30 A.M. to 11:30 P.M.

BUSES. The advantage of London's great bus system is that you get to see everything along the way. The disadvantage is that the system is impenetrably complex. If you're only in London for a day or two, forget it.

WHAT TO DO IN LONDON

Victorian-era Prime Minister William Gladstone once told a group of visitors that the best way to see London was from the top of a double-decker bus, and that is still the case today. **The Original London Transport Sightseeing Tour,** run by the city bus company, is a terrific 90-minute orientation of the best of the sights with great running commentaries. Distinctively painted buses leave from **Victoria Station, Piccadilly Circus** (from the corner of Haymarket), **Baker Street** (corner of Marylebone) and **Marble Arch** (at Speakers' Corner) roughly every half-hour from 10:00 A.M. to 5:00 P.M. daily (and later in summer at Victoria and Piccadilly). Fight for seats on the open top deck. Tickets are cheaper if purchased at the Regents Street BTA Information Centre, the London Transport Tours Office at Piccadilly, or at the Piccadilly, Oxford Circus, or Heathrow Tube station. No reservations are needed (for details, call 227-3456).

What you do next depends, of course, on your interests. And the choices are almost limitless. Established as *Londinium* by the Romans in A.D. 43, London has been growing ever since. Much of the city was leveled by the Great Fire in 1666, however, so anything you see today was probably built since then. Many old-looking buildings, like the Houses of Parliament, are reproductions. Since the Great Fire, the city has spawned some of the finest museums and galleries, the loveliest urban parks and residential squares, the best-recognized official buildings and monuments, and the most enticing shops in all of Europe.

But in the short time you have here, some dos and don'ts are in order. First, the don'ts:

♦ **DON'T bother with the changing of the guard at Buckingham Palace.** It's extremely boring and, unless it is the dead of winter or you're a professional basketball player, the crowds will block your view.

◆ **DON'T try to see the Crown Jewels.** Do see the Tower of London, if your taste runs to the grisly, but the line for the jewels is often hours long and the finale is somehow disappointing. Buy a booklet or a postcard instead.

◆ **DON'T try to get into the Houses of Parliament.** They're only open for tourists in the afternoon when the House of Commons is in session, and the lines are very long.

◆ **DON'T go into the splendid British Museum unless you intend to spend the rest of the day there.** There are some ninety different galleries in this monument to imperial sticky fingers; even those just devoted to ancient civilizations will captivate you for hours. (Open Monday through Saturday 10:00 A.M. to 5:00 P.M., Sunday 2:30 P.M. to 6:00 P.M.)

On the other hand:

◆ **DO visit St. Paul's Cathedral if you must choose between it and Westminster Abbey.** The abbey tends to be crowded, noisy, and uninspiring; the cathedral vast, hushed, soaring, and awe-inspiring—Christopher Wren's masterpiece and, miraculously, virtually the lone survivor of the blitz of December 19, 1940, which leveled much of "the City," as this part of London is known (that's why most of the buildings around St. Paul's are modern). If you do choose Westminster after all, take the hour-and-a-half "Supertour" operated by the vergers to really appreciate the abbey (call 222-7110 for times).

◆ **DO visit the Tate Gallery.** A short walk upriver from Parliament Square, the Tate displays primarily (but not exclusively) the work of British artists and houses the finest collection of J. M. W. Turner's work anywhere. It also has an excellent restaurant. (The gallery is open Monday through Saturday 10:00 A.M. to 5:50 P.M., Sunday 2:30 P.M. to 5:50 P.M.)

◆ **Most of all, DO walk through some of the neighborhoods and shop (window- or otherwise).** If you have time to do only one thing, after taking the London Transport bus tour, skip all the monuments and official "sights" and wander through the winding city streets and alleys. For wonderful shops, browse in Mayfair's Jermyn, South Moulton, Oxford, and Old and new Bond Streets; Knightsbridge's Beauchamp (pronounced "bee-cham") Place, Sloane Street, and Brompton Road; South Kensington's Fulham Road; and Chelsea's King's Road. For classic Georgian and Victorian townhouse neighborhoods, wander through Chelsea, Belgravia, and Mayfair. For theater and night life, it's Soho. For bookstores, go to Bloomsbury, near the British Museum. Or go to Camden Lock in Camden Town, just north of the zoo, for a walk along the Grand Union Canal or a ride on a canal boat. Pay attention to architectural details (and beware buses in their idiotic reverse-direction lanes!). Stroll through a park or two and feed the ducks. Duck into an old pub to refresh yourself. This is the real London.

🚗 THE THAMES VALLEY ALTERNATIVE TO LONDON

Distance: About 40 miles (64 kilometers) from Maidenhead
Roads: Fine, superbly scenic primary/secondary roads
Driving Time: 2–3 hours, depending on stops
Map: Michelin Map #404

> *. . . there is nothing—absolutely nothing—half so much worth doing as simply messing about with boats.*
> —Ratty (to Mole)
> Kenneth Grahame's *The Wind in the Willows*

Let's say you've already visited London on another trip. Or that, despite London's charms, you'd rather spend your last day in Britain out in the countryside. The valley of the meandering River Thames, with its pleasure boats and river locks, offers a delightful alternative to the city and will leave you within commuting distance of the airports tomorrow morning.

From either the **M11** or the **M1,** take the **M25** around to the west and south, in the direction of Heathrow. Then take the **M4** motorway **west,** away from Heathrow and in the direction of Slough and Bath. As you approach **Exit 6, Windsor Castle** rises across the fields to your left on a prominent hillside (to visit the castle take Exit 6 and follow the signs).

Leave the M4 at **Exit 7** and follow signs to the **A4** and **Maidenhead.** Immediately after you cross the bridge over the Thames at Maidenhead, turn **right** onto the **A4094** and follow the tree-shaded river as it bends to the north. Almost immediately, you reach **Boulter's Lock,** one of the many automated locks that permit boat traffic along the upper Thames. Stop and cross over to the island between the lock

"Messing about with boats" at Boulters Lock, on the River Thames at Maidenhead

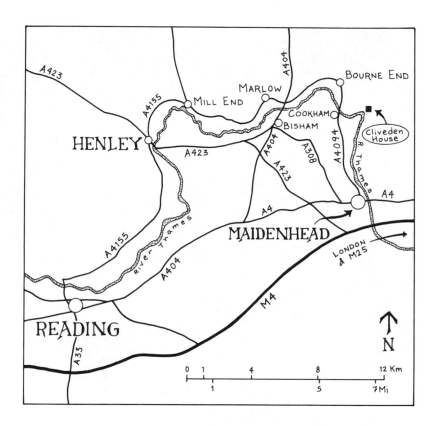

and the weir over which the river flows and watch the occasionally panicky business of filling the lock with boats and water.

Then follow the **A4094** north again to **Cookham,** a quaint old riverside village famous for its local artist, Stanley Spencer, and its ancient pub, the fifteenth-century Bel and the Dragon (Bel was a Babylonian deity), a contender for the title of oldest pub in Britain. There are lovely riverside walks from the village church. It was here that Kenneth Grahame grew up and the pastoral vision of *The Wind in the Willows* took hold. A few miles away is **Cliveden,** a famous stately home (with beautiful formal gardens) thought to be the model for "Toad Hall."

Continue on the A4094 to **Bourne End** and take the **A4155** toward **Marlow.** The A4155 parallels the river now as it twists west again, running through deep beech forests (the "Wild Wood" in *Wind in the Willows*) and across lush valley-bottom grain fields and grazing meadows. A handsome town with a terrific riverside pub, Marlow has about it that sleepy air common to towns along lazy rivers. The A4155 continues along the river through **Medmenham** and **Mill End,** before turning south with the river to **Henley,** site of the famous Henley Royal Regatta (traditionally held at the beginning of July).

At Henley, depending upon where you're spending the night, you can either stay on the A4155 to **Reading** and pick up the **M4** again, or cross the river and follow the **A423** and **A308** along the southern banks of the river back to **Maidenhead.**

CREATURE COMFORTS: THE LAST NIGHT

There are lots of guides to help you sort out a place to stay in London that meets both your geographical and budgetary requirements. Here are some alternatives to the usual London hotel or airport hotels.

An association of B&Bs in London's nicest inner suburbs, all close to Tube stations, offers an attractive and relatively inexpensive alternative to London hotels. For detailed listings and booking information, write **London Home-to-Home,** 19 Mount Park Crescent, Ealing, London W5 2RN, or call 081-567-2998.

If the idea of staying in the country, an hour or so from your airport, seems even more appealing, check the listings for the Thames Valley (for Heathrow) and Surrey (for Gatwick) in the Farm Bureau guide (see Further Reading).

◆DAY SIXTEEN

Home

Just as all international flights into London tend to arrive at the same time, they depart at the same time, too. Flights to the States, for example, all tend to leave between midmorning and early afternoon. That means there's going to be a huge crush of folks all trying to check in at once. In an effort to ensure that the benefits of the last two weeks aren't squandered by a couple of hours of frantic confusion, here are some tips for leaving London without losing your wits.

GETTING TO THE AIRPORT FROM LONDON

Between seasonal fog, occasional strikes, and the usual vagaries of airline travel, it pays to check in with your airline on the morning of your flight to determine its status. Your airline's number is either on your ticket envelope or in the phone book (or call Directory Enquiries, 142). If you need to call the airport directly, Heathrow is 759-4321, Gatwick 0923-28822.

Remember that you are expected to be **checked in** two hours before flight time. Given the length of the check-in lines, especially since airport security has been beefed up, you ought to arrive at the airport three hours in advance. If you have not checked in before the deadline, the airline is free to give your seat away to someone else. If you check in before the deadline and find your seat's been given to someone else anyway, or that the airline simply overbooked, then under International Air Transport Association regulations, the airline must (1) get someone who already has a seat to yield it to you, (2) book you on another flight departing to your destination with only a limited delay, or (3) put you up at a nearby hotel at their expense and pay you a very hefty fine, in cash, on the spot. The fine can be $400 per person. They won't volunteer this information; you have to know your rights.

GETTING TO HEATHROW. Unless you don't blanch at the prospect of dropping nearly £40 on a cab ride from central London, take the **Tube**—the Piccadilly (blue) Line to Heathrow (*not* Rayners Lane or Uxbridge). It takes about an hour and costs about £3. Baggage carts are available at the other end. If your hotel is near an **Airbus** stop, the bus is an attractive alternative. It also takes about an hour and costs about £5.

GETTING TO GATWICK. Only one real choice here, the BritRail **Gatwick Express** from Victoria Station, departing every 15 minutes and taking roughly 30 minutes (delays en route are not uncommon).

RETURNING YOUR RENTAL CAR

If you've kept your car until now, the drill is fairly simple, but takes a little more time. Assuming you're with someone else, drop them and your baggage, passport, and ticket at the departures terminal at your airport and have them get in the check-in line. Then take the car to the rental agency, stopping at a petrol station if you're expected to return the car with a full tank. After you've completed the formalities and have your receipt, they'll return you to the terminal, by which time your fellow travelers will probably just be reaching the check-in desk. Keep your receipt and be sure it has the details of your rental rate on it. (If the amount you're finally charged when your credit card bill comes in the mail is dramatically different, you'll need the receipt for your credit card company to fight it out.)

If you're coming from some distance and it's any day but Sunday, give yourself plenty of time. Traffic to and around the two airports can be heavy and delays are common. The signs to terminals, on the other hand, are extremely clear, so you're unlikely to get lost.

VAT REFUNDS

The British want to encourage you to shop in Britain, so many (though not all) shops participate in a scheme to refund you the **value-added tax (VAT)** you had to pay on your purchases (for goods, but not services like car rental). Most shops have their own VAT refund forms and stamped return envelopes, but you have to remember to ask for them and you usually have to spend more than £50 to qualify.

Pack any items on which you plan to claim a refund in your *carry-on bag,* so it doesn't get checked in as baggage. Then, once you've checked in, take your ticket, passport, and receipts to the VAT Customs Desk in the airport (ask at check-in if it isn't clearly marked). Customs will check the receipts and stamp the form. Then you mail it in a nearby mailbox. You *can* do this all after you get home, so long as your *own* customs officer checks and stamps the receipt. (And speaking of receipts, keep all your receipts handy in case you need them when you go through customs at home.)

Some weeks later, the store will mail you a VAT refund check, in pounds of course, and your bank will have to exchange it (although some larger establishments have finally begun to handle VAT through credit card credits). It is an awkward system, to say the least, but 17.5 percent is nothing to sneeze at, particularly if you've made some major purchases.

DUTY-FREE SHOPS

Both airports have huge duty-free shops and the bargains can be terrific. The emphasis is on liquor and tobacco products, though perfume, electronic gadgets, and some gift clothing are also featured. Look for the daily or monthly specials brochure and the discount coupons that duty-free shop representatives distribute in the waiting area. If the pound is weak compared with your own currency, you may well find significant bargains. More important, try not to get stuck with a lot of change. You will not be able to exchange British coins for currency when you get home. This is how the magazine and candy shops do so well.

HEADING HOME

Finally, don't press your luck at departure time. Remember that the gates are a *very* long way from the main departure lounge (and involve taking a shuttle train at Gatwick). If you cut it too short, the plane *will* leave without you.

Then sit back, watch the patchwork landscape slip beneath you, and try to persuade yourself that Dorothy was right when she told Toto there was "no place like home."

Further Reading

Backgrounders

Of the comprehensive guides to Britain or Wales, the *Insight Guides* series is the most imaginative and the most lushly illustrated. Separate books on *Great Britain, Scotland,* and *Wales* (published by APA Publications and distributed by Prentice-Hall Travel).

The finest regional guidebooks (with first-rate road maps) are the *AA/Ordnance Survey Leisure Guide Series.* Editions applicable to this itinerary include *East Anglia, Peak District, Snowdonia and North Wales, Brecon Beacons and Mid Wales, Forest of Dean and Wye Valley,* and *Cotswolds.* Published jointly by the Automobile Association and the Ordnance Survey.

Best book on natural history and wild areas: *Discovering Britain.* London: Drive Publications (for the Automobile Association) was published last in 1986. Check your local library.

Best books on London: *Insight Guides: London* (see above), and *London Access,* by Richard Wurman. New York: Access Press, 1993.

Accommodations Guides

FOR INNS AND SMALL HOTELS:

Brown, Karen. *English, Welsh, and Scottish Country Hotels and Itineraries.* Chester, Conn.: Globe Pequot Press, 1994.

Levitin, Jerry. *Country Inns and Back Roads: Britain and Ireland.* New York: Harper and Row, 1992.

Rubenstein, Hilary. *Europe's Wonderful Little Hotels and Inns: Great Britain and Ireland.* New York: St. Martins Press, 1994.

Stay at an Inn. London: British Tourist Authority, 1994.

FOR SELECT B&BS:

Country Lodging on a Budget: The Official Guide of the Farm Holiday Bureau U.K. 1991. London: William Curtis Limited, 1991. **Far and away the best B&B guide for the countryside.**

Brown, Karen. *English Country Bed & Breakfast.* Chester, Conn.: Globe Pequot Press, 1992. An excellent selection.

The Bed & Breakfast Guide to Great Britain. New York: Consumer Reports Books, 1992.

Welles, Sigourney. *The Best Bed and Breakfast in the World: England, Scotland, and Wales.* Chester, Conn.: Globe Pequot Press, 1994–95.

Good Room Guide. Excellent booklet listing first-rate B&Bs, published privately by Guestaccom, 190 Church Road, Hove, East Sussex, BN3 2DJ, or phone (0273) 722833.

YOUTH HOSTELS:

YHA 1992 Accommodation Guide. Available through Hostelling International/American Youth Hostels, P.O. Box 37613, Washington, D.C. 20013-7613, or phone (202) 783-6161.

Books on Food

FOR RESTAURANTS:

Jaine, Tom. *The Good Food Guide 1993.* London: Hodder and Stoughton (for the Consumers' Association), 1993.

FOR PUBS:

Aird, Alisdair. *The 1992 Good Pub Guide.* London: Ebury Press, 1992.

Hanson, Neil. *The Best Pubs of Great Britain.* Chester, Conn.: Globe Pequot Press (compiled by the Campaign for Real Ale), 1989.

Books on Walking and Climbing

Storer, Ralph. *100 Best Routes On Scottish Mountains.* Seattle: The Mountaineers, 1987.

Wilson, Ken, and Gilbert, Richard. *Classic Walks: Mountain and Moorland Walks in Britain and Ireland.* London: Diadem Books, 1982.

Useful Addresses

British Tourist Authority Overseas Offices

UNITED STATES:

551 5th Avenue
Suite 701
New York, NY 10176
1-800-462-2748
In NYC: (212) 986-2266

CANADA:

111 Avenue Road
Suite 450
Toronto, Ontario M5R 3T8
(416) 925-6326

AUSTRALIA:

210 Clarence Street
Sydney, NSW 2000
(02) 267-4555

NEW ZEALAND

Dilworth Building
Third Floor
Cnr. Queen and Customs Street
Auckland 1
(09) 3031 446

National Tourist Boards

English Tourist Board
Thames Tower, Black's Road
Hammersmith, London W6 9EL
(071) 846 9000

Welsh Tourist Board
Brunel House, 2 Fitzalan Road
Cardiff CF2 1UY
(0222) 499909

Scottish Tourist Board
23 Ravelston Terrace
Edinburgh EH4 3EU
(031) 332 2433

National Parks Covered in This Book

Yorkshire Dales National Park
Yorebridge House, Bainbridge
Leyburn, N. Yorkshire DL8 3BP
Tel.: (0969) 50456

Lake District National Park
Busher Walk
Kendal, Cumbria LA9 4RH
Tel.: (0539) 24555

Northumberland National Park
Eastburn, South Park, Hexham
Northumberland NE46 1BS
Tel.: Hexham 605555

Other Helpful Organizations

The National Trust
36 Queen Anne's Gate
London SW1H 7AS
(071) 222 9251

National Trust for Scotland
5 Charlotte Square
Edinburgh EH2 4DU
(031) 226 5922

Countryside Commission
John Dower House
Crescent Place, Cheltenham
Gloucestershire GL50 3RA
(0242) 521381

Countryside Commission for
Scotland
Battleby, Redgorton
Perth PH1 3EW
(0738) 27921

Ordnance Survey
Romsey Road, Maybush
Southampton SO9 4DH
(0703) 792763

Automobile Association
Fanum House
Basingstoke, Hants. RG21 2EA
(0256) 20123

Ramblers' Association
1/5 Wandsworth Road
London SW8 2XX
(071) 582 6878

Index

ABOUT THE AUTHORS

Bill North is a writer and independent public policy consultant.
Gwen North is a consultant in fashion merchandising. Maryland residents, the Norths are avid travelers who visit Great Britain several times a year. For years they have been developing travel itineraries for their friends, tailored for independent, sophisticated travelers with wide interests but limited vacation time. The increasing demand for these itineraries led to *The Two-Week Traveler Series.*